Contents

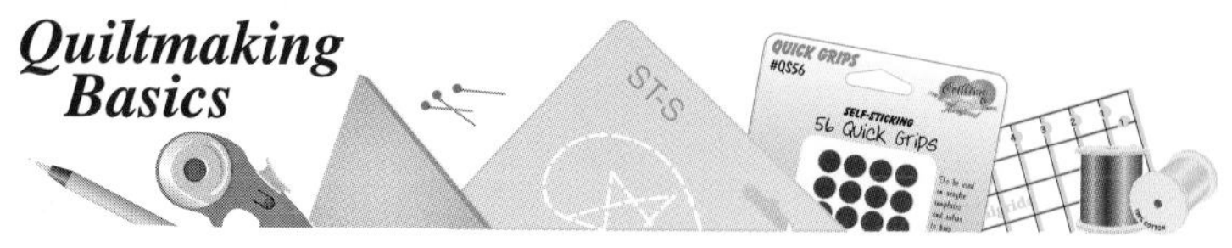

How To Use This Book

This book contains step-by-step instructions for each design.

A. Before starting, read through entire instructions so you get an idea of the complete process.

B. There are color photos to look at if picking fabric is difficult for you. Check yardage charts for each quilt before purchasing fabric. Make sure to prepare your fabric as suggested.

C. Templates are printed in actual size at the end of this book. Acrylic templates can be purchased at your local quilt shop or from "Quilting From The Heartland", P.O. Box 610, Starbuck, MN 56381 U.S.A. 1-800-637-2541 or 1-320-239-4044

Preparation of Acrylic Templates

Templates come with protective paper on each side; simply peel off before using. They are pink in color (so you won't lose them in your fabric), as well as transparent which allows you to take advantage of certain fabric designs.

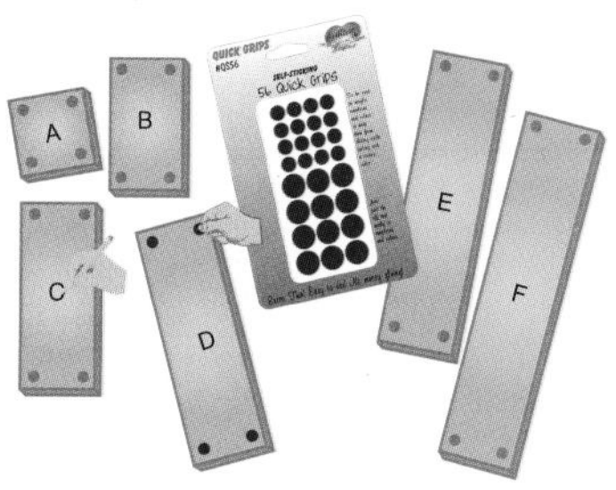

For the best accuracy while cutting with the Rotary Cutter, apply **Quick Grips** to each corner of the template; if it's a larger template, put one in middle along edge. Quick Grips are small circles of felt with adhesive backing. They keep templates from sliding on your fabric while cutting. **Please Note!** If you don't put the Quick Grips on the far corners, the fabric will move when you approach corner with cutter.

To identify templates easier, label them with letters. Use a permanent marking pen or pen and masking tape.

Preparation of Fabric

I prefer to use 100% cotton fabric because it is lightweight making it easy to quilt through three layers of the quilt sandwich. Cotton is easy to manipulate when matching points and flexible when working with curves. If you are going to use blends, choose all fabrics of the same blend.

Separate fabrics by color and wash in cool water with a mild soap that contains no bleaching additives. My favorite soap to use is **Orvus® W A Paste**. The cleaning agents are biodegradable, as well as gentle on fabric. Use only one tablespoon to approximately six gallons of warm water. Rinse well with plenty warm water. If fabric still bleeds after one washing, you may consider a second wash. Line or machine dry.

Caution! If you use a steam iron when you are piecing a quilt and you haven't pre-washed the fabric, your cut pieces will shrink unevenly, making them difficult to work with.

Press and Starch

I have started to use spray starch on most fabrics that go into the quilt. Starch makes cutting and sewing much easier. It also acts as a stain guard, making it easier to remove pencil lines. A light mist is adequate for most quilting projects, but if pieces are small, spray both sides of fabric.

Starch will also prevent pieces from getting pulled into needle hole when sewing.

It is cheaper to mix your own starch with equal parts of Sta-Flo liquid starch and water. Put it in a mister and lightly mist fabric before pressing it.

Grain of Fabric

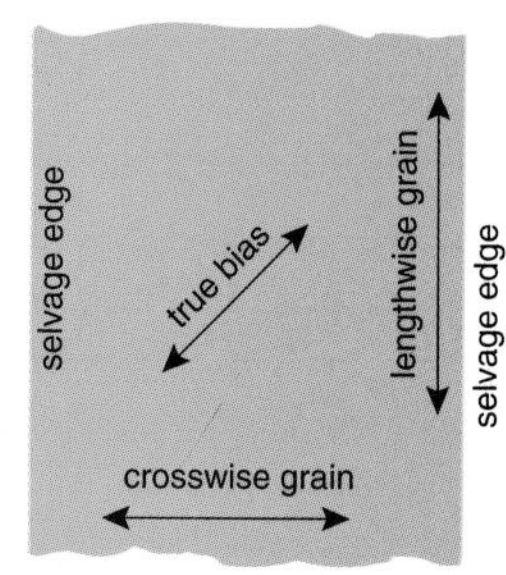

Lengthwise grain runs parallel to edge of fabric and crosswise grain runs from selvage to selvage. They are both considered to be on straight of grain. True bias is cut at a 45° angle and it is stretchiest part of fabric. Avoid having bias edges of fabric on outside edge of quilt block. This will help keep quilt square; also, it will hang better if it is a wall quilt.

There are times when I ignore this rule, especially if there is a design in the fabric that I want to capture. Because templates are transparent, you can place them in exact position before cutting. You can create some great designs, especially from border prints and stripes, but you can cut only one at a time. It will look as if a mouse has been into your fabric when you have finished cutting.

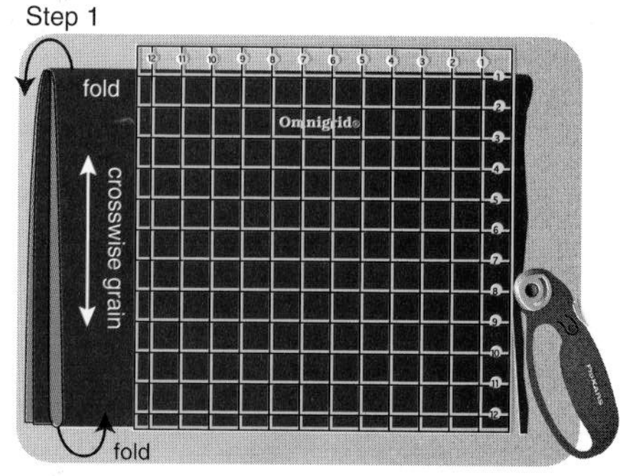

Straightening Fabric

Step 1. Fold fabric in half, matching selvage edges. Fold fabric a second time matching first fold to selvage edges. Put folded fabric on mat board so it extends to right for right-handed people and to left for left-handed people. Place bottom edge of 12 1/2" x 12 1/2" Omnigrid® ruler along fold of fabric, in far enough from uneven edge so you can cut it off. Make clean cut through fabric, starting in front of fold, cutting to opposite edge with one clean (not short and choppy) stroke. Try not to disturb fabric after edge is straightened. Bi-fold (fold on top of itself) fabric on top board so it can turn easily without moving fabric.

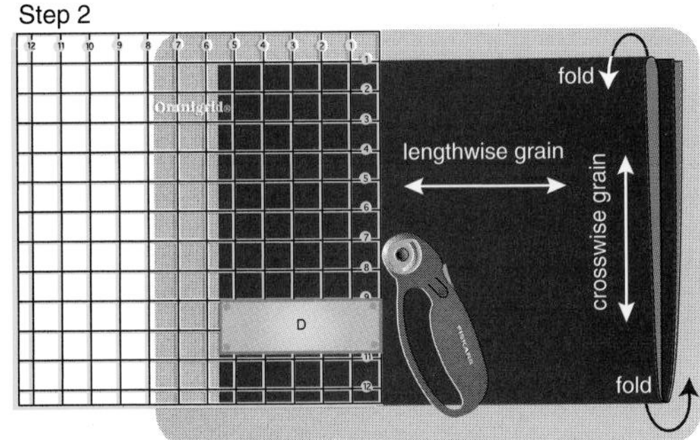

Cutting Strips for Large Logs

Step 2. If you need many logs from each fabric cut strips to accommodate length instead of width. This saves fabric.

Keep fabric folded in fourths. Make sure fabric is lying straight, so you don't end up with zig zag strips. Place a 12 1/2" x 12 1/2" Omnigrid® ruler on top of folded fabric and cut strips needed for templates. For example, cut strips for template D 5 1/2" wide.

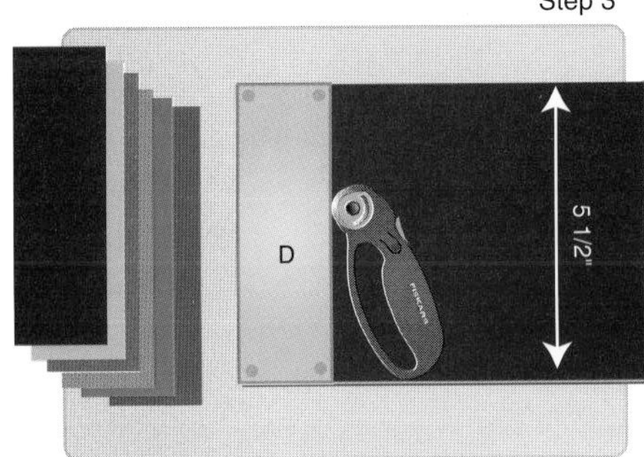

Cutting Large Logs

Step 3. If same template is used for many pieces such as in the Chicken Doorstop, you can save time by cutting many pieces at a time. Place strips on top of each other. Line up edges. Place template on top of strips and cut number needed.

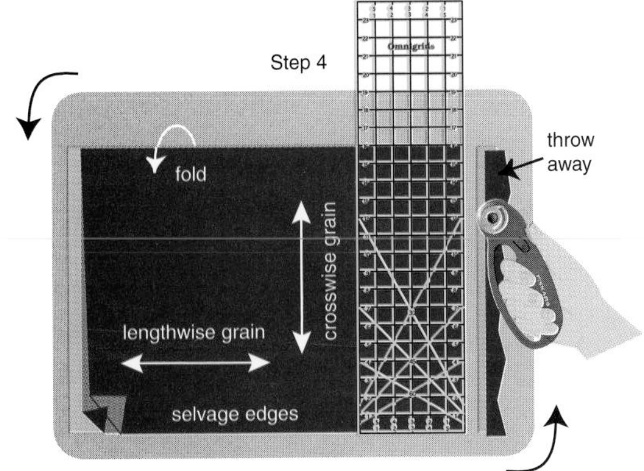

Straightening the Fabricwith 6"x 24" Ruler

Step 4. When same shapes are cut from more than one fabric used in the quilt, you can save time and accuracy by straightening more than one at the same time. Fold each fabric in half and place one on top of the other, lining up selvage edges. I like to work with folded fabric because layers seem to stabilize each other, especially if they are freshly ironed.

Place bottom edge of ruler on selvage edge. Start cutting about 1" from selvage edge going backwards off fabric. Starting in the same place, continue to cut away from yourself when trimming off uneven edges. Try not to disturb the fabric after it is straightened. Bi-fold the fabric on top of the board before turning it.

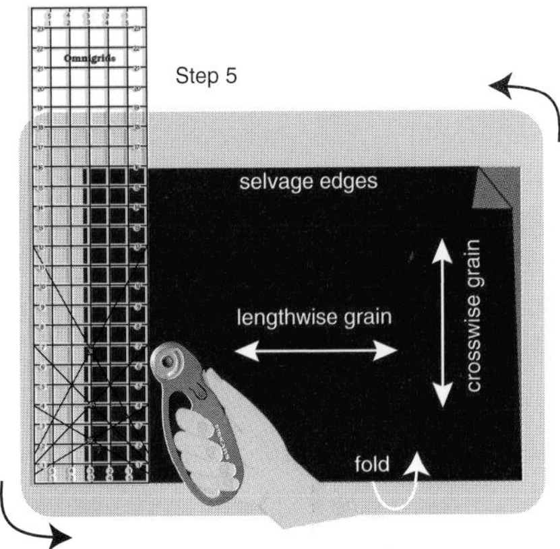

Cutting Strips with 6"x 24" Ruler

Step 5. Move ruler to the proper position to get width needed for strips. Cut required number of strips.

When you get more experienced with this method of straightening fabric and cutting strips, you can layer as many as six fabrics on top of each other.

If you are using a 6" x 12" Omnigrid® ruler, you will have to fold the fabric in half matching the selvage edge, and in half again. **Note!** Make sure your fabric is lying straight while cutting strips with the 6" x 12" ruler, so you don't end with zig zag strips.

After you have mastered cutting strips, it's easy to recut them into squares with a 6" x 12" ruler.

Seam Allowance

Sew all seams with a **scant 1/4" seam allowance** to make up for amount of fabric used in seam line. The settings I use to get scant 1/4" on the #1 Husqvarna 1200 are as follows: program stitch length for 2.5, stitch width 3.0, and mirror image stitch width to move needle to right needle position.

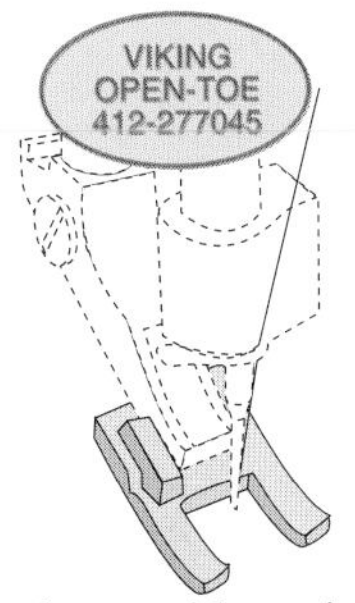

Thread and Feet

I prefer to use open-toe or edging foot for piecing. On open toe foot the portion of foot directly in front of needle has been removed to give an unobstructed view of stitch. Edging foot has a guide on right side that prevents fabric from moving too far to right. If you never sew over pins, this foot is perfect.

Use **100% merc. cotton thread,** size 50 to match 100% cotton fabric for care and strength. Cotton thread is strong, yet fine, for accurate piecing.

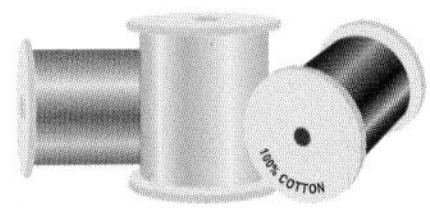

Invisible thread works well when there are many colors in quilt. It is available in clear or smoke. Like fish line, it is very strong and comes in different weights. Sunlight will break down nylon fibers over time so use it discretely.

Cotton thread will match fabric for strength and care. If you want to hand quilt down to the next generation, use cotton because it will last as long as the fabric.

Free motion quilting takes the most skill and works best for continuous line designs, stippling, outlining flowers, and feathered designs. It doesn't work well for long straight lines.

Attach darning foot to machine and lower feed dogs so you can freely manipulate fabric. Practice controlling speed of machine on a scrap of fabric before starting on a finished quilt top. Set machine for straight stitch and put stitch length at zero. Leave long enough tail when beginning and ending so you can bury thread just like you do when hand quilting.

Because there is so much happening at one time, it's easy to get tense. Remember to breathe and relax when machine quilting. After all, this is fun! Don't turn fabric; instead, move it forward, backward and from side to side.

Look where you're going, not at needle. If you sew too slowly, stitches will be long and if you sew too fast there will be too many stitches per inch. Practice improves your skills. Have fun with it. Just like hand quilting, every stitch won't be perfect.

If you want to sew straight lines, the walking foot works well. It can be used for cross hatching and stitching in the ditch. The machine will do the work and you will have perfect stitches. If you are working on a large quilt it will be hard to pivot because of all the bulk.

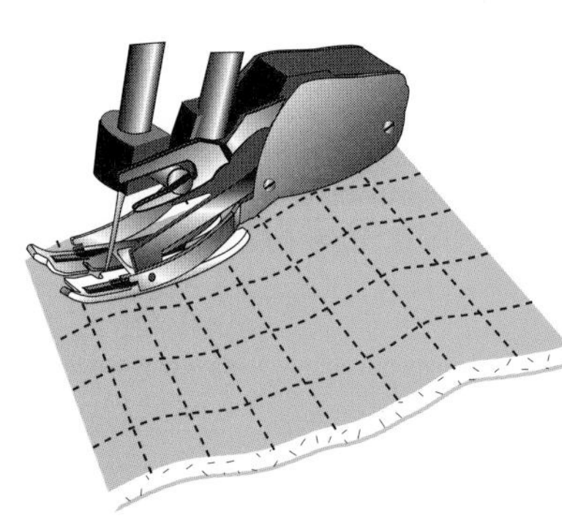

Does Your Machine Eat Fabric?

Try one or more of these tips if you are having trouble with fabric getting pulled into feed dogs.

1. Switch to a single-hole needle plate.
2. Use an anchor cloth as a leader when starting to sew. Anchor cloth is a small square of fabric folded in half. Start sewing on anchor cloth and butt the next set of pieces up to it as you sew. Beginning stitches on patchwork will be more secure and won't pull apart as easily as first stitches sewn. Cut anchor cloth from beginning of your work and sew off onto it when ending. You won't have to hold threads when starting with this method. This will also save time and thread.
3. Spray starching fabric before cutting pieces stabilizes fabric and makes stitching easy.

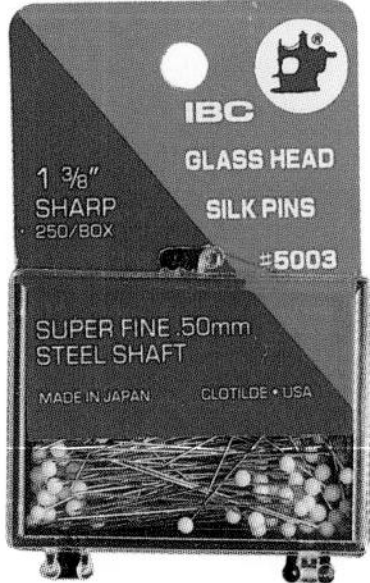

Silk Pins

There is a big difference in pins. Some are as big as nails. I prefer glass head silk pins with a super fine .50mm steel shaft. They are fine and never leave holes. Silk pins slide easily into fabric because of the fine shank. Silk pins are best, if it is necessary to sew over pins.

Use a stiletto instead of your pointer finger to guide fabric in front of needle when machine piecing. You won't worry about pieces scooting to one side at end of seam, when using a stiletto.

Pressing Techniques

There is a lot of debate about which way to iron seams when putting blocks together. There are advantages to both and I suggest you try both ways and decide for yourself which one you prefer. I don't necessarily use the fastest method, but I use the one that makes the block look best when finished. Sometimes both methods are used in the same quilt.

It is faster to iron seams to one side and seams are a little stronger, but you have more bulk in one place which makes it difficult to match some designs with triangles and hexagons. It takes more time to press seams open, but you will have a flatter quilt top making it easier to hand quilt. I will share with you which method I prefer for each quilt in this book.

No matter which direction you iron seams, always take time to ***finger press seams first*** before ironing. To finger press, use your pointer finger to scratch fabric in direction you want it to go as you move it along seam allowance. Your finger will act as a mini iron and is often enough to do a good job.

Finger pressing gives you accuracy and speed when ironing and helps eliminate pleats in seam wells.

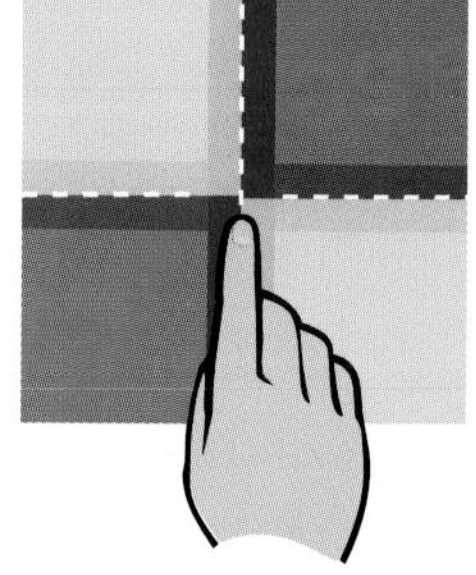

After you have finger pressed seam, press it gently with a steam iron, always on wrong side. Sliding iron back and forth can cause bias edges to stretch and block could be distorted. **Whichever method of pressing you use, be sure to press as you go. It is harder to match unpressed seams and crossing over them can cause seam wells at intersections.**

If you press seams to one side, press them towards darker fabric whenever possible to avoid shadows under light pieces.

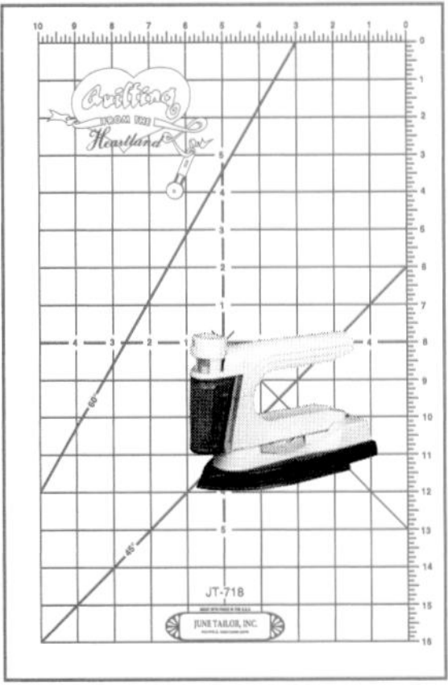

Place a pressing mat near your sewing machine so you don't have to leave sewing area every time you want to press a seam. I don't use large ironing board until blocks are being connected. I use small Clover travel iron at the sewing machine for pressing seams. It gets plenty hot and does a good enough job.

Much of the time I press pieces together before starting to sew. This creates a temporary bond of pieces making it easy to keep edges aligned as they are fed under the presser foot. Then ***finger pinning*** units together is enough. It takes time to insert pins and they can get in the way.

Portable Sewing Table

If you don't have a sewing machine cabinet, you would like this portable sewing table because it maximizes space around the free arm and it is easy to take to class.

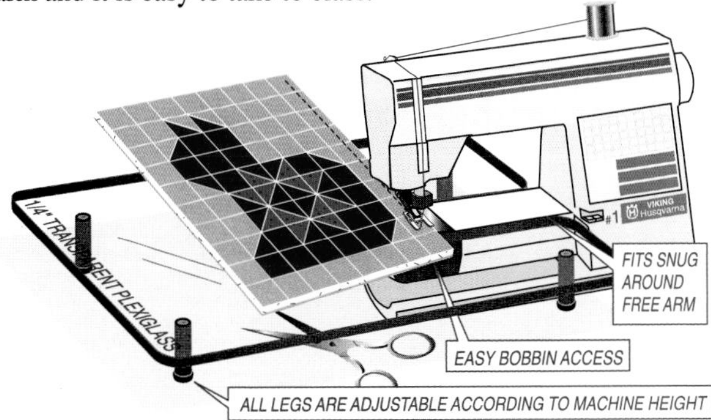

Chain Sewing

To save time and thread, chain sew pieces together whenever possible. At end of a seam, do not back stitch or cut thread. Feed next pair of pieces under presser foot as close as possible to first pair. Continue to feed pieces as close as possible. After all pieces have been sewn, remove chain and clip threads between pieces.

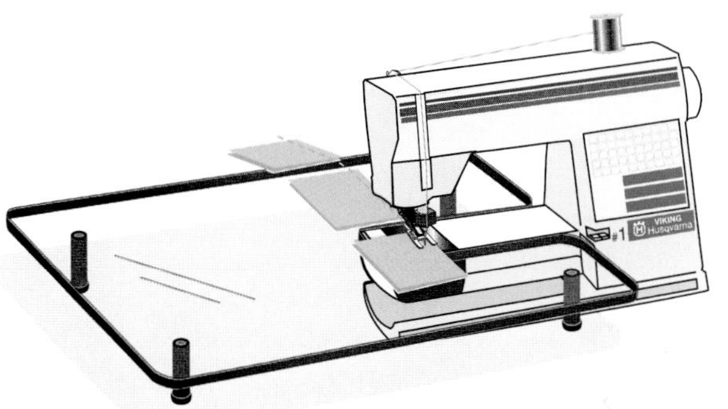

Flannel Board

Use a flannel board at cutting table when planning your next quilt. Mine has a pocket to insert a 17" x 17" Q-Snap frame to make it into an easel or a handle to hang on door or wall hook. It is easy to transport from cutting table to sewing machine or take to classes.

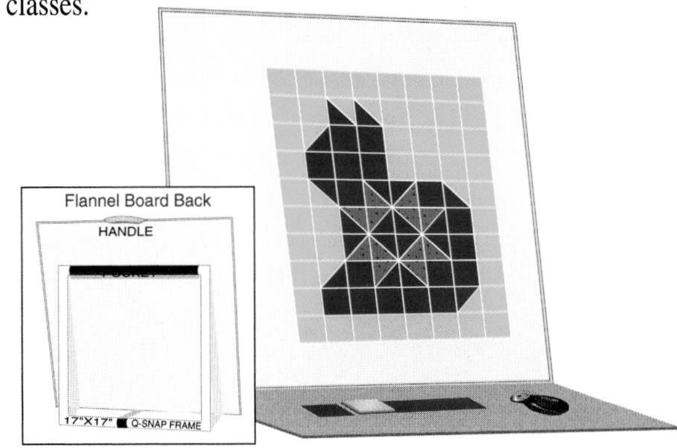

Borders

Every quilt needs one or more borders to announce its completion. Think of the border as a picture frame. If border fabric is plain, it becomes a showcase for quilting.

There can be one or more fabrics used in border and it can be mitered or squared. I prefer the look of mitered corners unless there is a corner stone in the border. The corner stone can be a pieced block or a plain square (see diagram below.)

When working with border, I lay strips of fabric along edge and use what feels right. Sometimes two borders look better than one. If you use two borders, they look best if they are of different widths. You might decide to introduce a large print in border that wasn't used in quilt.

When possible, pick quilting stencil before cutting borders so you know how wide to cut strips. It's easier to mark if you purchase matching border and corner sets. Make sure width of stencil fits within border. Last 1/4" of border around outside edge should not be counted because it will eventually be covered with binding.

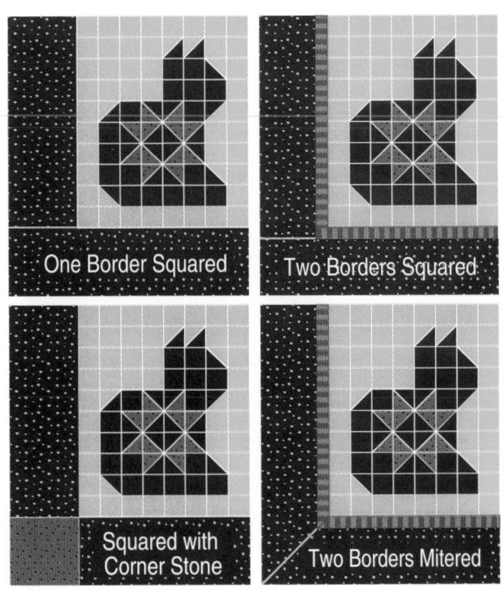

Borders with Mitered Corners

Allow extra length for mitered corners. Measure distance from top to bottom on both sides of quilt. If your measurements are different, take average length. To find out how much extra is needed, fold cut strip on the diagonal. I cut strips 6 1/2" wide for most outside borders. Next, subtract from top and bottom the 1/4" that is used in seam.

Match center of border strip to center of quilt edge. Hold in place with a pin. Insert another pin 1/4" from top and bottom end of quilt. Evenly insert more pins along edge. Sew this seam with quilt on top so intersections you want to sew over are visible. Stop sewing 1/4" from each corner on top and bottom of quilt. After all sides are attached, seams will touch in corners. Attach border on other side in same way. Repeat step to add top and bottom border.

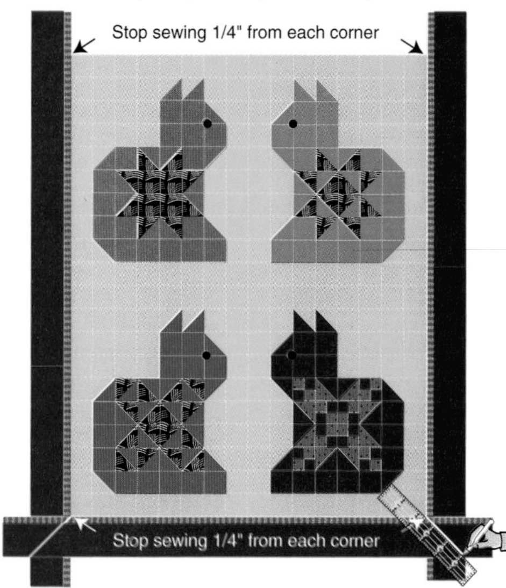

After all four sides have been attached, iron seam allowance towards border. Cross one border over the other making a perfect 90° corner. One at a time, make a chalk line on right side of both top and bottom at a 45° angle. Match these lines and pin to hold in place. Sew this seam starting at outside point and back stitch at inside corner. Corner should lie flat. Trim off excess fabric.

Marking Quilting Design

Before making quilt sandwich, mark quilting designs on quilt top. Using pre-cut stencils is an easy, fast and economical way to transfer quilting designs. Plastic stencils have a series of slots, wide enough to allow points of pencils to mark through onto fabric. Bridges are left between slots to hold stencil together. You can join broken lines after stencil is removed to make a continuous quilting line or join them during quilting process.

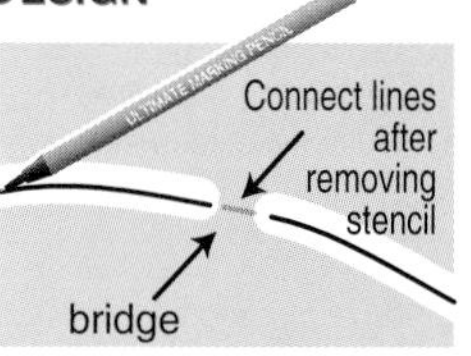

Consider open areas that need quilting. Quilting will show up more on a solid fabric than on a busy floral. If you use a fabric with very little print or even better, a solid, for back of quilt, it will be reversible. Choose stencil to complement quilt. Mark lightly through slots following lines until design is completed.

Prepare Quilt Back

If light fabrics were used in quilt top, don't use dark for quilt back because it will show through. Before making quilt sandwich (front, batting, and backing) you will need to make the quilt back. The back should be 2" - 3" larger (on all four sides) than pieced top. Measure finished quilt top and add 4" - 6" to length and width. If you are making a wall quilt less than 40" wide, you won't have to sew strips of fabric together for backing. Cut length needed. If quilt is wider than 40", you will have to sew strips together. Sew seams with a 5/8" seam allowance and trim to 1/4". Iron seam open.

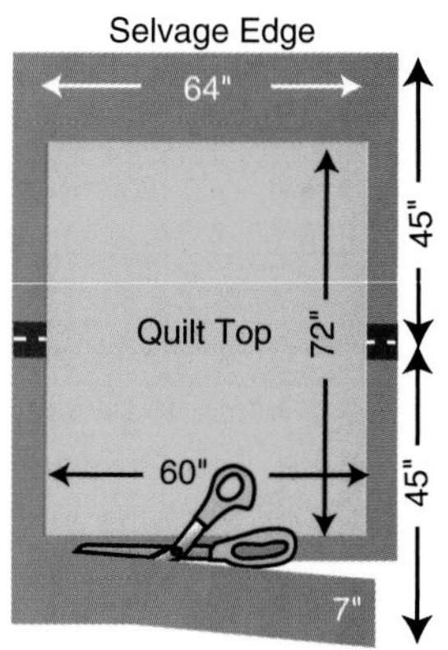

Measure quilt top for which you are making back and figure out best use of fabric. Length and width of quilt will determine whether you put seam lengthwise or crosswise. Center quilt over back and leave equal amounts of extra fabric on each side.

Quilt Sandwich

After quilting design is marked on quilt top, make a quilt sandwich by placing back of quilt on bottom with wrong side facing up. The middle is batting and pieced quilt is on top, right side facing up. Work on a table top or a tile floor if available. Smooth out and secure bottom layer in place (wrong side facing up) with masking tape. Batting and pieced top is secured in place with pins.

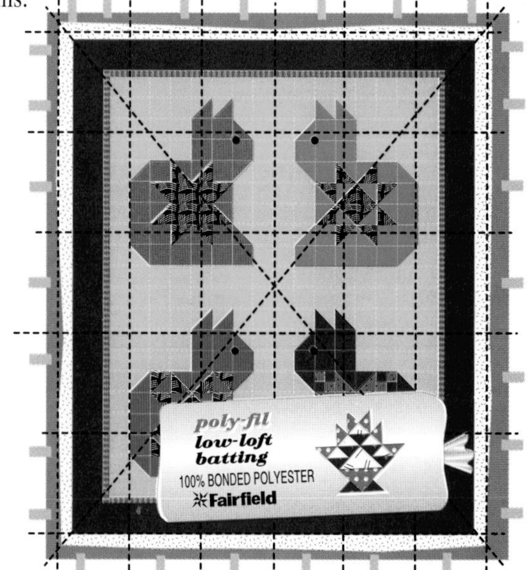

I prefer Fairfield low-loft batting for both hand and machine quilting. It's easier to get even stitches with light batting and finished quilts drape nicely over beds.

Baste quilt with a large needle diagonally, vertically and horizontally. You can also pin-baste with rust proof safety pins.

Basting Quilt Sandwich on Table Top

Fold top of quilt in half and mark center on all four edges. Do the same with batting and backing.

Mark center of table top in three places with a toothpick held in place by masking tape. Toothpicks make a bump that can be felt through quilt sandwich layers. If quilt is longer than length of table, put a tooth pick in center of table edge.

Fold back of quilt in half, wrong sides together. Match centers of back to toothpicks on table. Unfold back with wrong side up and secure ends with masking tape. If back is longer than table, secure it with clips.

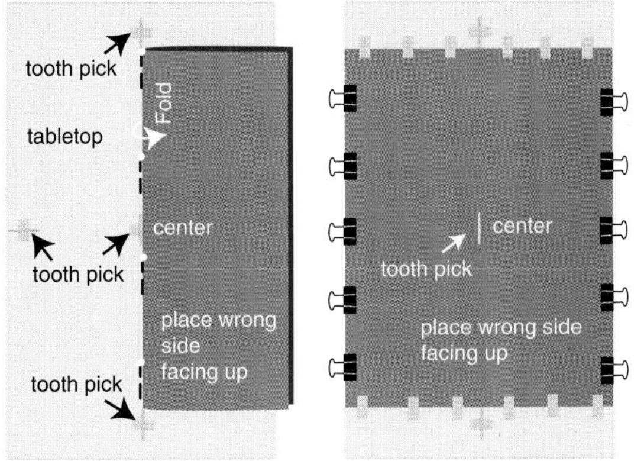

Fold batting in half and match to center bumps. Let batting drape over table top.

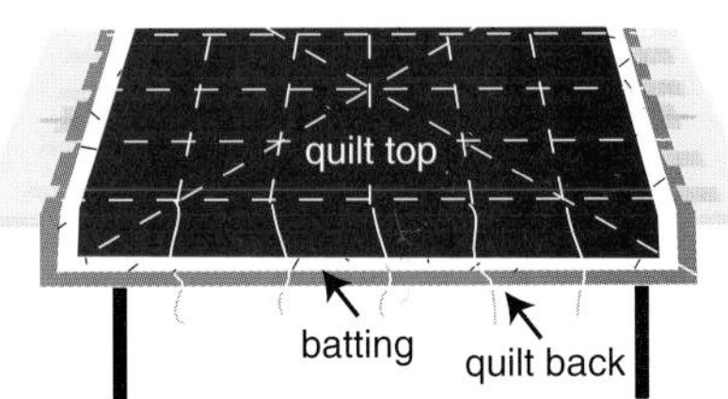

Fold quilt top in half, right sides together and match the fold to center bumps. Unfold quilt top over table top and smooth it out. Now you are ready to baste. Start in the center and work your way out. If your quilt is larger than the table top, remove clamps after it is basted and readjust quilt sandwich on table top.

Turn excess backing along outside edge over batting and baste it in place with binding clips, you have a temporary binding. This prevents batting from getting snagged during quilting process.

Binding

To keep quilt and batting from shifting while you attach binding, machine sew with a walking foot or hand baste 1/8" from edge.

Cut enough 2" strips on the straight of grain or bias for binding.

Step 1. Cut off both ends of all 2" strips at a 45° angle. Now bulk of seam will be evenly distributed. Sew strips together and press seams open. At beginning, fold 1/4" back and press.

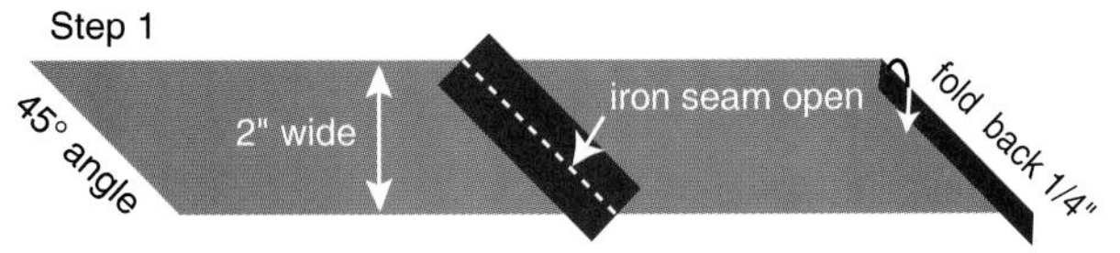

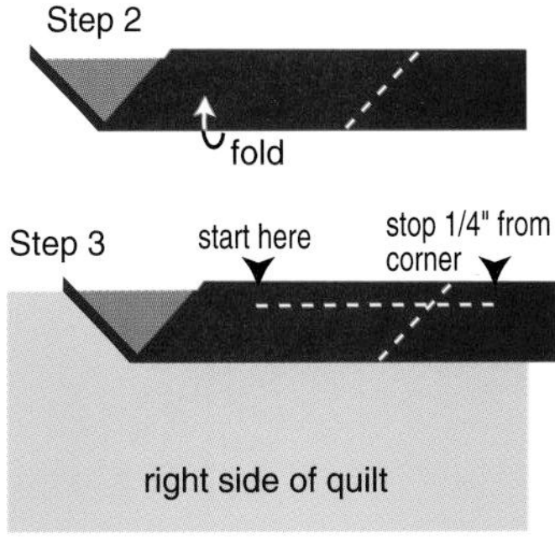

Step 2. Fold binding in half and press.

Step 3. Starting at end of binding with 1/4" folded back, place binding on right side of quilt. Make sure a seam does not fall on a corner; if it does, find a new place to start. Match edge of quilt to cut edge of binding and start sewing 1" after 1/4" fold so end of binding can be slipped inside for a nice finish. Sew 1/4" from edge and stop sewing 1/4" from corner of quilt edge and back stitch. Cut thread.

Step 4. Turn your work and fold binding back. Binding edge and quilt edge should make a straight line when folded regardless of the angle of the quilt corner. This fold will start the miter on the corner.

Step 5. Place your finger on first fold and flip binding down to make the second fold even with binding; this will complete miter. Finger pin and start sewing from the outside edge to 1/4" of next corner. Repeat steps #3 - #5 until you are around entire quilt.

Step 6. Turn binding on the right to back side of quilt to form miter.

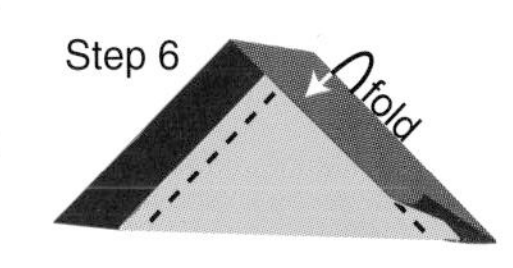

Step 7. Fold other side over to complete mitered corner. Bulk in corners will automatically end opposite each other on top and bottom. Using a matching thread, hand sew with a blind stitch.

Hold binding in place with pins or binding clips as you stitch. If you use binding clips you won't have to worry about being poked with pins.

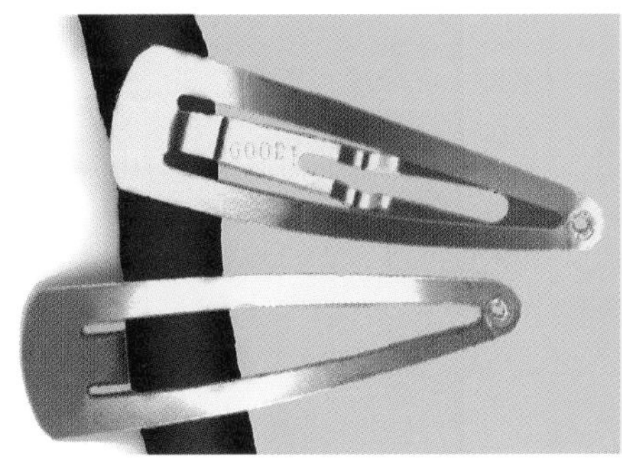

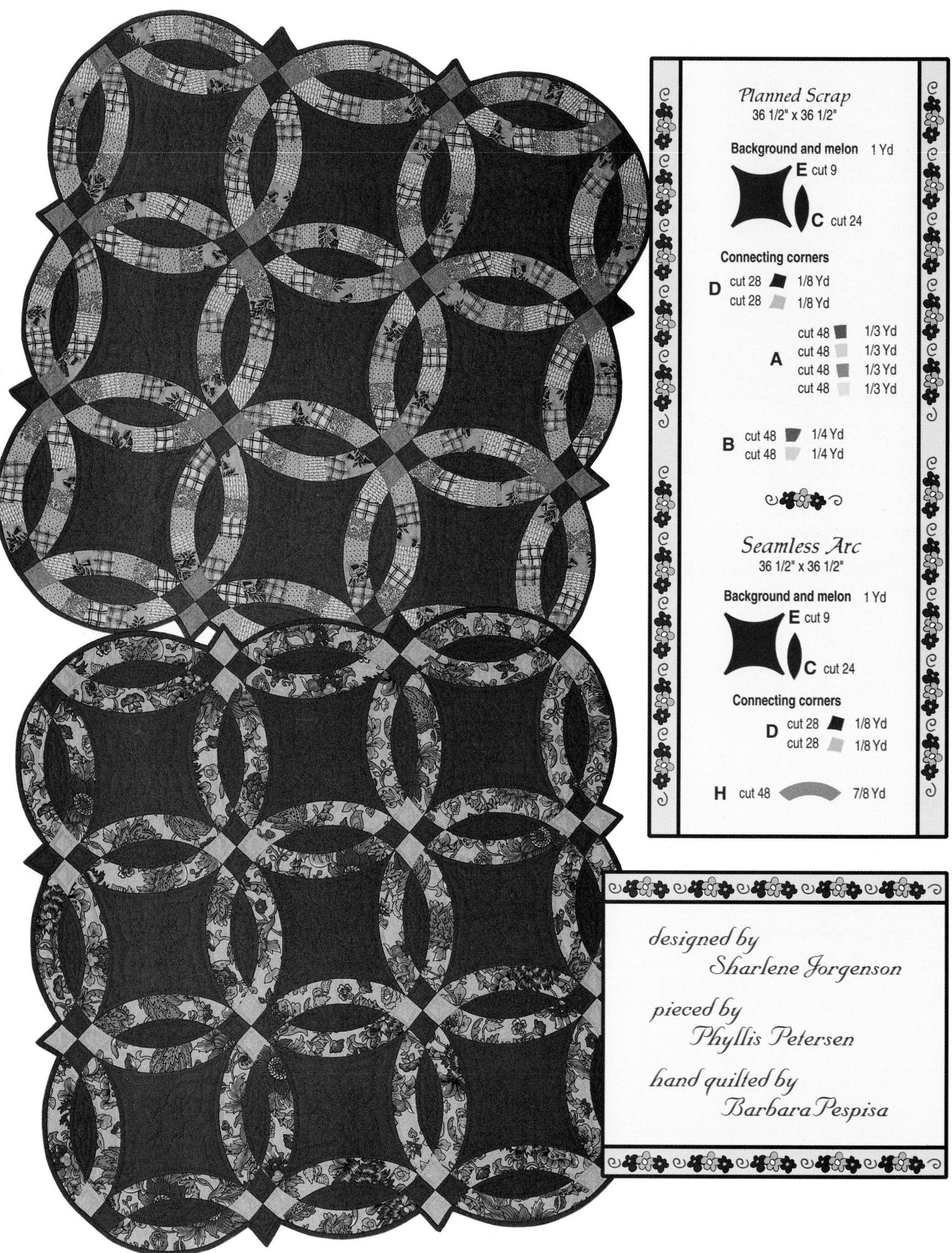
Planned Scrap
36 1/2" x 36 1/2"
Background and melon 1 Yd
E cut 9
C cut 24
Connecting corners
D cut 28 1/8 Yd
cut 28 1/8 Yd
A cut 48 1/3 Yd
cut 48 1/3 Yd
cut 48 1/3 Yd
cut 48 1/3 Yd
B cut 48 1/4 Yd
cut 48 1/4 Yd
Seamless Arc
36 1/2" x 36 1/2"
Background and melon 1 Yd
E cut 9
C cut 24
Connecting corners
D cut 28 1/8 Yd
cut 28 1/8 Yd
H cut 48 7/8 Yd
designed by
Sharlene Jorgenson
pieced by
Phyllis Petersen
hand quilted by
Barbara Pespisa

Country French Double Wedding Ring

Shopping List

- QS1 Double Wedding Ring Templates
- Quick Grips
- Omnigrid® Rulers 6" x 24"
- Fiskars® Rotary Cutter
- IBC Glass Head Pins 0.50mm steel shaft
- Fairfield poly-fil low-loft batting
- ST1-24 Stencil

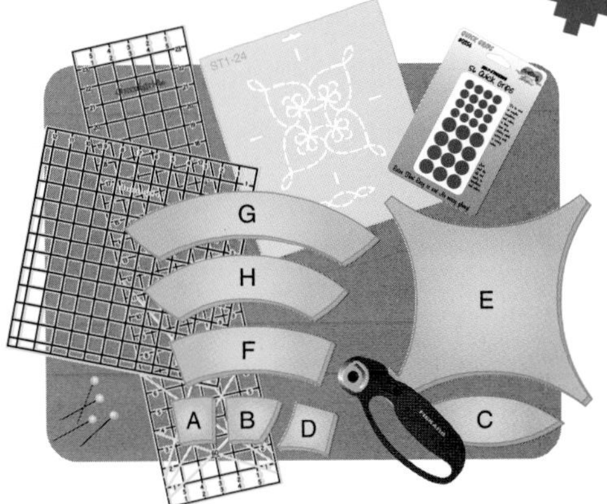

Read pages 2-9 before starting.

Choosing Fabric

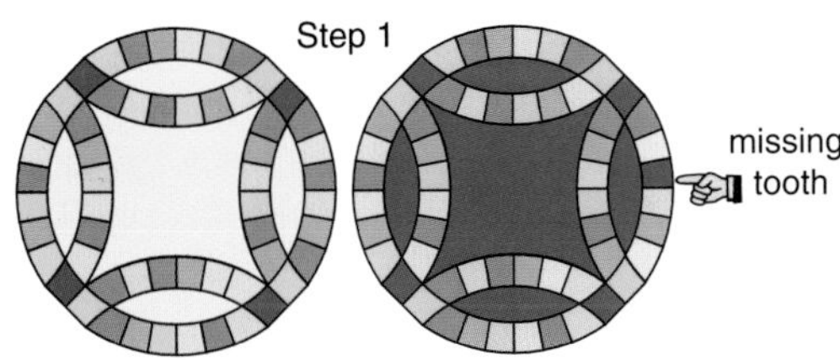

Step 1. First decide if you want a light background with dark rings or a dark background with light rings. Use light to medium scraps in arcs if background is dark, to avoid the missing tooth effect. The Country French wall quilt on page 8, was made with "Cumberland" fabric designed by Fons & Porter for Benertex Inc. Choose fabrics of high contrast for connecting corners to separate circles in the design.

Cutting Instructions

Prepare and straighten the fabric as suggested on pages 2-3. Prepare templates as suggested on page 2. Use templates G, A, B, C, D and E when cutting the Scrap Double Wedding Ring.

Step 2. Place template G on top of 6 layers of fabric. Don't worry if there isn't enough fabric to fill the arcs because you will discard the unfilled pieces when you sew. Don't worry about the grain line when cutting these pieces.

If you're using 12 1/2" strips, bi-fold them on top of mat board to make it easier to turn board as you cut. ***Do not disturb this arc until you have completed Step 3.***

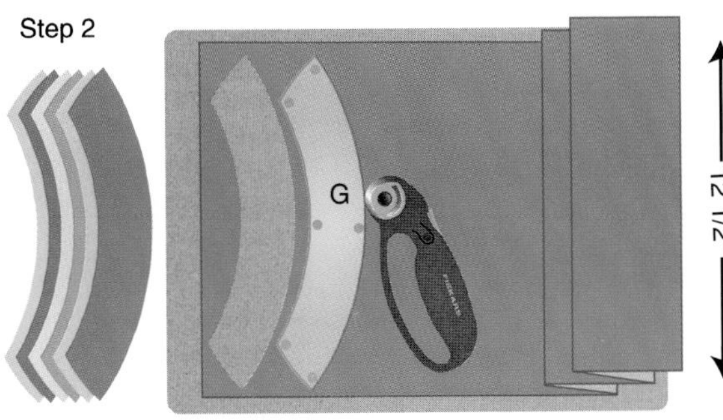

Step 3. Place template B on end of arcs cut in step 2. Match edges of template to edge of arc. Make first cut along straight edge of template B.

Next use template A to cut four center wedges. ***Template B should fit exactly on top of piece that is left.*** If it doesn't, something has moved while cutting and you need to find pieces that were cut wrong. You get 36 pieces each time, or enough for 6 arcs, if there is enough fabric scraps to fill all arcs.

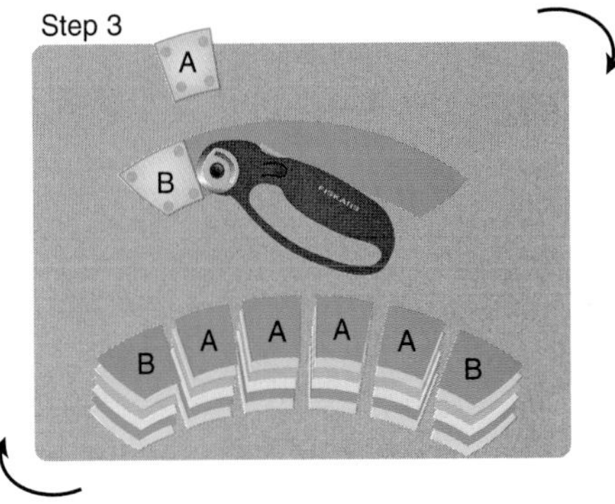

Separate A's into four containers as you are cutting so it is easier to evenly distribute colors in the quilt. B's don't have to be divided as they will work out automatically.

Cutting Connecting Corners

Step 4. Look at pages 2-3 to see how to straighten fabric and cut strips. Bifold 2 strips of each color on top of a small mat board to make it easier to turn as you cut around template. You may cut connecting corners on straight of grain or on the bias. Place D on top of strips as shown in diagram, to cut on the bias. Bias D's are easier to sew into the quilt making small amount of fabric wasted worth while. To cut connecting corners on straight of grain, line up a straight edge of template D with bottom edge of strips cut 2 1/2" wide.

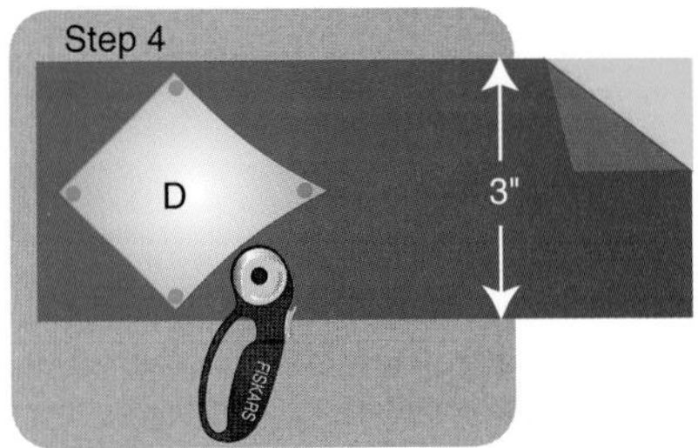

Cutting Backgrounds and Melons

Step 5. To cut backgrounds and melons, fold fabric in half and then in half again, so you have four thicknesses. Bifold fabric on a large mat board so board turns easier as you cut around templates.

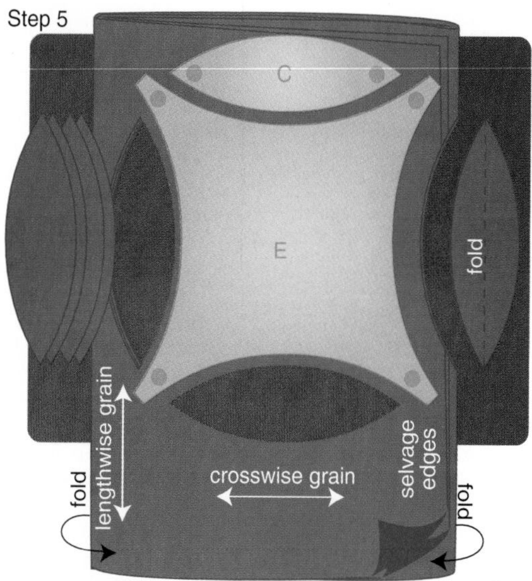

Place template E on fabric first, then see if template C will fit on all four edges. If it doesn't you have to cut one out of folded edge. Cut around E first. Then cut C's from leftover pieces. Use small mat board to cut C's so it is easier to turn your work as you cut. There will be very little waste of fabric when cutting E's and C's together.

Sewing Test

Step 6. Even though the 1/4" seam allowance is included in templates, you can't sew with the full 1/4" seam. Sew with a scant 1/4" seam allowance to make up for fabric used in seam allowance.

Look at steps 6-9 before taking sewing test. Sew one arc together like diagram. Each arc has 4 A's in center and a B at each end.

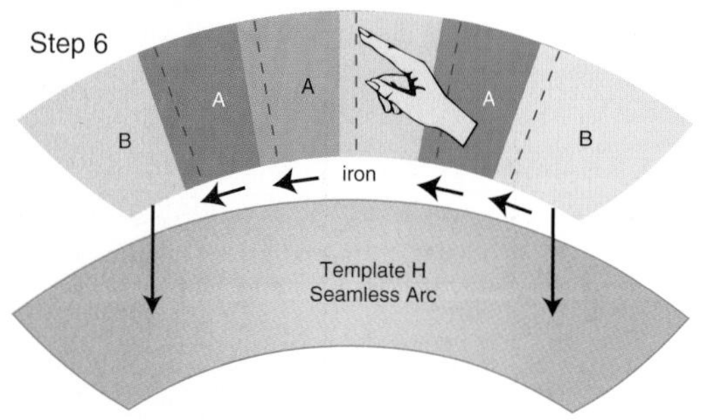

Finger press seams to left before pressing with iron on wrong side. Place sewn arc on top template H (seamless arc template), to see if all six sewn pieces equal the template. If not, adjust seam allowance. Melons will not lie flat if seam allowance is incorrect.

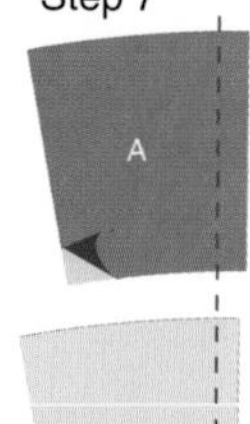

Sewing Arcs

Step 7. To save time and thread, chain sew A's together with a scant 1/4" seam allowance. There is no special order; however, there should be a contrast from one piece to the next so they don't mush together in the arc.

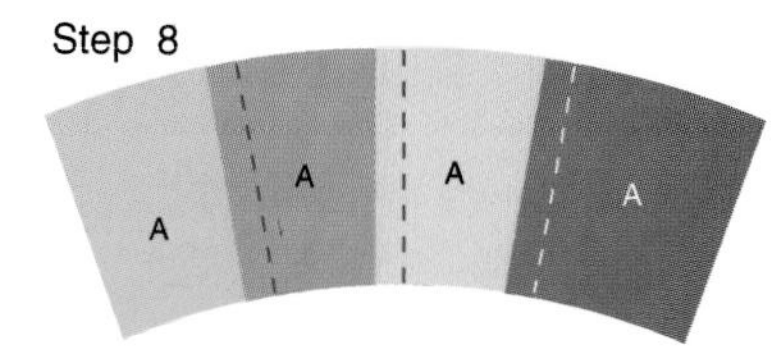

Step 8. Chain sew A's into groups of four.

Step 9. Right sides together match straight edge of B to A. Add one B on each end of arc. Finger press each seam to the left first; then, press seams with an iron.

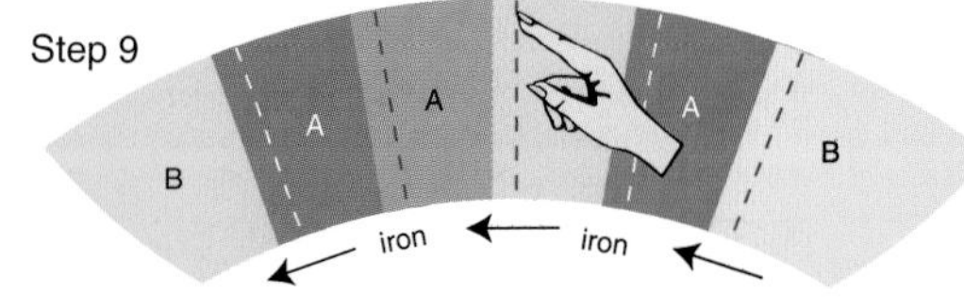

Step 10. Attach connecting corners (D) with different colors on opposite ends. Match curve of D to curve of B. Make sure you put the same color on the same end of arc each time.

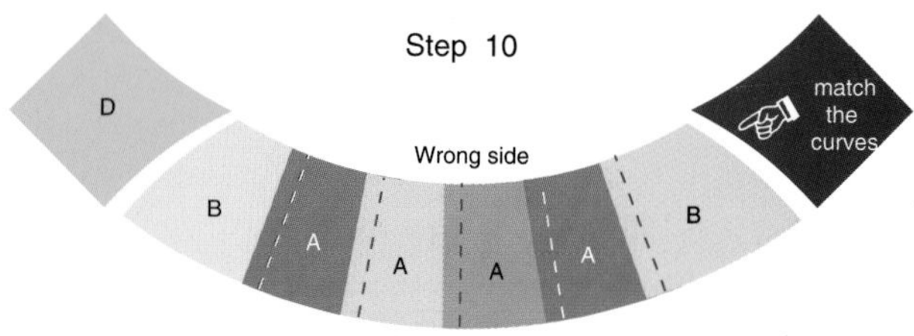

Step 11. With right sides together, place D on top of B. The D piece will extend 1/4" over the top edge when it is lined up correctly. ***Do not back stitch.*** Without using pins, sew a few stitches and stop with needle in down position. Lift presser foot.

Readjust edges of D to fit curve of B on underside and sew a few more stitches. Leave needle in down position and lift presser foot. Adjust edges of D to line with B the rest of the way. Finish seam. ***Do not back stitch***. Repeat this step on opposite end of arc.

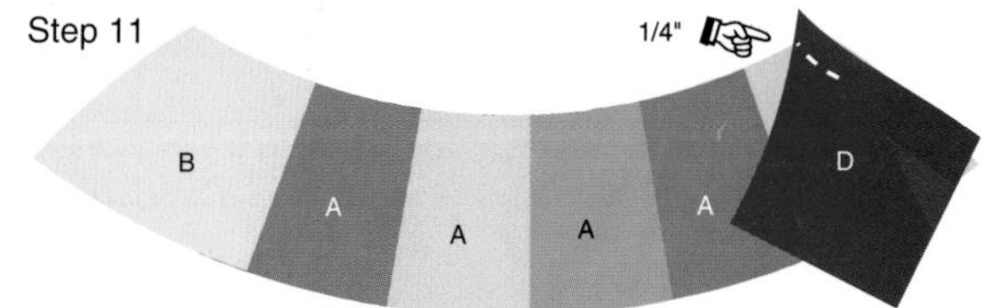

Step 12. Iron the seams of the D's towards the center. Do not stretch the arc when pressing the seams.

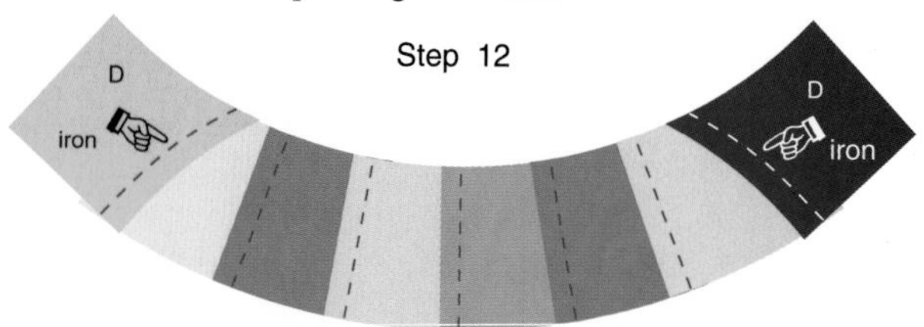

Step 13. Fold melon in half. Cut small notch on folded edge to mark center on both sides. Be careful not to cut into seam line. You could also mark point with a fabric marking pencil. Next, make a dot with a marking pencil 1/4" from sides ***(not from point)*** of C piece.

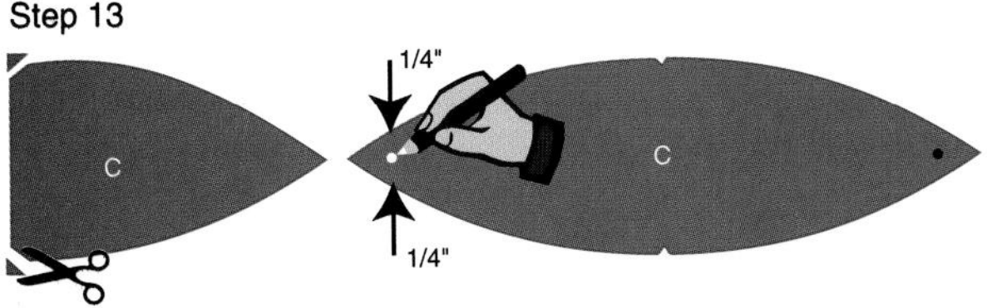

Step 14. To arcs without D's add C melon. Put right sides together. Place pieced arc on top melon. Match center seam of arc to notch of melon. Insert pin to hold. Place pin at each end. Melon overlaps edge by 1/4" when pinned because the 1/4" seam allowance is included. Put one more pin between middle and end on both sides. Sew seam with pieced arc on top for best results. Because you ironed seams of arc to the left you won't have to sew against them now.

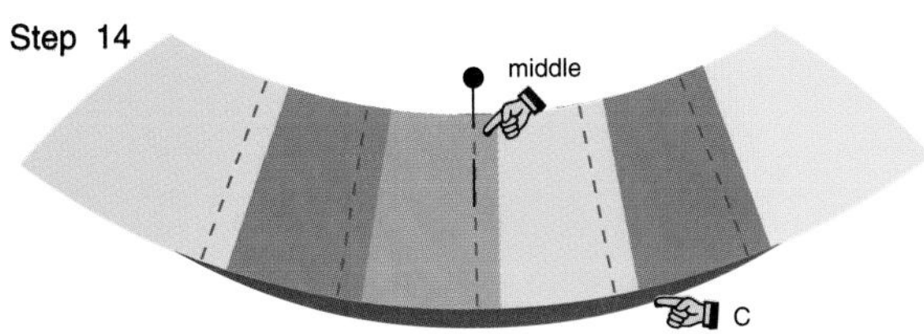

Step 15. Finger press seam towards C melon, then press on back side with iron. Ears of the melon will be extended 1/4". Cut off ears to eliminate bulk in seams.

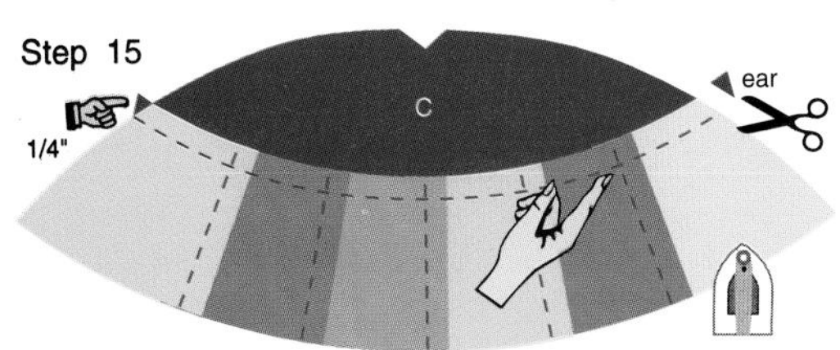

Step 16. With right sides together, place pieced arc with connecting corners on top melon. Match center seam to notch of melon. Silk pins are best for pinning.

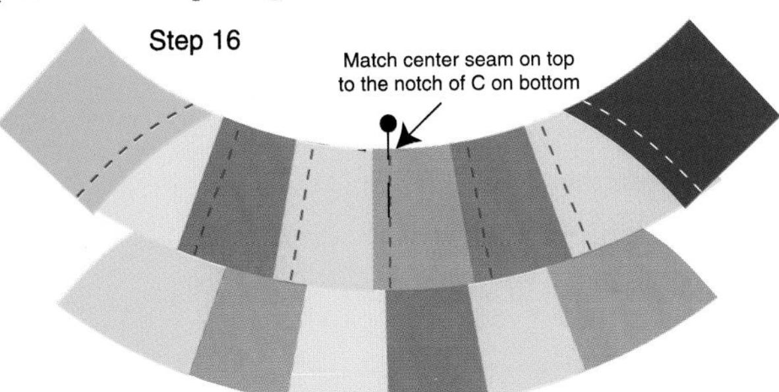

Step 17. Look at arrows & stick a pin on seam line 1/4" in from edge between piece D & B on top. Bring it through 1/4" in from edge on seam line between C and B on bottom. Do not flip this pin backwards into fabric; it is just holding pieces in place temporarily until you insert a pin on either side of it. Before you remove center pin, make a mark there with a pencil. Remove center pin before you sew seam. Place pins at ends of D pieces and several places along the edge. Refer to diagram.

Do not back stitch at beginning or end of seam. Sew directly over intersection you marked with a pencil between D and B. Press this seam towards C. If melon does not lie flat, your seam allowance has been too big or too small.

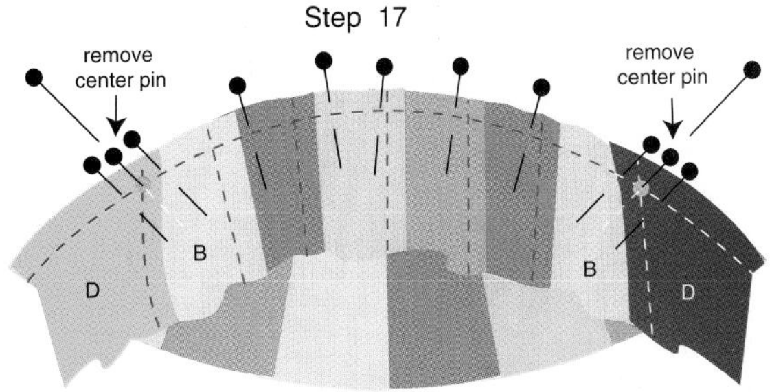

Step 18. Fold E into fourths. Cut a small notch on the fold. Careful! Don't cut into seam allowance. This is only for marking purposes. On all four tails of E make a dot with a fabric marking pencil 1/4" from all three edges.

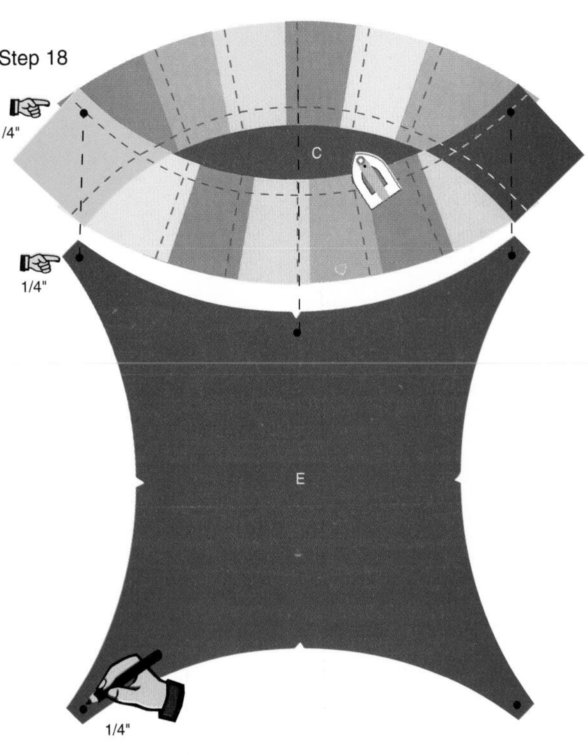

Step 19. With E on top, match center seam line of pieced melon to notch on E. Pin both corners at dots of background E to melon on seam line 1/4" from edge between B and D. Back stitch to point where pin goes in. Sew to other corner and back stitch. It's important to sew only to point where pin enters for perfect corners. Never sew to the end of E.

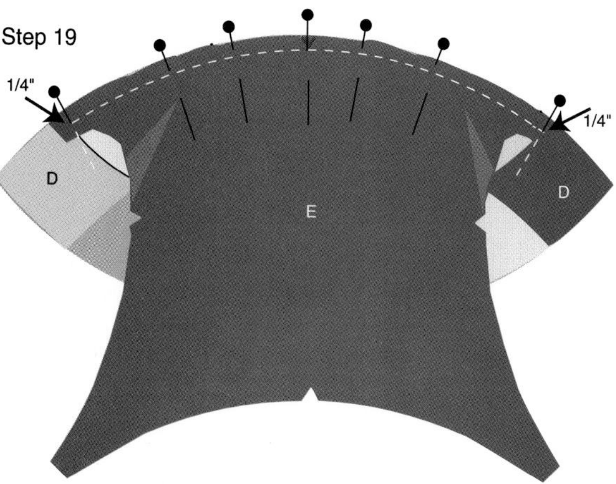

Step 20. Make sure you have the right connecting corners together when you start attaching them to E.

Always sew with E on top and never sew to end of E tails as indicated by arrows. I guide the fabric in front of the presser foot with a stiletto as I sew. Fold seam back in corners where the arrow is pointing.

Do not sew connecting corners (D's) together yet. This will be done after rows are connected. Press these seams towards E.

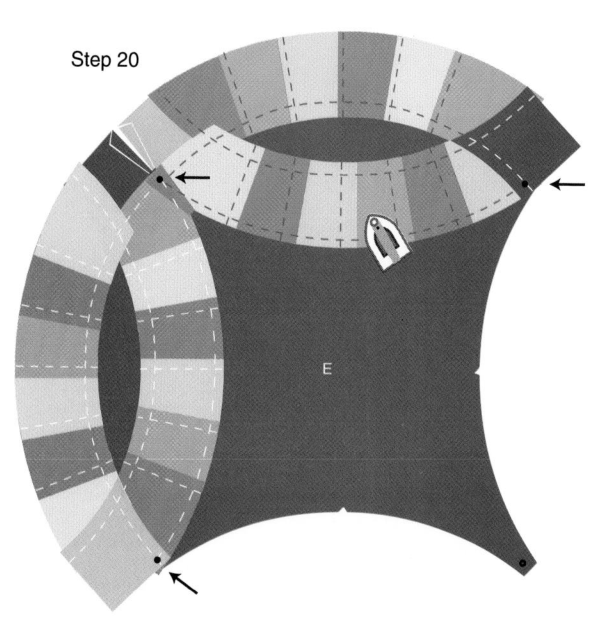

Connecting Circles

Step 21. After you have made one complete circle, make the connecting circle with three sides. Lay out the melons ahead of time so colors of connecting corners alternate correctly. You don't want to spend time ripping. When you add the connecting circle, sew with the E background on top and stop at each dot. ***Do not sew connecting corners yet.*** You can adjust the quilt to any size by adding circles.

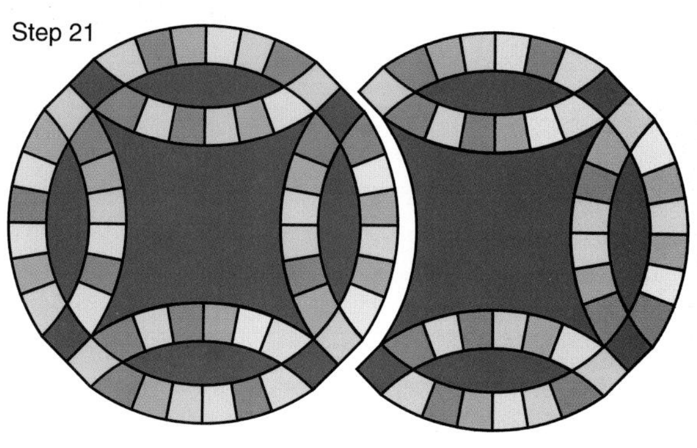

Connecting the Rows

Step 22. With right sides together, place the E's of the first row on top of the 2nd row and match up the center seams of the melons to the notches on the E pieces. Put a pin in each center and at each corner, connecting the dots on the E to the seam line between D & B. Treat each circle as a separate seam and back stitch at each dot. Do not sew through the tails of the E piece and do not sew the connecting corners until the row is completed.

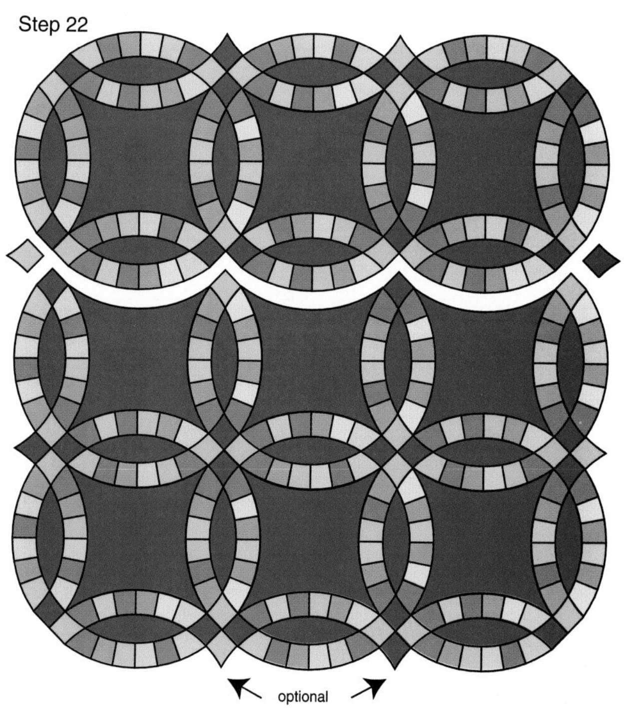

Step 23. The very last seams are the connecting corners at intersections of circles. First, sew two sets of seams across from each other indicated by arrows. When you sew these seams, start from center, sew towards dot and backstitch. Notice how the tail of E is not included in the seam. Bend it back out of the way when you approach the corner. Next, sew the last seam across the middle, flip-flopping the seams of the intersection in opposite directions. Back stitch at each end of this seam. Press tails of the intersection in opposite directions. Back stitch at each end of this seam. Press tails of E open and flat like the drawing shows. Notice how seams meet at dot.

Adding connecting corners on the outside edge of the quilt is optional. These are added after the quilt has reached its finished size. Look at the diagram to the left.

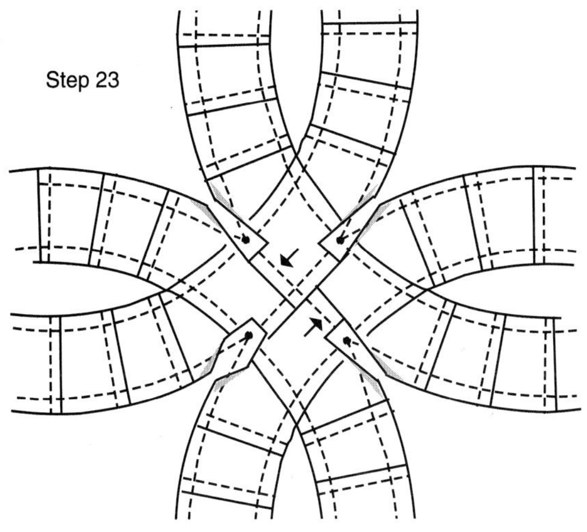

Finishing Touches

Read page 6 to make finishing touches.

Binding Your Quilt

To keep layers of quilt sandwich from shifting while attaching binding, hand baste or sew along outside edge with a walking foot 1/8" from edge. Trim excess batting and back fabric away from edge before attaching binding.

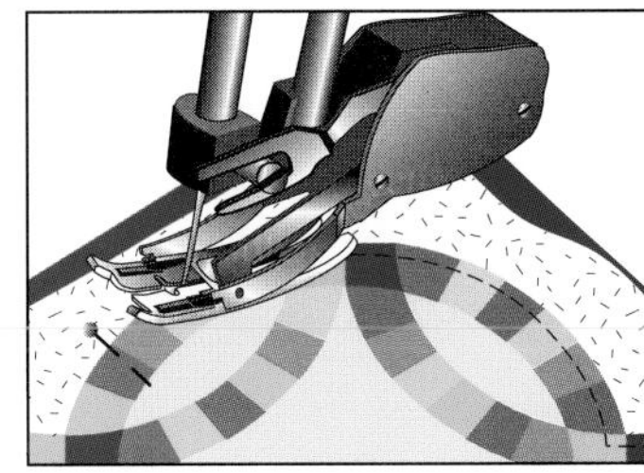

Step 1. Cut 2" strips on the bias. Trim both ends of all strips at a 45° angle so the bulk will be evenly distributed when attached. Sew strips at a 45° angle so bulk will be evenly distributed when attached. Sew strips together and press seams open. Fold 1/4" back at the beginning and press.

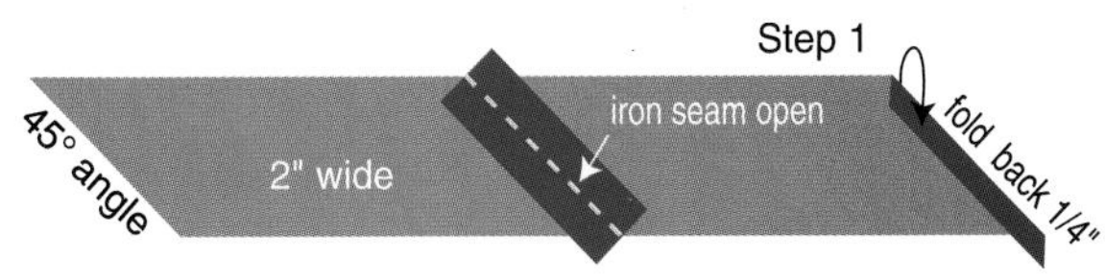

Step 2. Fold the binding in half and press.

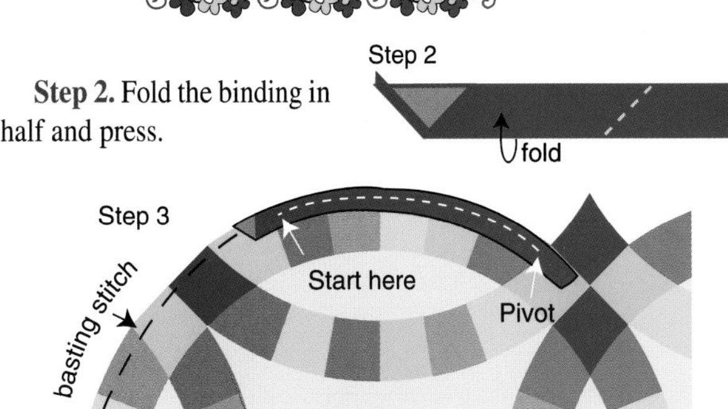

Step 3. Start at the end with the 1/4" folded back. Place on right side of quilt and make sure a seam does not fall on a corner. If it does, find a new place to start. Match quilt edge to cut edge of binding. Start sewing 1" after 1/4" fold so end of binding can be slipped inside for a nice finish. ***Do not stretch*** binding as you sew around curves.

When you get to an inside curve, stop needle in down position. Lift presser foot.

Step 4. Readjust fabric and sew to 1/4" from point of connecting corner. Back stitch and cut thread.

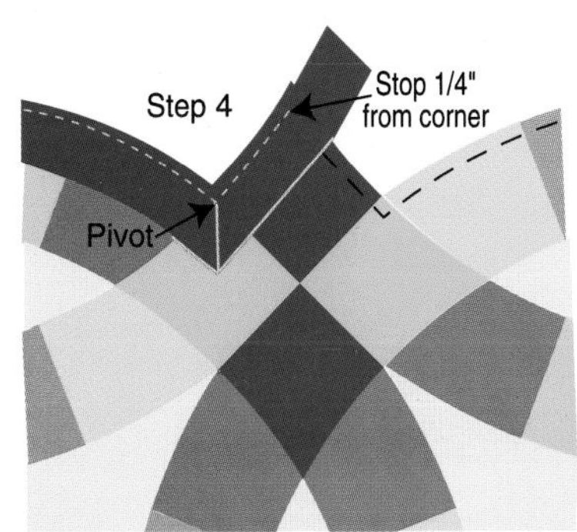

Step 5. Turn your work and fold binding back. Binding edge and quilt edge should make a straight line when folded regardless of the angle of the quilt corner. This fold starts the miter on the corner.

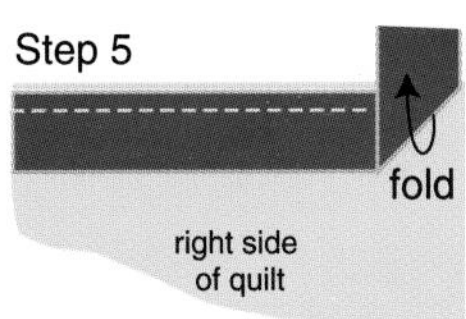

Step 6. Place your finger on first fold and flip binding down to make second fold even with binding; this will complete the miter. Finger pin and start sewing from outside edge and pivot on next inside corner. Repeat these steps until you are around complete quilt.

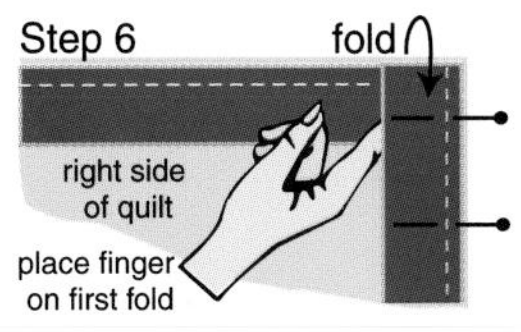

Step 7. Turn binding to back side of quilt to form the miter.

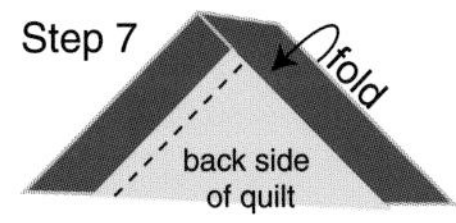

Step 8. Fold other side over to complete mitered corner of connecting corner. Bulk in corners will be opposite each other on top and bottom. Use matching thread and sew with a blind stitch.

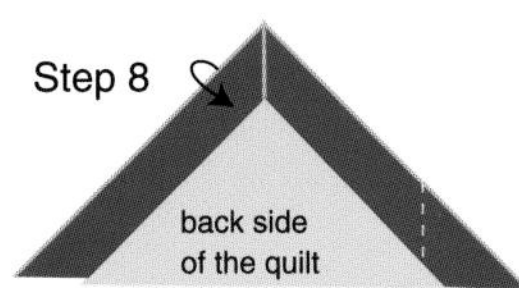

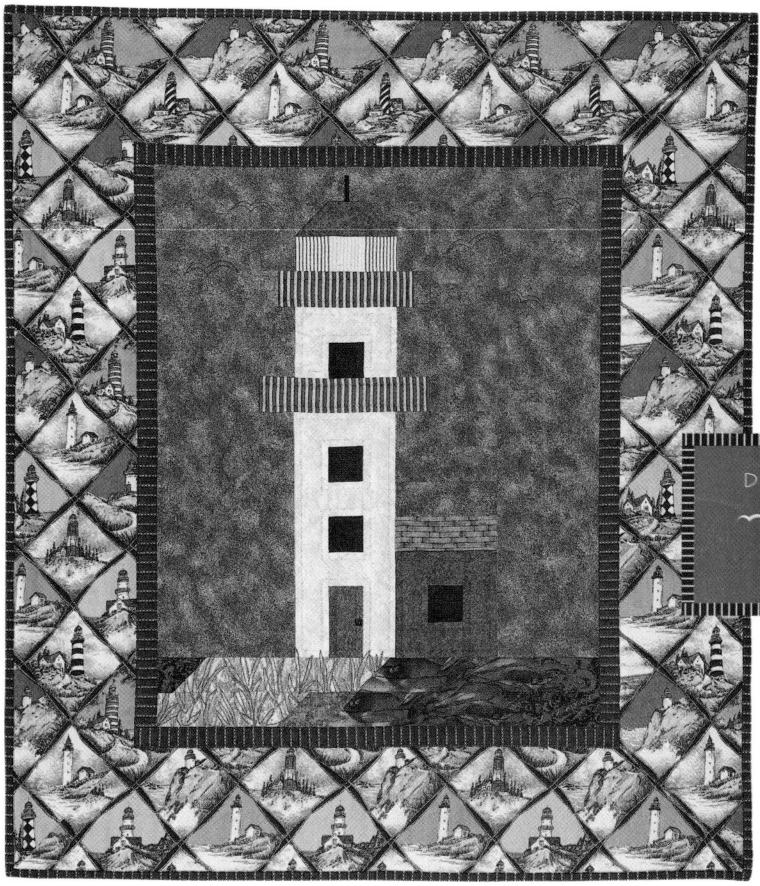

DESIGNED & PIECED BY SHARLENE JORGENSON
MACHINE QUILTED BY PHYLLIS PETERSEN

DESIGNED BY SHARLENE JORGENSON
PIECED BY PHYLLIS PETERSEN
MACHINE QUILTED BY MARCIA STEVENS

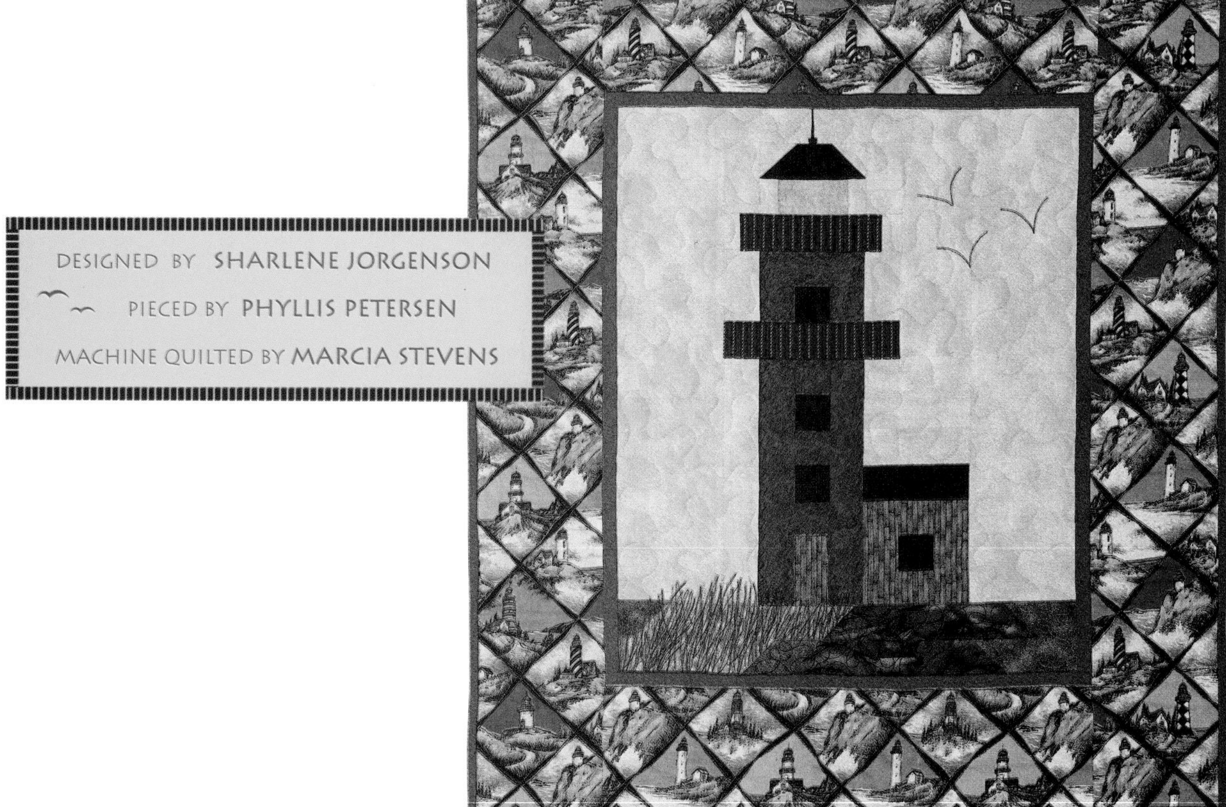

SHOPPING LIST
- QS28 Log Cabin Templates
- Quick Grips
- Omnigrid® Rulers 6" x 24"
- Fiskars® Rotary Cutter
- IBC Glass Head Pins 0.50mm steel shaft
- Fairfield poly-fil low-loft batting

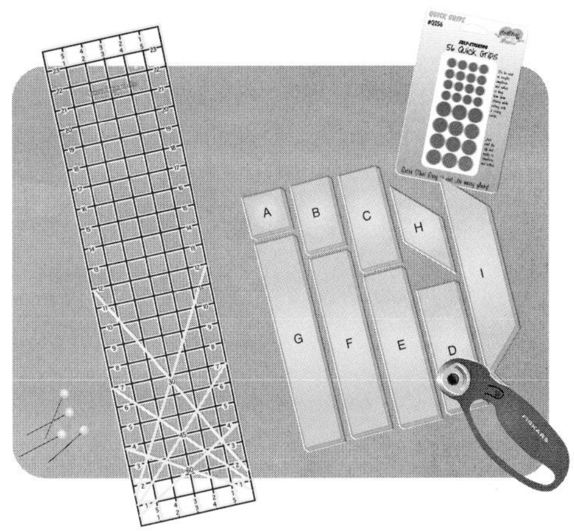

Read pages 2-7 before starting.

THE LIGHTHOUSE

First choose border fabric to create the palette. Because I couldn't make up my mind, I purchased three different fabrics that could be used for the border. All three fabrics included the same colors so I didn't have to make the final decision until the quilt was ready for the border.

Next pick a fabric without much texture for the sky so it doesn't matter which direction the logs are cut. If the quilt has a light sky fabric, pick fabrics for a dark light house and if you pick fabric for a dark sky the light house looks better made from a light fabric. I was lucky to find a fabric that resembles stucco for both the ivory and red part of the Lighthouse. Striped fabric was used for both cat walks and wood grain fabrics were used for roof and door. I found fabrics with perfect textures for the grass, rocks and water. The water should be darker than the sky to establish a shore line. After experimenting with different border widths, I decided to use a striped fabric for the inside border (cut 1" wide). When it ended up as a small wall quilt I was able to eliminate two large scale border fabrics. The outside border was cut 5" wide.

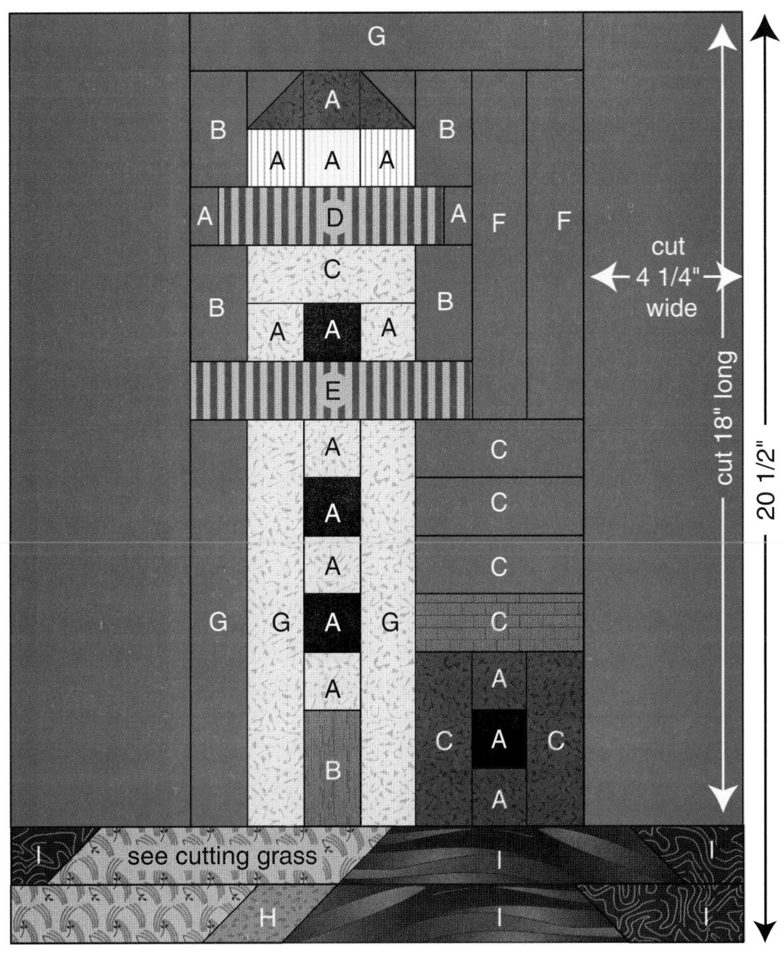

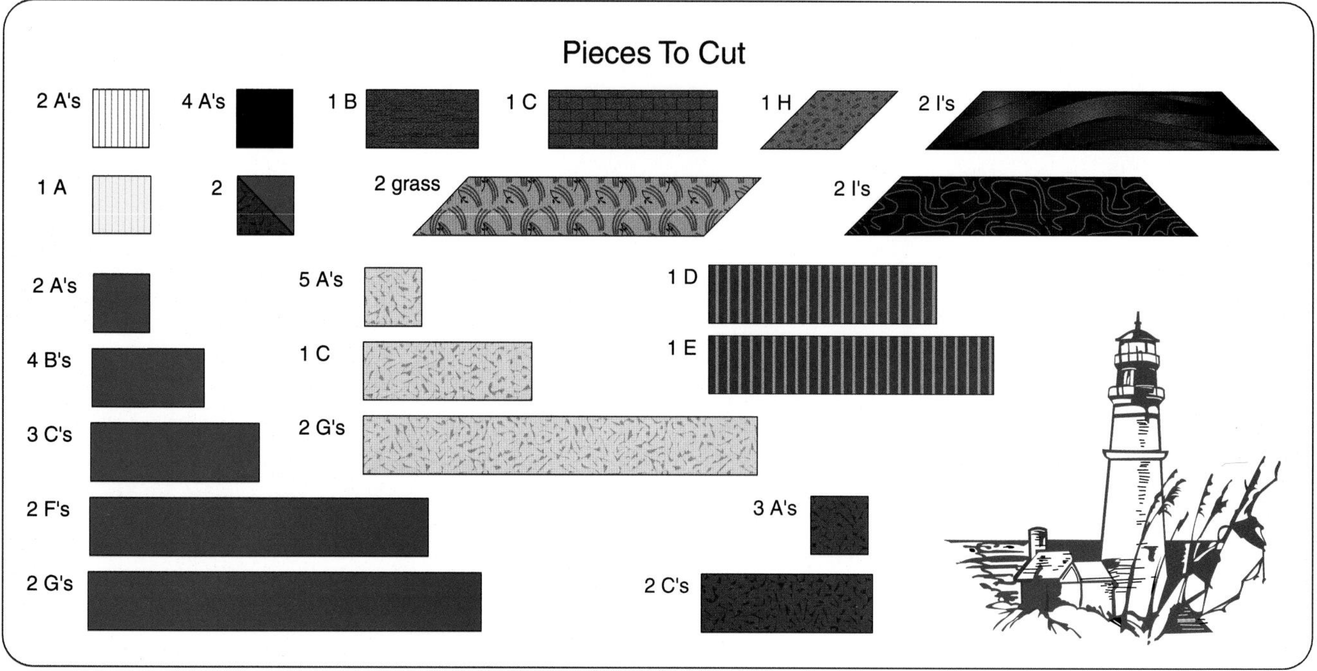

Cutting Strips

Step 1. To save fabric when cutting pieces for a design that needs only a few pieces from each print, cut strips width of template.

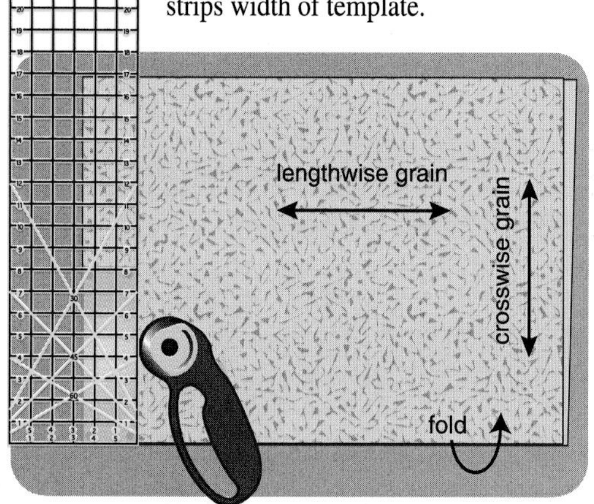

Step 2. Diagram below shows different pieces being cut from same strip to save fabric when cutting pieces for light house.

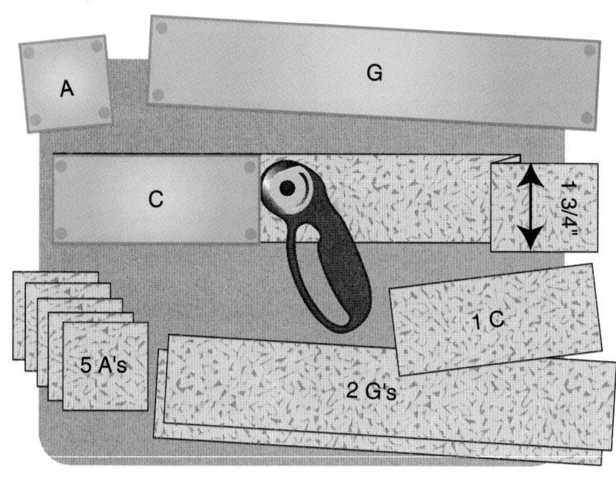

Cutting Bias Strips

Step 3. Because such a small amount of fabric is needed for roof of lighthouse, I purchased a fat quarter. Place roof and sky fabric right sides together as shown in diagram below. Match 45° line of ruler with bottom edge of fabrics. Cut one strip 1 3/4" wide.

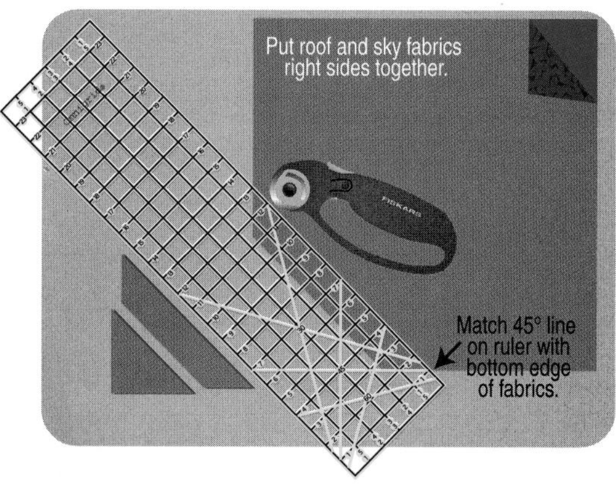

Step 4. Sew bias strips together. Finger press seams open before pressing with iron. Place template A on top of strips. Match corners of template to seam line. Cut only one at a time.

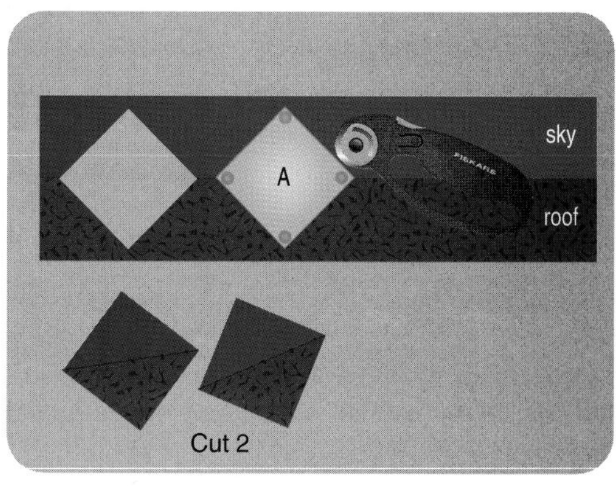

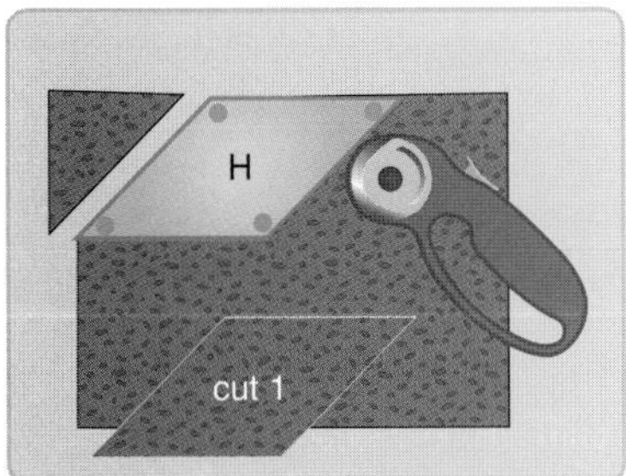

Step 5. Place stone fabric on a small mat board so it is easy to turn your work as you cut around the template. Cut one H for stones to go between grass and rocks on the shore.

Step 6. Buy fat quarters for water and rocks because such a small amount is needed. Cut strips 1 3/4" wide from water and rock fabric. Place template on strips and cut 2 of each.

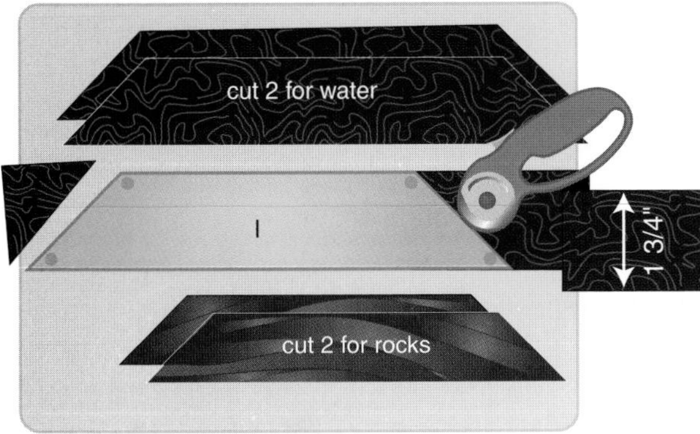

Step 7. Use template I to cut grass. Start with a strip 1 3/4" wide. I improvised by flipping the I template 180° to get the diamond needed for the grass. You can experiment with different lengths. Pieces don't have to be same length because excess will be cut off in step 20. See diagram below.

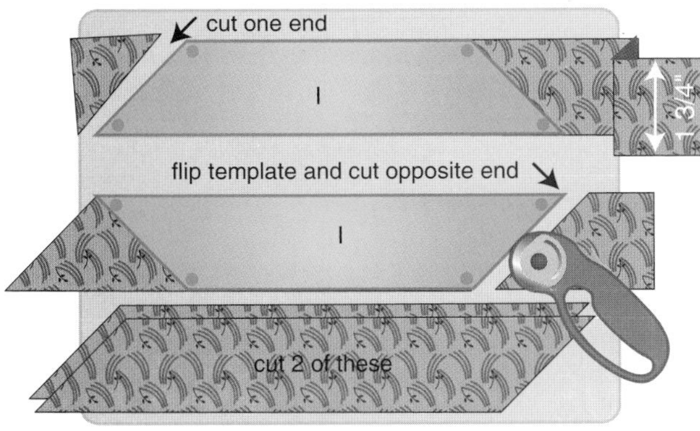

Sewing Instructions

Step 8. Sew all seams with a scant 1/4" seam allowance to make up for fabric used in seam line. Two A's sewn together should equal B template. If not, adjust your seam allowance before continuing.

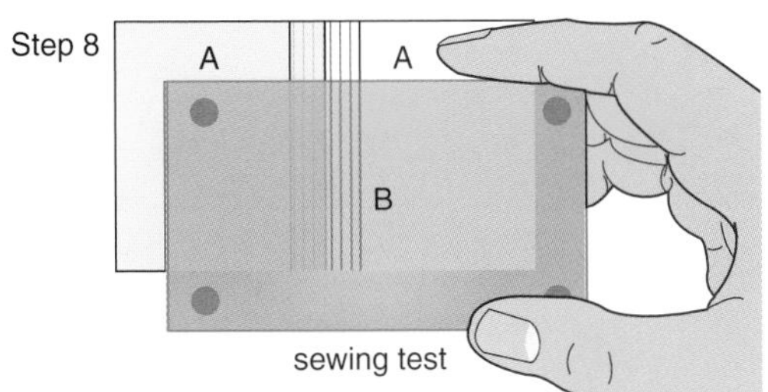

Step 9. Construction of lighthouse starts with the roof. Right sides together put half square triangle unit cut in Step 4 on top of an A square. Make sure unit is turned in right direction. Match corners. Do not back stitch at beginning or end of seam. Start sewing on an anchor cloth so beginning stitches on patchwork won't pull apart as easily as first stitches sewn. To prevent uneven seams, guide pieces in front of presser foot with stiletto to end of seam. Finger press seams open before pressing with an iron. Intersections should be 1/4" from edge.

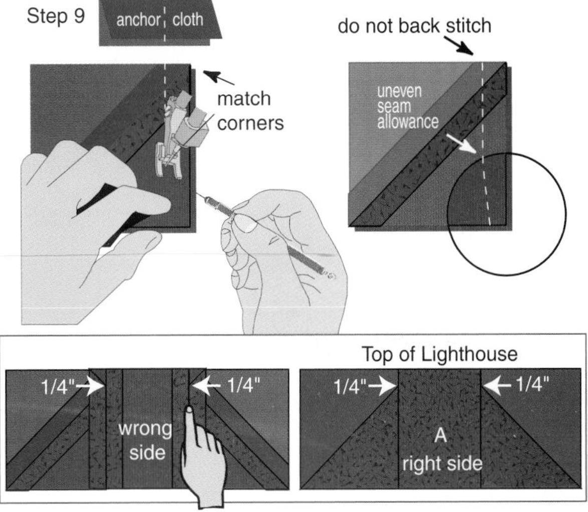

Pinning Options

Accurate pinning is the key to getting seams perfectly matched. I show you two methods of matching seams and suggest you try both and pick one that works best for you. Seams are pressed open with both methods. Pressed open seams take more time but results are a quilt that lies flat and hangs straight.

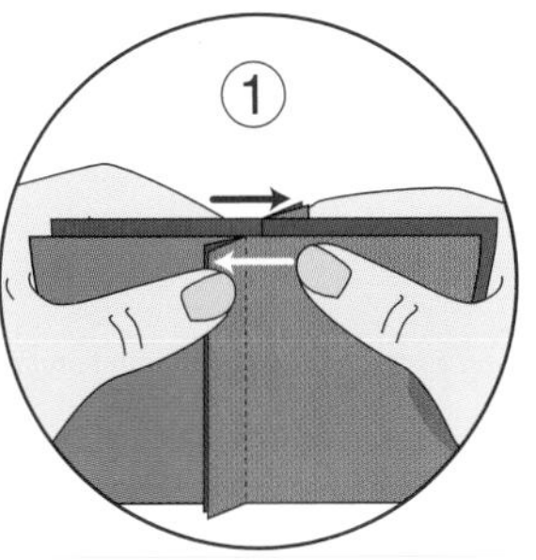

1. To make it easier to match seams pressed open, tip seam allowances in opposite directions.

2. Slide intersecting seams together. Raised area of opposing seams helps to make a perfect match.

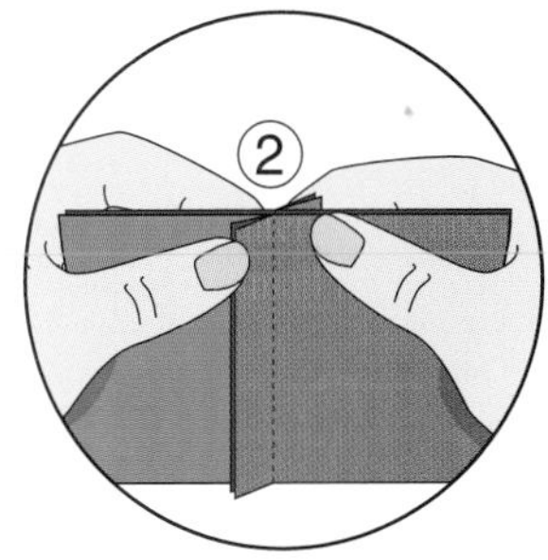

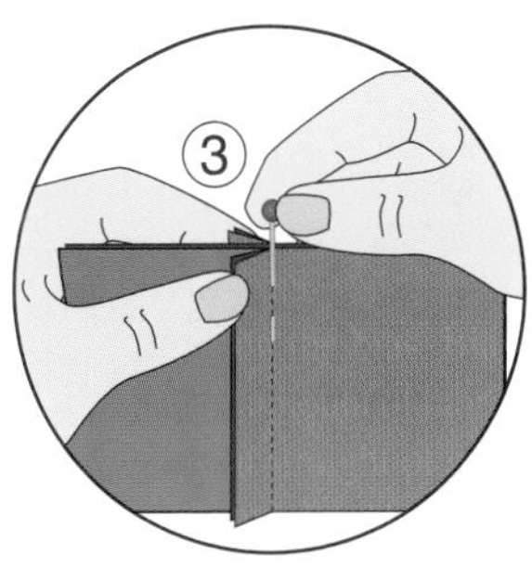

3. Without disturbing match, tip bottom seam allowance in same direction as top seam allowance and firmly hold in place. Secure match with pin on seam line through the block, not the seam allowance.

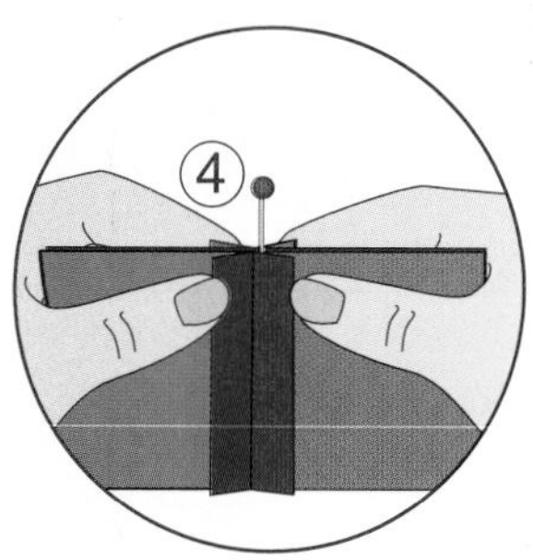

4. Pin is hidden when seam allowance is flipped open. Sew slowly when sewing over pin. The seam is stitched as an opened seam. The results are a flat block when pressed. Step 10 shows second method for matching intersecting seams.

Step 10a. Connect three A's together for light section. Put yellow A in center. Press seams open. Three A's sewn together should equal C template.

b. Right sides together put roof section on top of light section. Make sure seam is sewn on *bottom edge* of roof unit. Insert pin 1/4" from edge through top and bottom. Leave this pin standing.

c. On both sides of standing pin insert another pin through seam allowance to hold intersection in place. Remove standing pin before sewing.

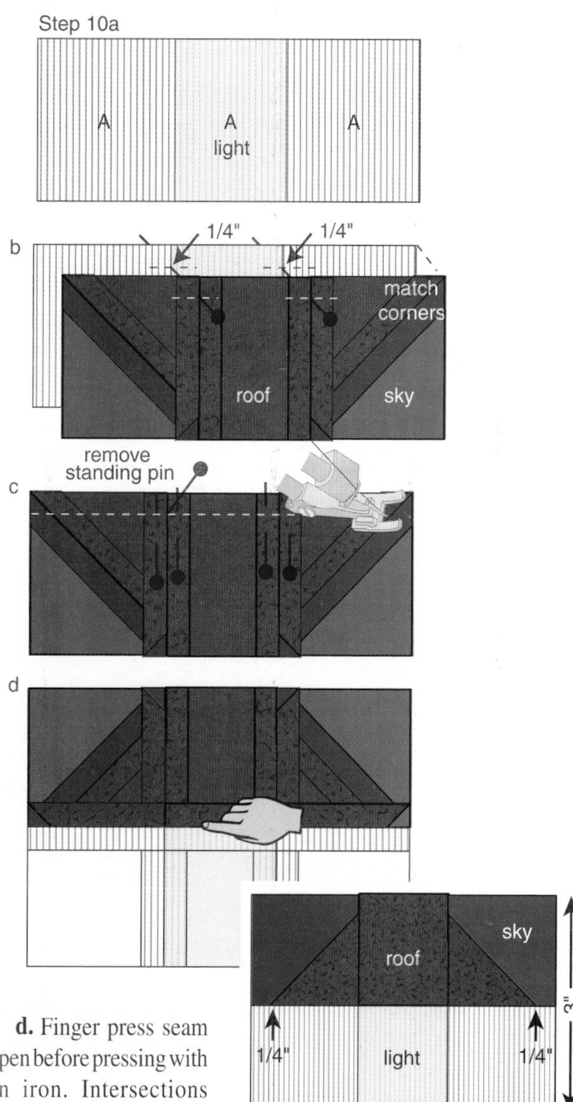

d. Finger press seam open before pressing with an iron. Intersections should be 1/4" from edge.

Step 11. Right sides together add B sky piece to both ends of block. Sew seam with B on bottom so intersection you want to sew over is visible. Sew directly over intersection. Finger press seam open before pressing with an iron.

Step 12a. Right sides together add sky piece A to both ends of D cat walk. Press seams open.

b. Place template E in center of unit

c. Remove both ends with rotary cutter.

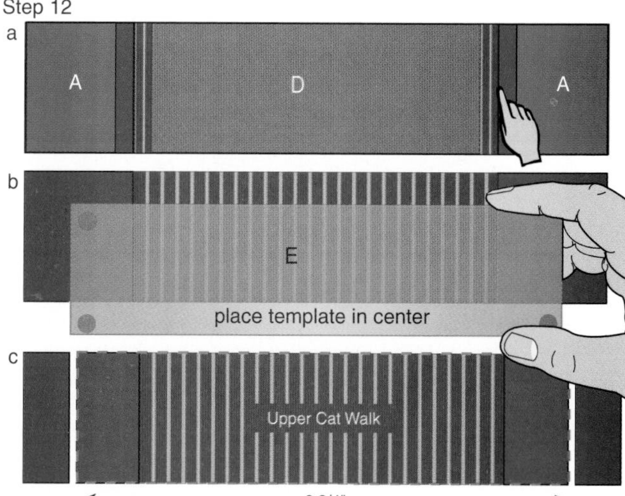

Step 13. Add cat walk made in step 12. Press seam open.

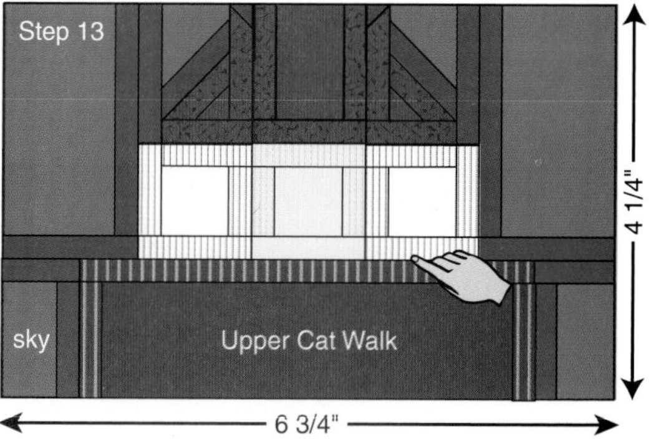

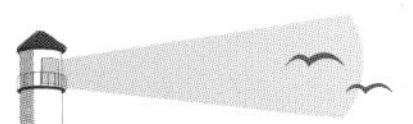

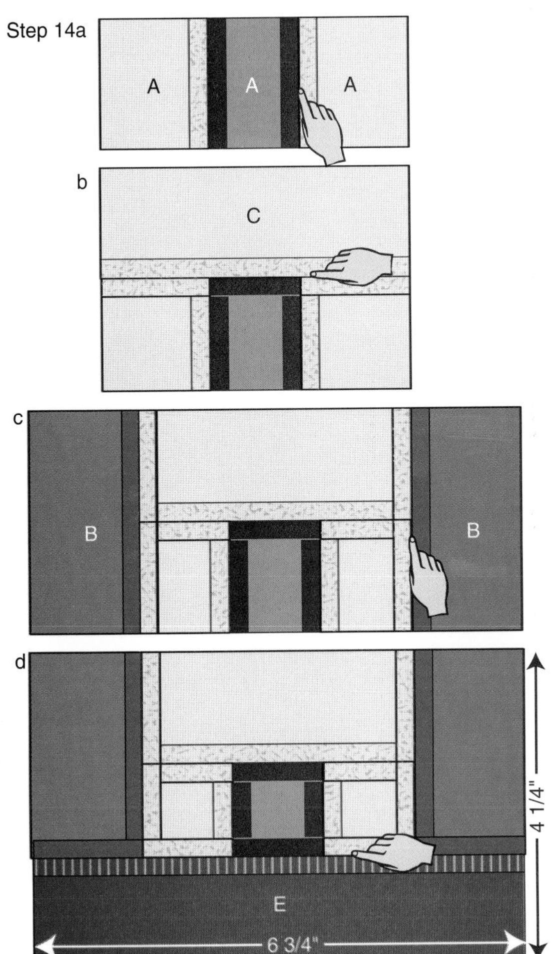

Step 14a. Put a black A (window) between two light A's. Press seams open. These pieces sewn together should equal the C piece.

b. Add a light C to top edge. Press seam open.

c. Add sky B piece to both sides of unit. Press seam open.

d. Add cat walk E piece to bottom edge.

Step 15. Connect units made in Steps 13 &14. Press seam open.

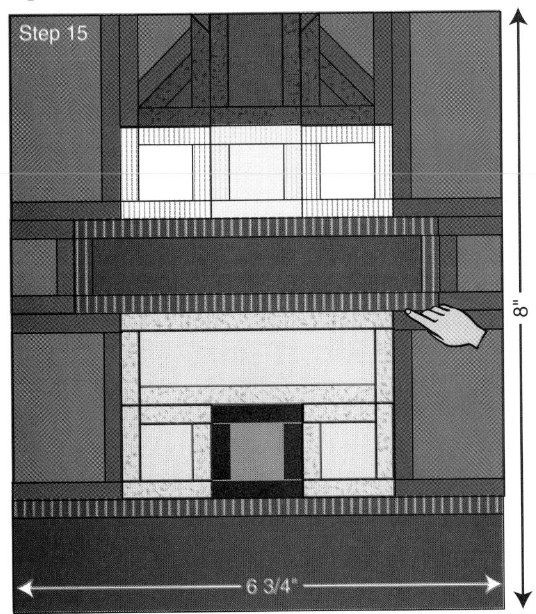

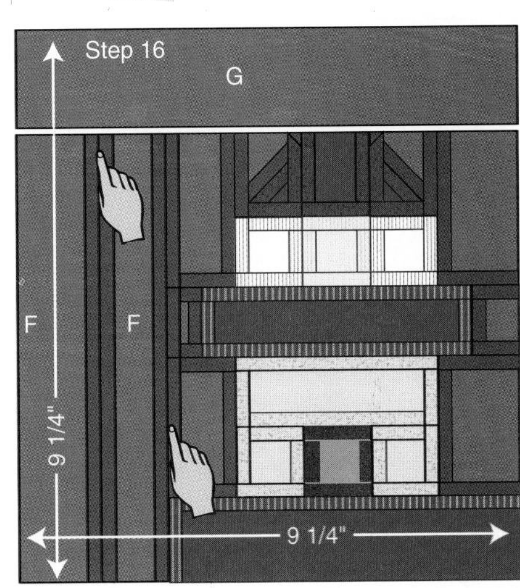

Step 16. Add two F's from sky fabric to edge of unit as shown. Press seams open. Next add a sky G piece to top edge. Block should be a 9 1/4" square after G is added.

Step 17. Start building bottom of lighthouse by connecting pieces as shown in diagram Press all seams open.

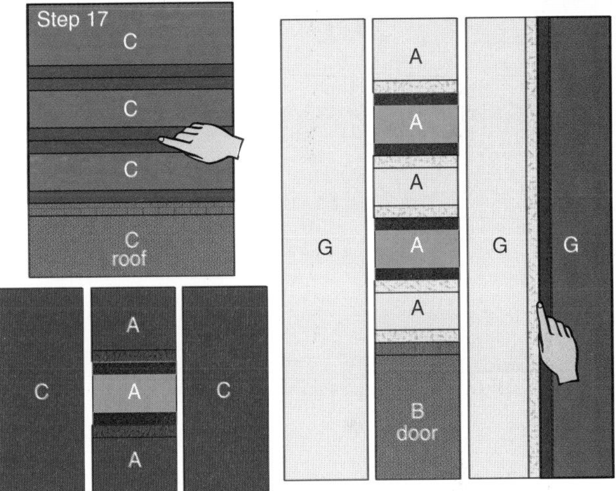

Step 18. Continue to connect pieces together as shown. Press seams open. Block should be a 9 1/4" square after center seam is sewn.

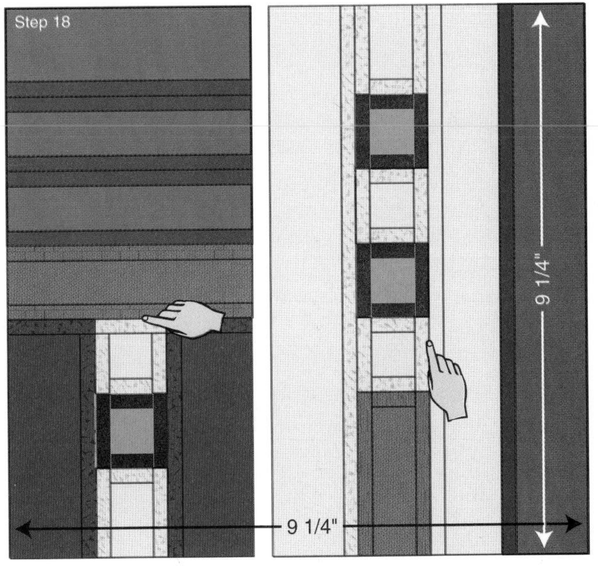

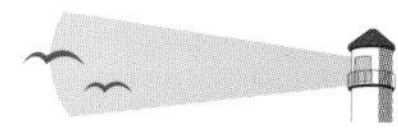

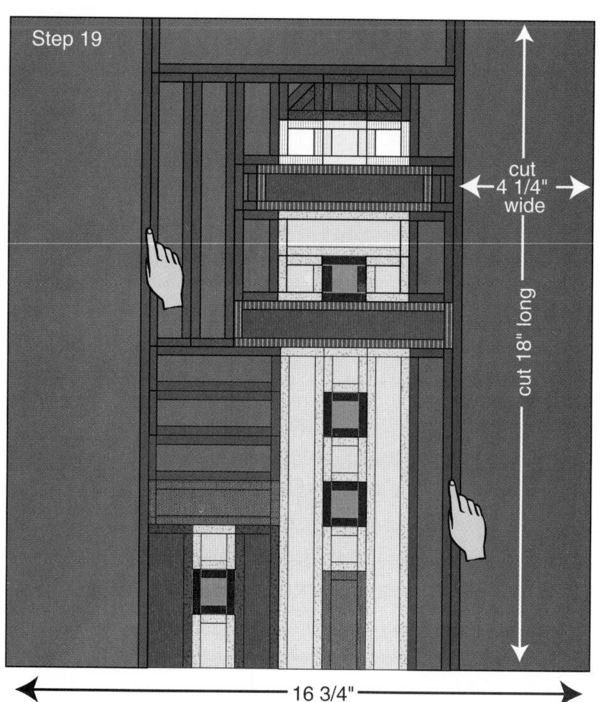

Step 19. Connect top of lighthouse from Step 16 to bottom of lighthouse completed in Step 18. To each side add a strip of sky 4 1/4" wide and 18" long. Press all seams open.

Sewing Foundation For Lighthouse

Step 20

a. Connect water, grass, and rocks into rows. Finger press seams open before pressing with iron.

b. There is only one intersection to match when sewing this seam. Right sides together. Insert pin 1/4" from edge through top and bottom to match seams. Flip pin into fabric and sew seam.

c. Press seam open.

d. To find the desired placement for the foundation, I moved it back and forth under the lighthouse before trimming both ends with a rotary cutter. Foundation should be 16 3/4" long when trimmed.

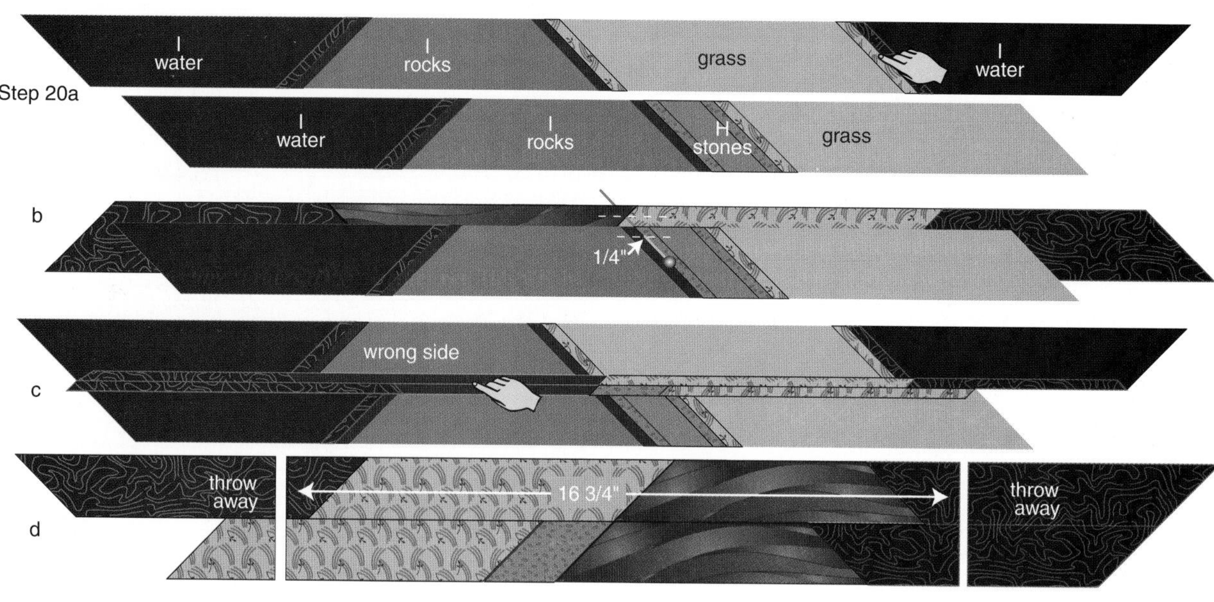

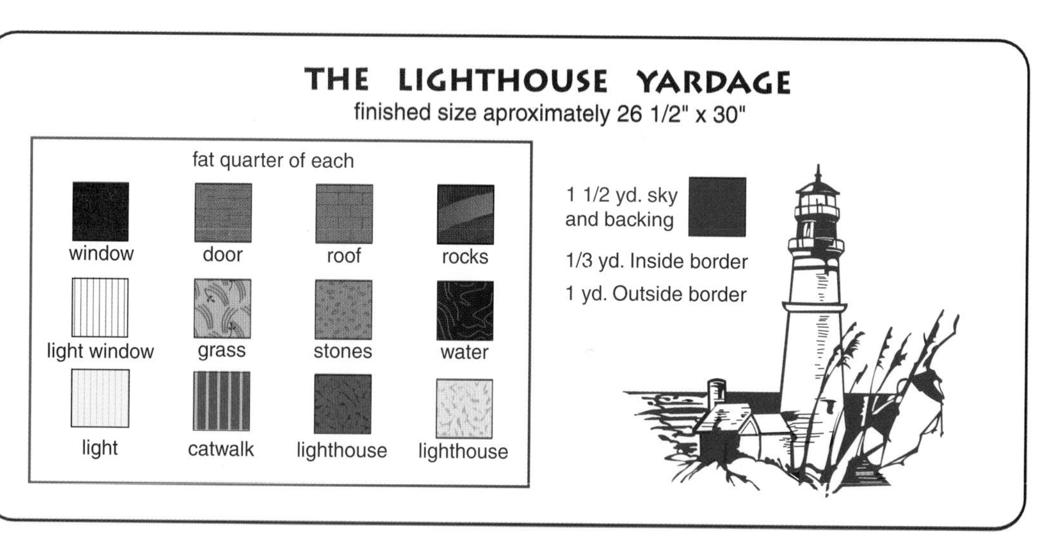

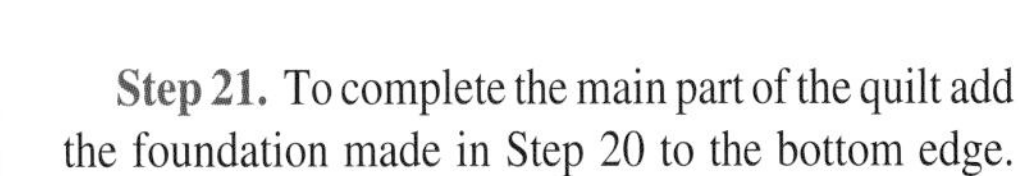

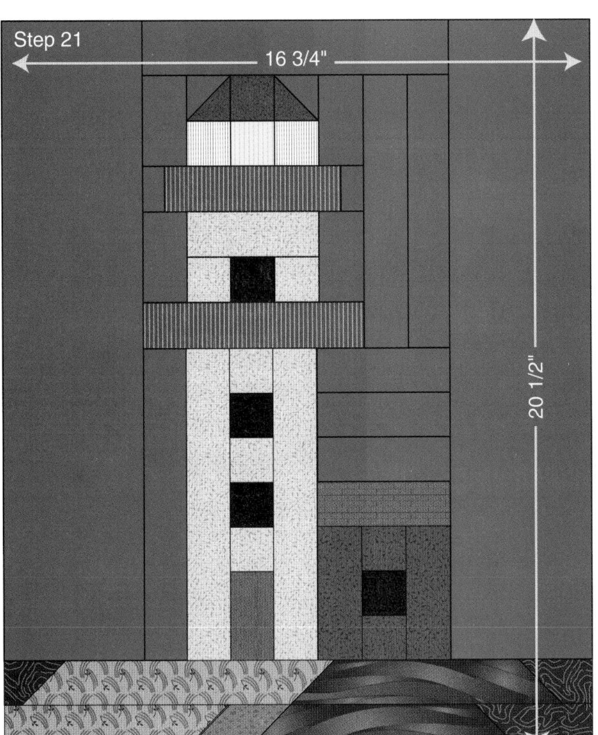

Step 21. To complete the main part of the quilt add the foundation made in Step 20 to the bottom edge. Press seam open.

Finishing Touches

Step 22. I cut strips for inside border 1" wide from a striped fabric. Cut strips for outside border 5" wide.

After borders have been added it's time to be quilted. My quilt was machine quilted. Different sizes of sea gulls were drawn in the sky and quilted with a white Sulky thread. We ignored some of the seam lines and treated each color as one piece. Top stitching was done 1/4" from the edge as shown in the diagram. Different colors were used to match each area. Brown and green thread were used for the grass to add dimension and a button was added for the door knob. Large meandering was done in the sky. For the meandering we used a thread a shade darker than the sky fabric. Crosshatching seamed to be the perfect solution for the outside border because we could follow the design in the fabric. The fabric used for the inside border was repeated for the binding.

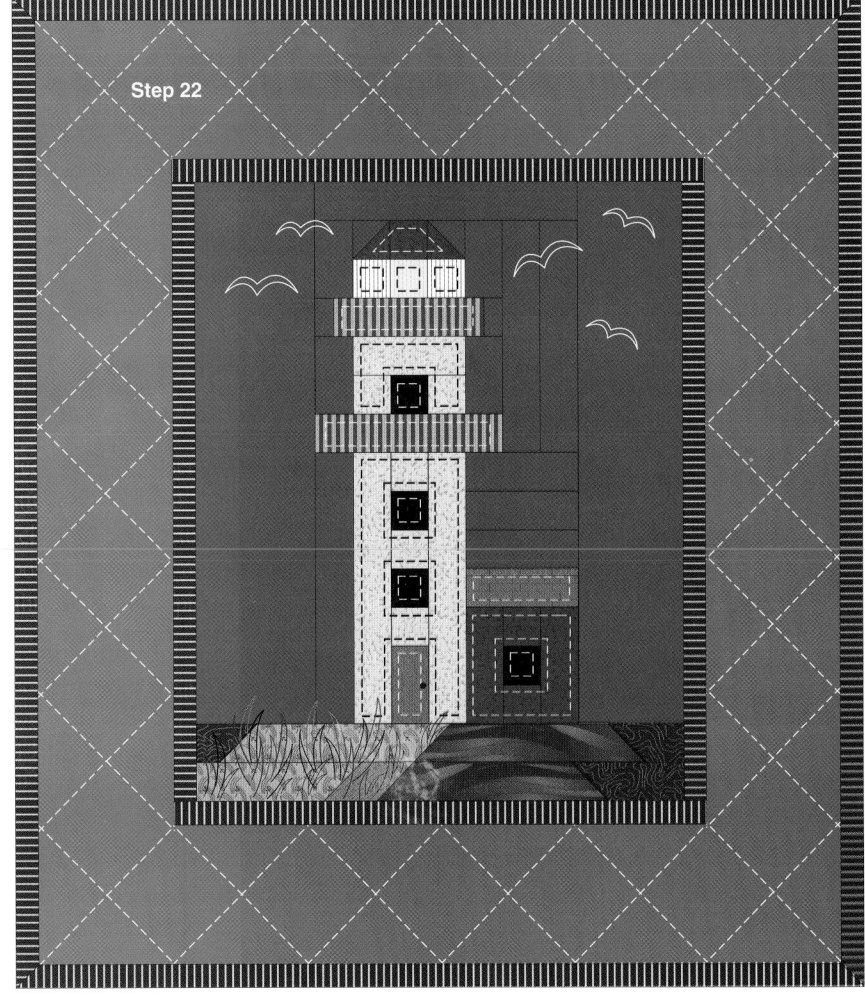

The Story

In 1995, I took a group of American quilters to Norway. We had a marvelous time seeing the sights, visiting Norwegian quilters and buying fabric. Our grand finale was a weekend quilting retreat with Americans and Norwegians. We held two days of classes, showed and told and spent our off moments in the little merchants mall. I hate to admit in print that by then I was down to my last kroner but the fabric had been so-o-o beautiful. Two women from Sandefjord came in with a basket full of the most wonderful little chicken pin cushions. I scraped the bottom of my purse and borrowed from my daughter to buy a chicken. When I got home I figured out how to make them by sewing log cabins on paper. First I gave them as gifts, then I sold the extras at quilt guilds. Wonderful chicken names started to inspire color choices-"funky chicken," "spring chicken," "little red hen," and "chicken cordon bleu" to name a few. I never planned to teach chicken making but I was in desperate need for a quick fun class for the Pt. Bonita Quilt Retreat and the chicken filled the bill. Since then the chickens have spread like wild fire and the variations have been exciting. It didn't occur to me to make a pattern for what wasn't my own original idea. But I have seen some of the second and third generation chickens and realized I could help with the log cabin papers, a little ultra suede for the comb and beak instructions.

Doreen Speckmann

After seeing Doreen's chickens I called her and told her that we had templates for the miniature Logs and she said it was perfect to speed up production.

> Dear Shar,
> Just got the templates and chicken design. I think these were made for each other. I've used the paper piecing because it was fine for the small stuff. But you know, I'd rather use templates any day. I'll have time to play with them at Sievers this week. Didn't have time to make you a chicken – busy, busy.
>
> Yours
> Doreen

Let us know if you have any ideas to add to this hybrid we've hatched.

Doreen passed away very suddenly and was never able to see my final interpretation of this wonderful design. The quilt world will miss her creativity, friendship, and sense of humor.

Sharlene Jorgenson

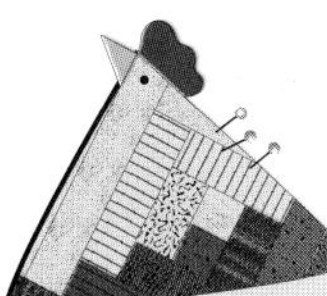

Chicken Pin Cushion

Shopping List

- QS33 Miniature Log Cabin (pin cushion)
- QS28 Log Cabin (door stop)
- Quick Grips
- Omnigrid® Rulers 6" x 24"
- Fiskars® Rotary Cutter
- IBC Glass Head Pins 0.50mm steel shaft
- Fairfield poly-fil low-loft batting
- Six light and seven dark fabric scraps
- Crushed walnut shells, rice, aquarium gravel or wool

Chicken Pin Cushion

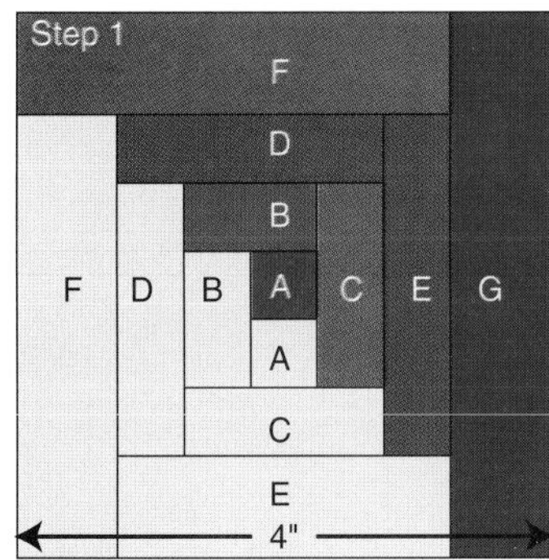

Step 1. To make a pin cushion use templates A, B, C, D, E, F and G from QS33 miniature Log Cabin templates. To make a door stop use QS28 large Log Cabin templates. I used only scraps for my chickens. Each block is 4" before it is made into the pin cushion.

Stabilizing fabric with spray starch before cutting makes it easier to control small pieces when sewing.

Cutting Instructions for Pin Cushion

For more cutting instructions see page 3.

Step 2. Cut strips 1" wide for pin cushion. Cut different pieces from same strip to save fabric. To make 1 chicken, cut two light and two dark pieces with each log template. One exception is, only dark G's are used. See diagram in step 1. I used six lights and seven darks.

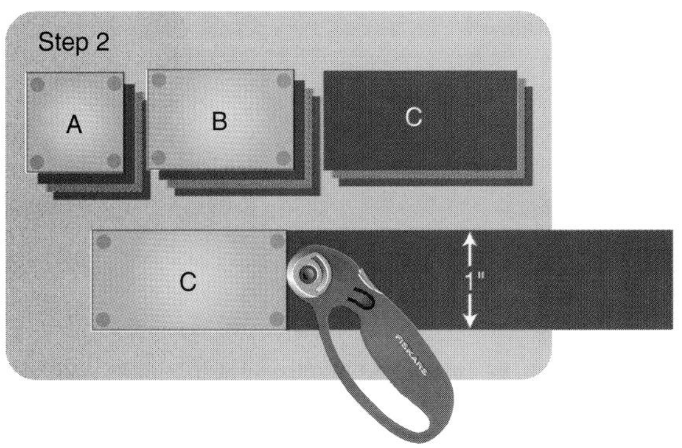

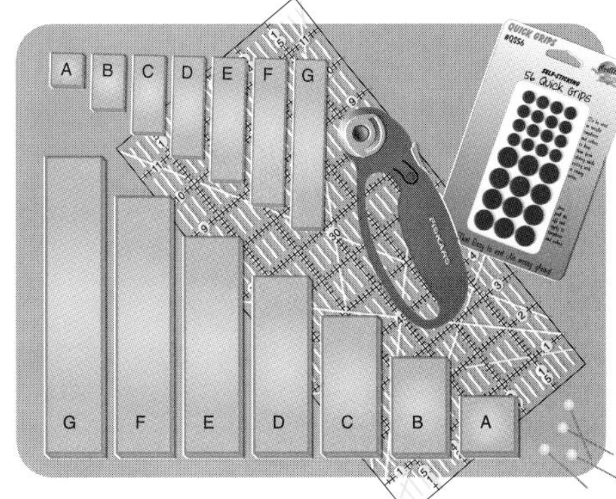

Sewing Test

Sew all seams with a scant 1/4" seam allowance to make up for fabric used in seam line. Two A's sewn together must equal B piece. I find it very helpful to use a stiletto to guide small pieces in front of needle when sewing.

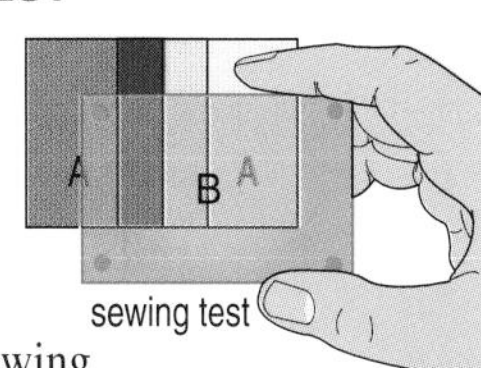

Sewing Instructions

Follow order of Construction on page 24 for pin cushion. Start each block in center. It doesn't matter if you add logs going in clockwise or counter clockwise direction, but you want to make them both the same for each chicken. ***After you have made one round ,always add next log to side that has two seams to cross over (see #5 on page 24).***

Step 3a. Put a light and dark A right sides together. If you start sewing on an anchor cloth, beginning stitches on patchwork will be more secure and won't pull apart as easily as first stitches sewn. Do not back stitch at beginning or end of seam because it will be crossed over by next seam. Back stitching creates bulk in corners. If you are making more than one chicken, chain sew to save time and thread. Clip threads between units.

b. Finger press seam open. Place a light B on left side of A unit.

c. Right sides together, put a light B on bottom. Match corners before sewing.

d. Finger press seams open.

e. Turn unit to right side. Red A is in upper right corner.

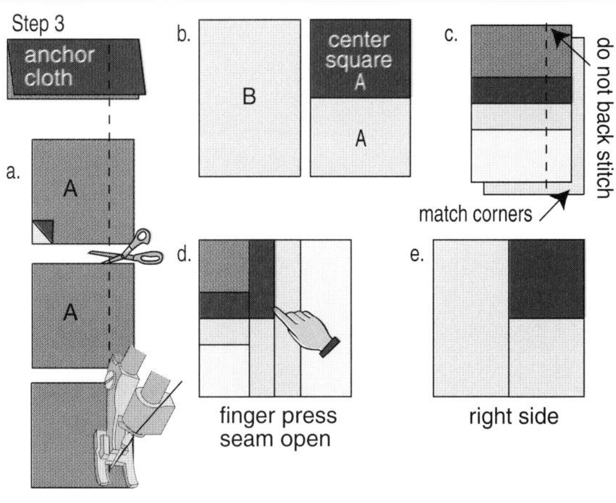

Order of Construction for Traditional Log Cabin Block

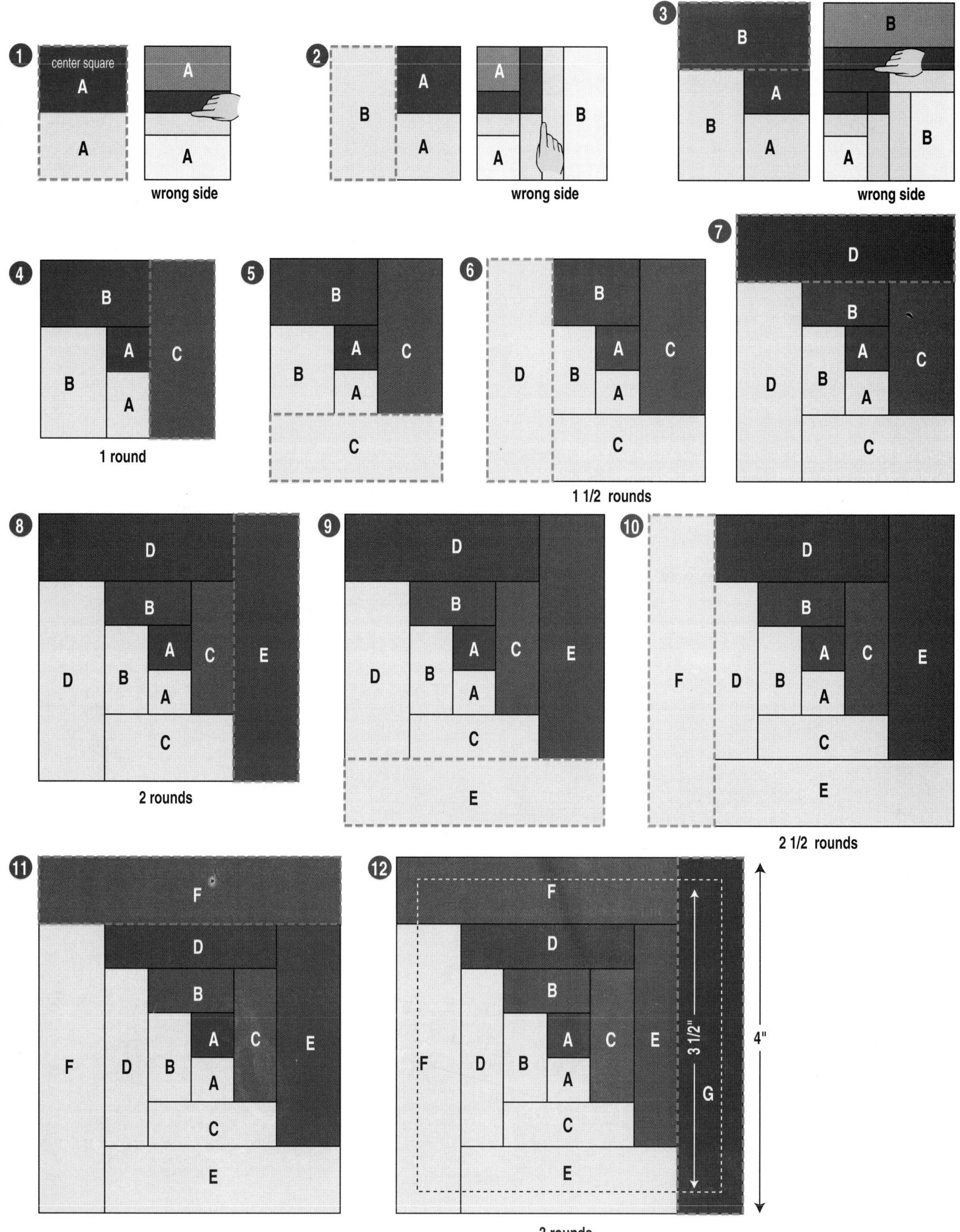

See # 3 (wrong side of block) on page 24. After seams have been pressed open you can no longer see wrong side of center A piece. Block should measure 4" when Step 12 is completed. After block is used in a pin cushion it measures 3 1/2". Make 2 blocks for each pin cushion.

Step 4. Patterns for comb and beak are actual size. Cut one red comb and one yellow beak for each chicken out of felt or ultra suede. It is easier to cut them freehand. Enlarge patterns for door stop.

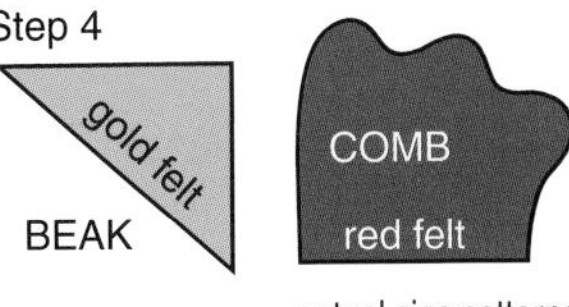

Step 5. To make a rooster pin a comb and beak to dark corner on one block. It will be a hen if beak and comb is put in light corner. Make sure comb doesn't get into beak seam allowance.

Right sides together put another block on top. Match light and dark corners. If you don't, a funky chicken will be hatched.

Secure with pins. Sew seam 1/4" from edge. Back stitch at beginning and end of each seam. See diagram for sewing instructions. Start sewing up the back and stop with needle in a down position between comb and beak. Lift presser foot, readjust fabric and sew to next corner. Pivot again and sew to dot. Leave an opening about 1 1/2" long. Leave fourth side open.

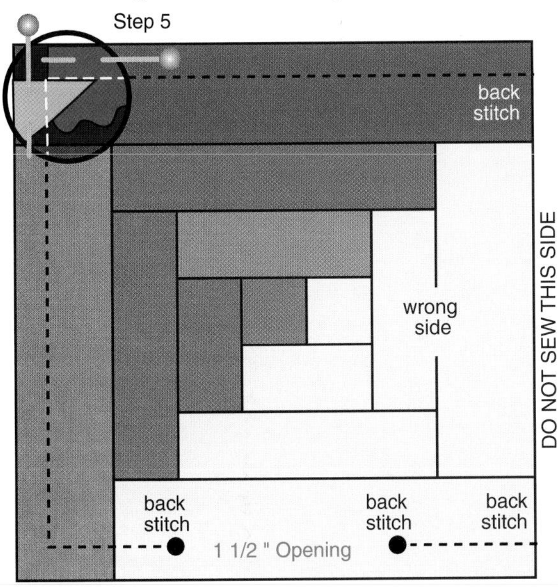

Step 6. Choose two contrasting colors for tails. Cut a 2 1/2" square for large tail and a 2 1/4" square for small tail. Cut both squares in half diagonally. Match edges and secure with pins. Leave longest (bias) edge open and sew on two edges. Trim corners and turn to right side. Press flat.

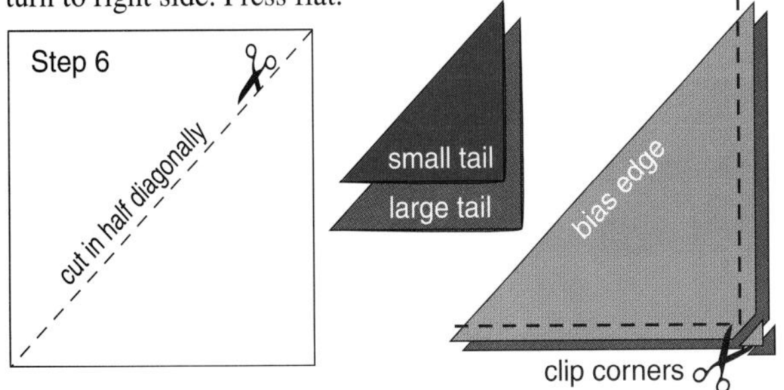

Step 7. Place smaller tail on top and baste together. To find center of tails fold in half. Match center of tails to seam line and pin in place on top of open side. Small tail is on top next to seam.

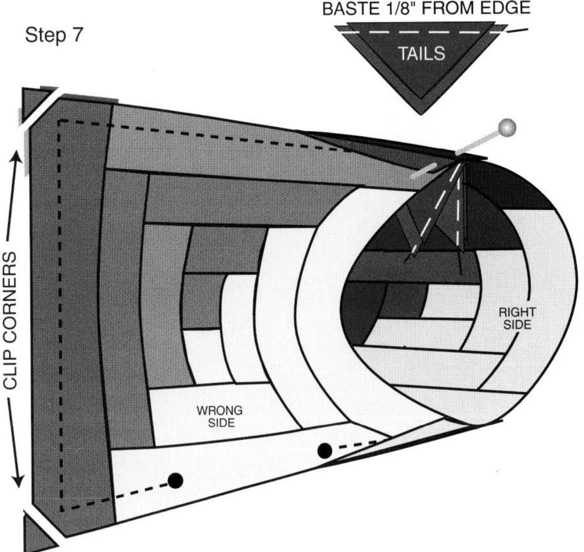

Step 8. To form body of chicken squash seams together. Match seams. Sew across end. Back stitch at beginning and end of seam. Clip corners before turning through opening.

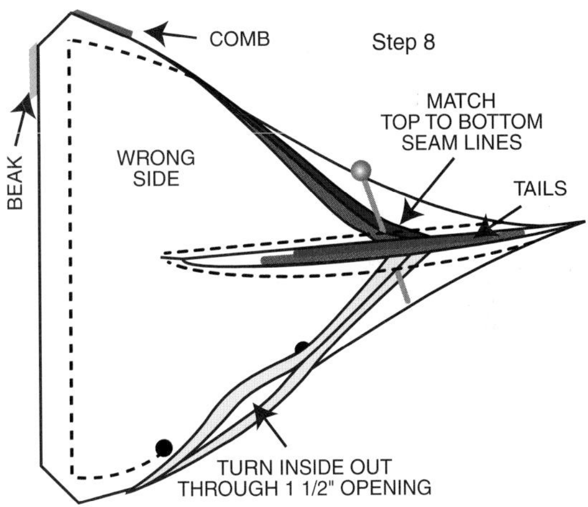

Make a funnel with plastic and fill chicken as full as possible with crushed walnut shells (my favorite), rice or aquarium gravel. Wool is also a great filling.

Whip stitch opening together. To complete pin cushion, attach small beads for eyes. This is a perfect gift for a quilting friend and it is an inexpensive bazaar item to make.

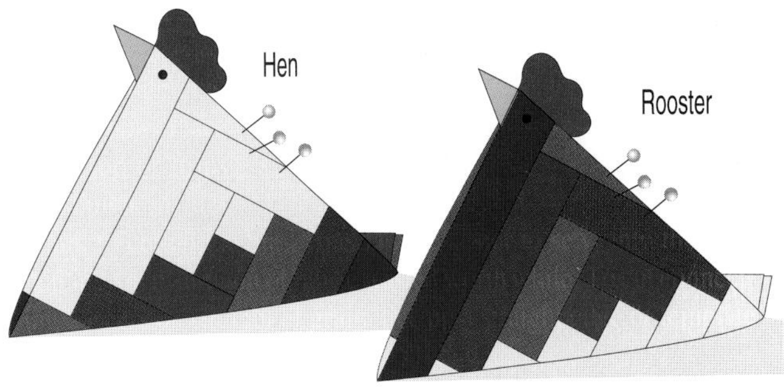

✻ Use this pattern with the large logs (QS28) to make door stops.

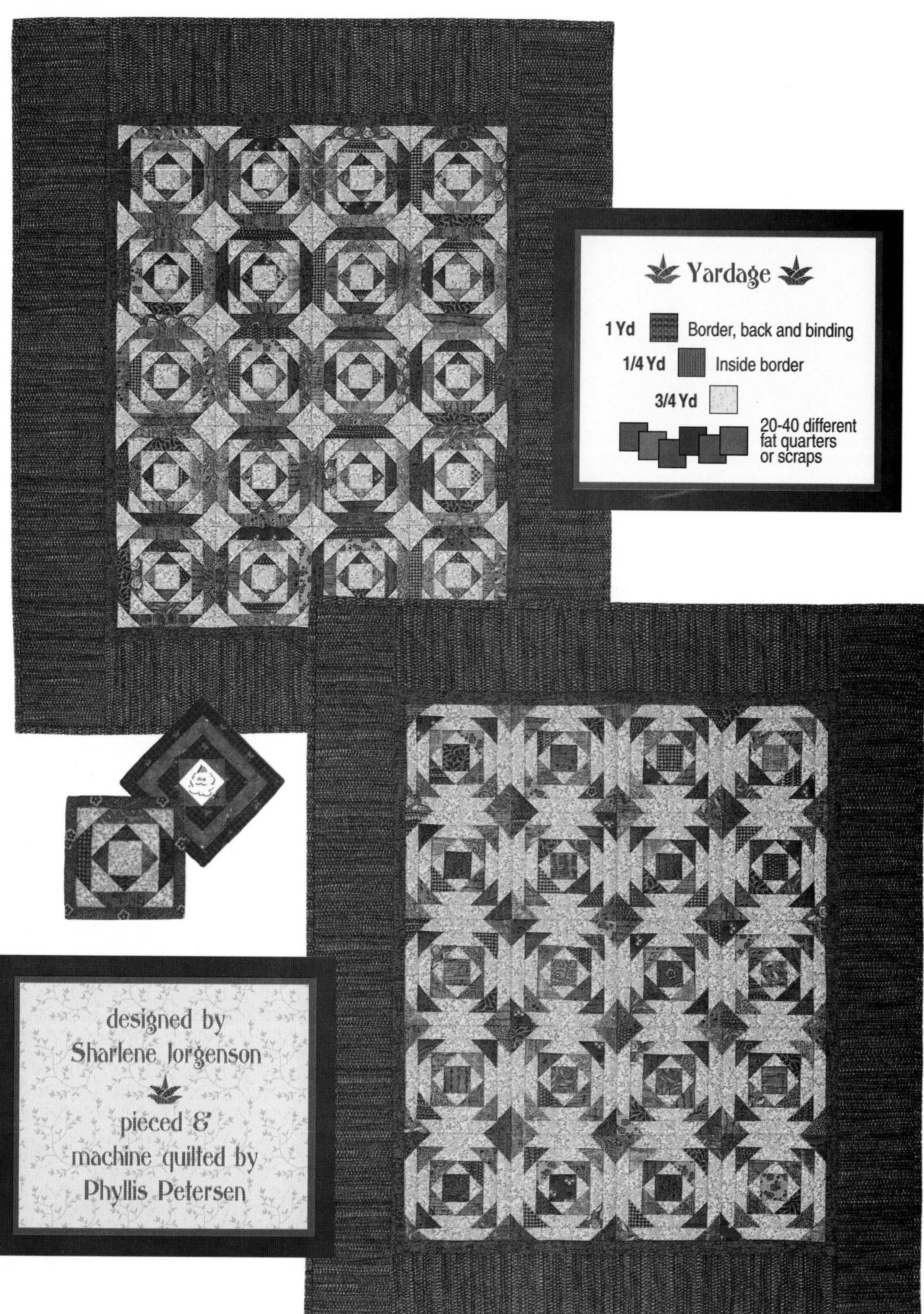
Yardage
1 Yd Border, back and binding
1/4 Yd Inside border
3/4 Yd
20-40 different fat quarters or scraps
designed by
Sharlene Jorgenson
pieced &
machine quilted by
Phyllis Petersen

Shopping List

- ▲ QS33 Miniature Log Cabin templates
- ▲ Quick Grips
- ▲ Omnigrid® Rulers 6" x 24"
- ▲ Fiskars® Rotary Cutter
- ▲ IBC Glass Head Pins 0.50mm steel shaft
- ▲ Fairfield poly-fil low-loft batting

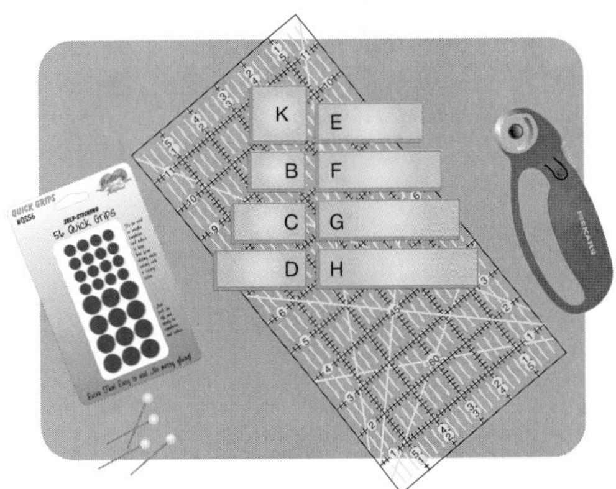

Read pages 2-7 before starting.

About Pineapple Log Cabin

The light and dark are reversed in quilts on page 26. The one on upper left has the same light fabric for all background logs and different colors in each center and corner. The other example has same light fabric in every center and corner and each log is a different scrap. Even though scraps were used, it was important to decide on a palette. In the beginning I thought purple and blue didn't belong in these quilts, but decided they added life after making a couple of blocks. If a fabric seems to ruin the quilt remove it and save pieces for another quilt. I used approximately 40 different prints in these quilts. You will be able to keep control of the design if all prints portray the same mood. For example it will look confused and haphazard if you mix contemporary prints with traditional ones.

One block can be made into a coaster or Christmas ornament. See page 26. The size of the coaster and ornament can be altered by the number of rounds added to the block.

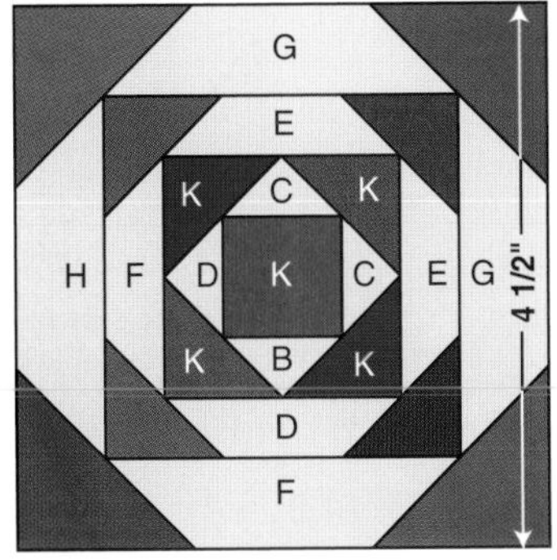

When making miniatures, I chose small scale prints. It was easy to select fabrics for this quilt because I harvested scraps left over from the Barn Dance quilt made in a previous series. Most of the fabrics come from the Barn Dance collection by Benertex.

Cutting Instructions

See fabric preparation on page 2. It is much easier to work with small pieces if fabric has been starched before pieces are cut. To make the Pineapple Log Cabin, use templates K, B, C, D, E, F, G and H from the miniature Log Cabin template set. In these instructions the same light fabric was used for all logs and 40 different dark prints were used for centers and folded corners.

Step 1. To straighten fabric and cut strips see page 3. To save time place up to six strips 1 1/2" wide on top of each other. Bifold strips on a small mat board. Place template K on top of strips and cut pieces until strips are used up. To keep colors evenly distributed, separate pieces into piles. Work with one pile at a time and put the rest into a transparent envelope. Template K is used for both the center square and folded corners of each block. For this quilt 208 K's are needed for 16 blocks.

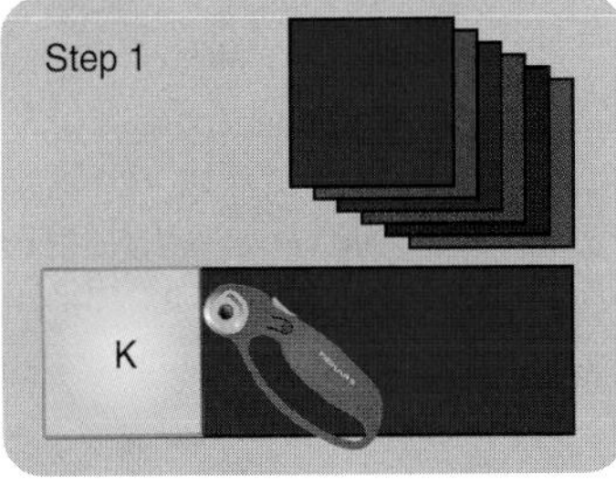

Step 2. To save fabric cut strips to accommodate the length of logs instead of width. Place up to six strips of the same fabric on top of each other. Cut logs until strips are used up. Repeat this step until you have cut light logs with templates B, C, D, E, F, G and H.

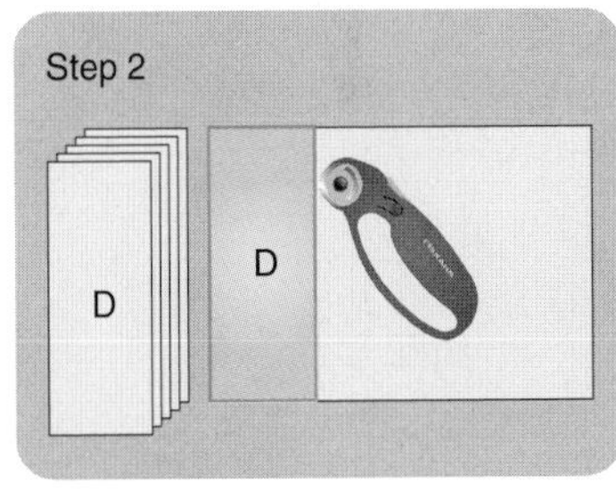

Sewing Test

Step 3. Sew all seams with a *scant 1/4"* seam allowance to make up for fabric used in seam line. Right sides together, place B on top of K. Sew seam and press open. Place template C on top. If it is same length you passed the sewing test. If you continue without passing your problem will get worse each time you add another log.

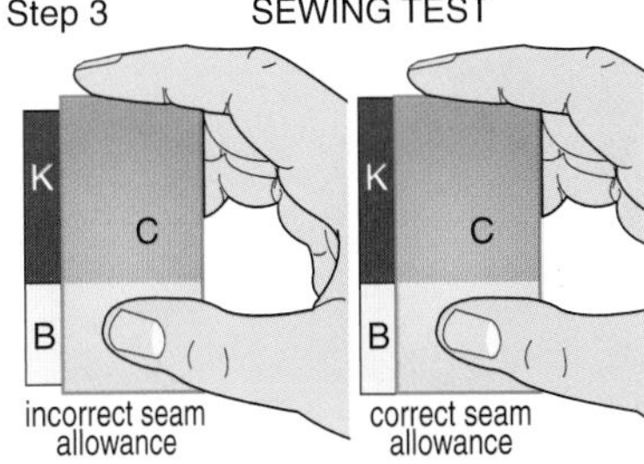

If you want a motif centered in a Christmas ornament, take advantage of the fact that templates are transparent. Center template K over featured design. Design must be small enough so it doesn't get into seam allowance. Fussy cut around K template with cutter. Cut one at a time.

Sewing Instructions

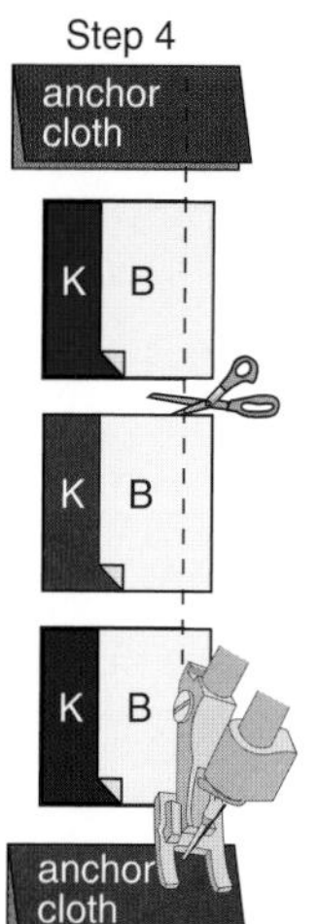

Step 4. Right sides together chain sew 16 B's (all the same fabric) to K's (all different fabrics). If you start sewing on an anchor cloth, beginning stitches on patchwork will be more secure and won't pull apart as easily as first stitches sewn. Do not back stitch at beginning or end of seams because it creates bulk in corners. Last stitches are sewn on a second anchor cloth.

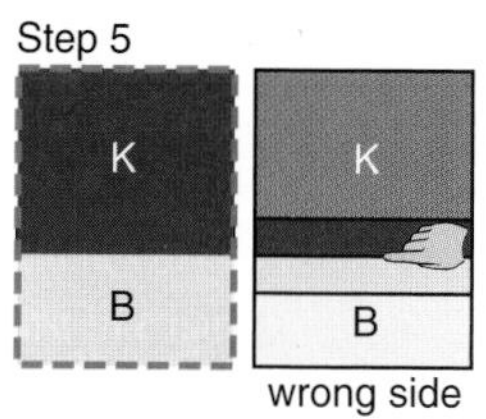

Step 5. Finger press seams open before pressing with an iron.

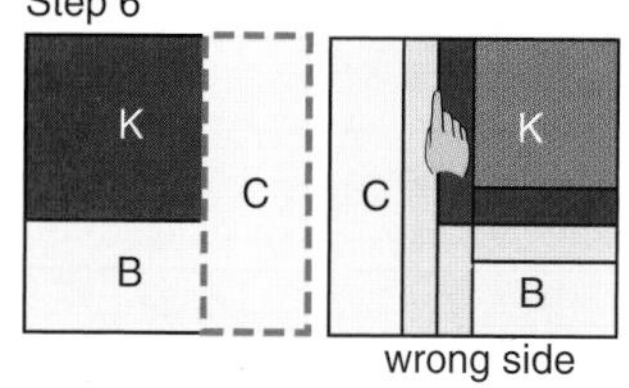

Step 6. Always add C log to *same edge on all blocks.* If C is too long or to short you have sewn with *wrong* seam allowance. Press seams open.

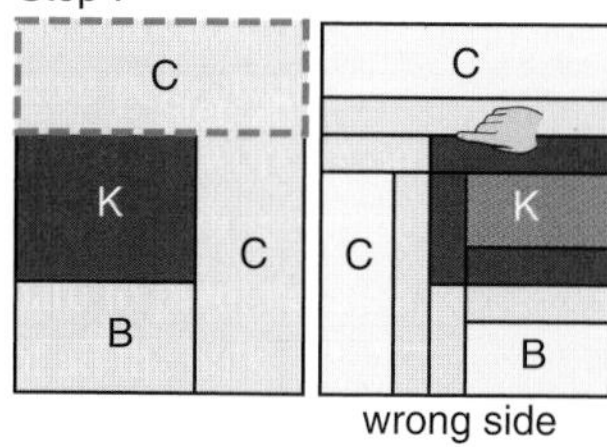

Step 7. Right sides together add another light C log. *Make sure it is always added to the same side.* Press seam open.

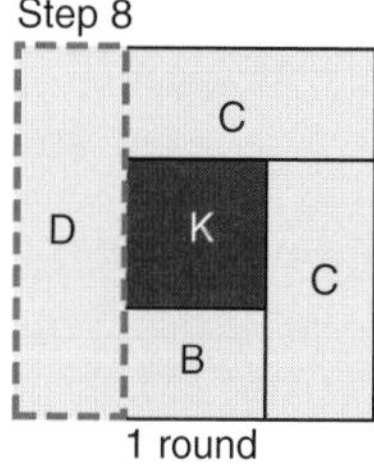

Step 8. Add a light D log to finish first round. Press seam open.

Step 9. Fold K in half diagonally to form a triangle. Match edges before pressing. Hold corners down with stiletto to prevent yourself from getting burnt when pressing in a crease. I pressed one of each (40) color so I had an assortment to pick from when making blocks. Folded squares make this quilt three dimensional.

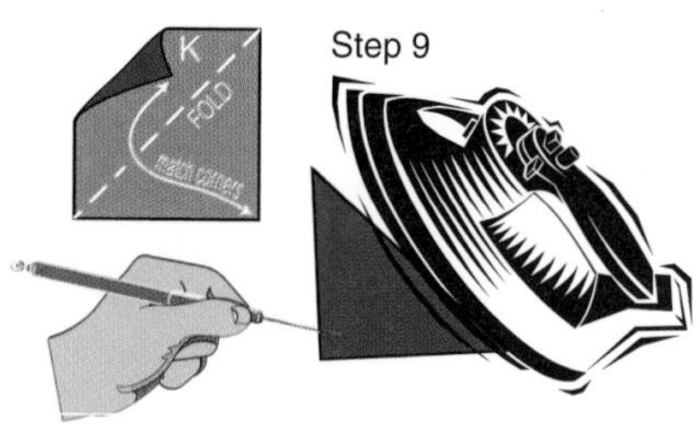

Step 10 a. On edge that has B log place a folded K on each corner. Secure with pins. K's will intersect 1/4" from edge at center point.

b. Place a light D log on top of folded K's. Guide pieces with stiletto as you sew. Do not back stitch at beginning or end of seam. Make sure edges of folded K's match edge of block when approaching center point of seam. Instead of trying to put in so many pins, insert stiletto inside fold of K to push it into position. If edges are lined up correctly and you sew with a perfect scant 1/4" seam allowance, seam will be sewn directly over point folded K's intersection .

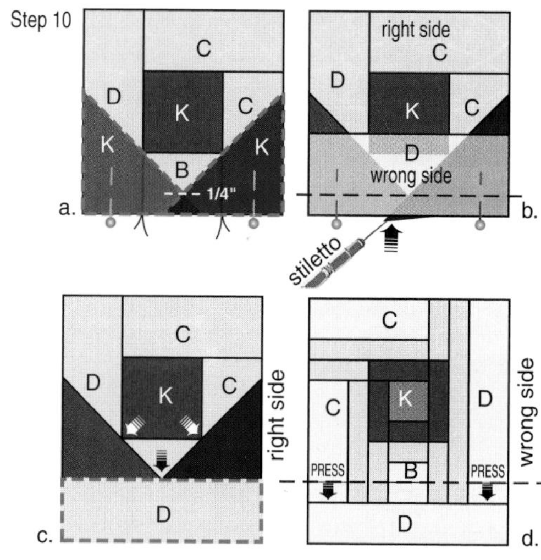

c. Now all seams will be pressed outward instead of open. If seam is correctly sewn there will be a perfect intersection (see black arrow). Also corners of center K square will meet edge of folded K's (see white arrows).

d. Diagram shows back side of block after seam is pressed.

Step 11

a. Place next folded K in upper right corner.

b. Place light E log on top.

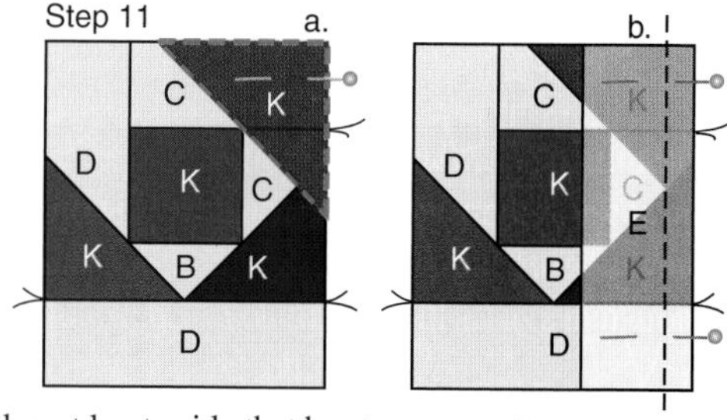

Tip! Always add next log to side that has two seams to cross over. Guide fabric with stiletto as you sew.

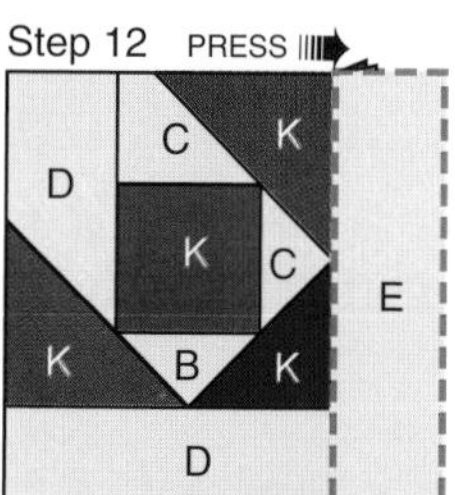

Step 12. Finger press seam towards outside edge of block before pressing with iron.

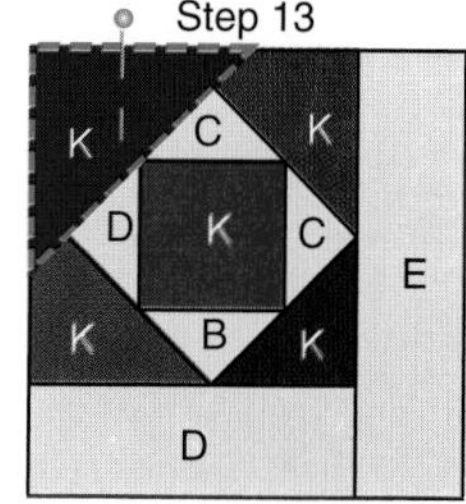

Step 13. Pin next K in corner.

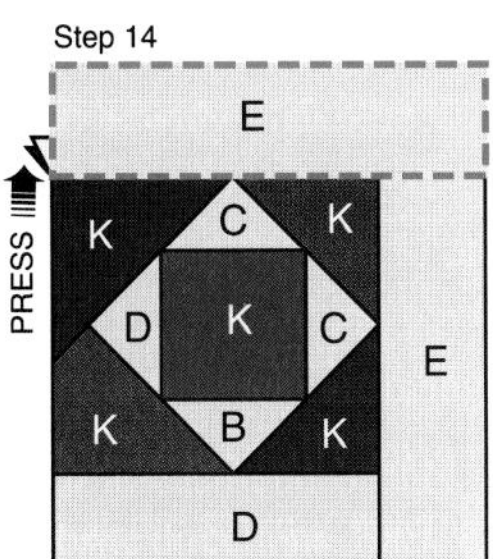

Step 14. Right sides together add E log. Press seam outward.

Step 15. Right sides together add light F log. Press seam outward. This completes second round.

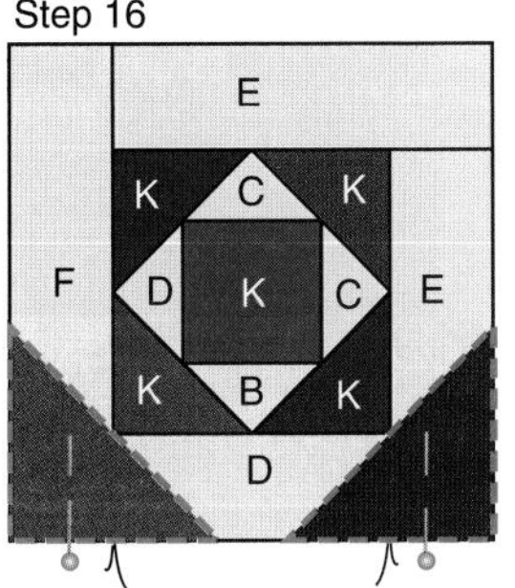

Step 16. Add two more K's to bottom of block. Secure with pins.

If you want to make a Christmas ornament or coaster, put a K in all four corners. We made a second block for back of Christmas ornament. Back of coaster is just a square of fabric. Stitch 1/8" from edge before attaching binding.

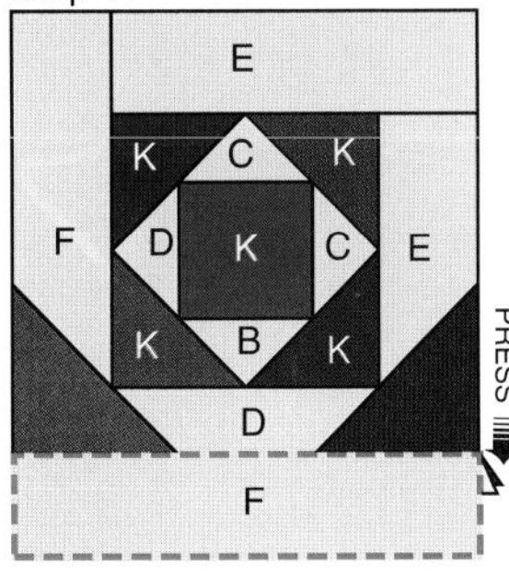

Step 17. Right sides together add light F log. Press seam outward.

Step 18. Add another K's to upper right corner of block. Secure with pins. Add a light G log. Press seam outward.

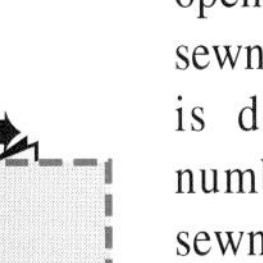

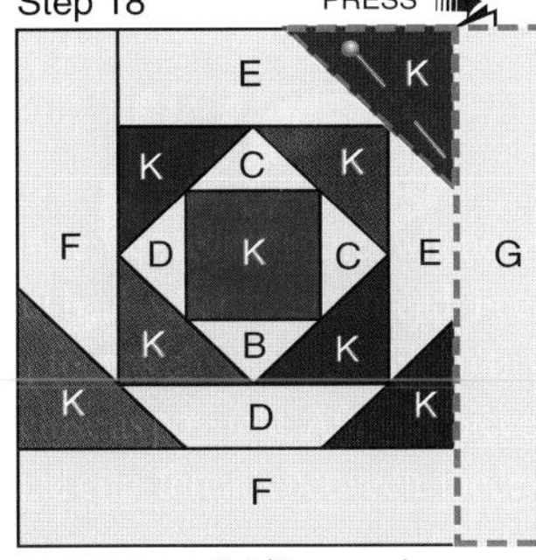

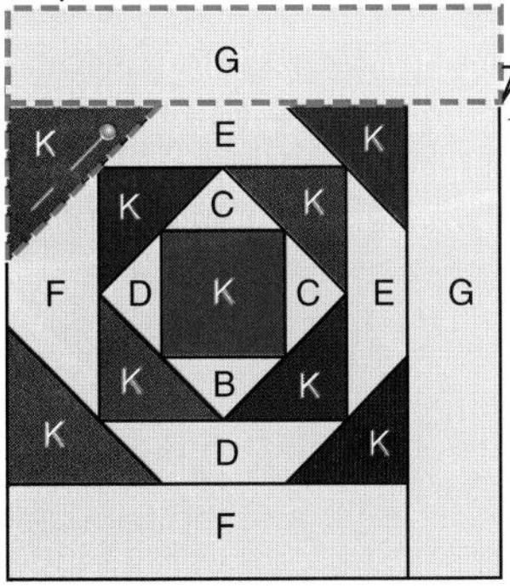

Step 19. Add another K to upper left corner. Secure with pins. Add another light G log. Press seam outward.

Step 20. Add light H log. Press seam outward.

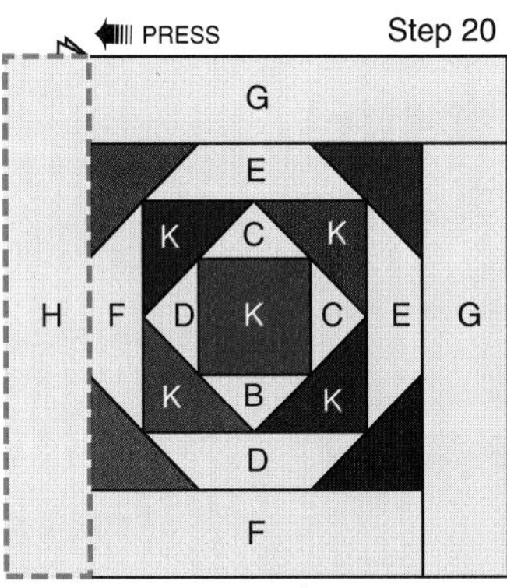

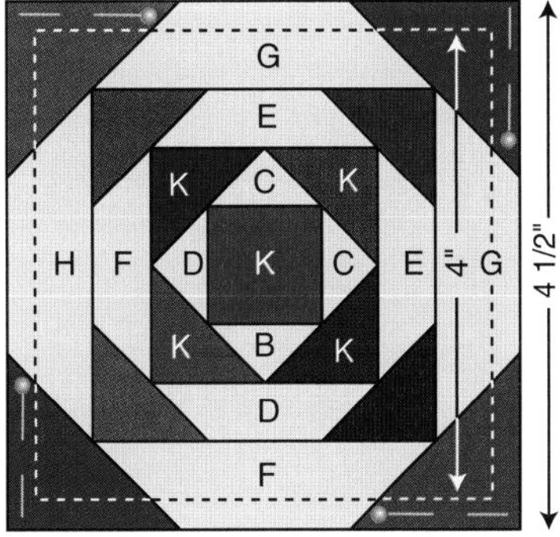

Step 21. Place a folded K on each corner. Make sure edges match edge of block. Stitch 1/8" from edge. There are 16 blocks in both quilts shown on page 26.

Connecting Blocks Into Rows

Step 22. Arrange all blocks on flannel board to evenly distribute colors. Place two blocks right sides together. Fold top corner back and match folded edges of K pieces. Insert pin along fold. This is a great tip to insure perfect points on right side after seam is sewn, Repeat on opposite corner. Press seam open after seam is sewn. Width of quilt is determined by number of blocks sewn together. We had 4 blocks in each row. Make 6 rows.

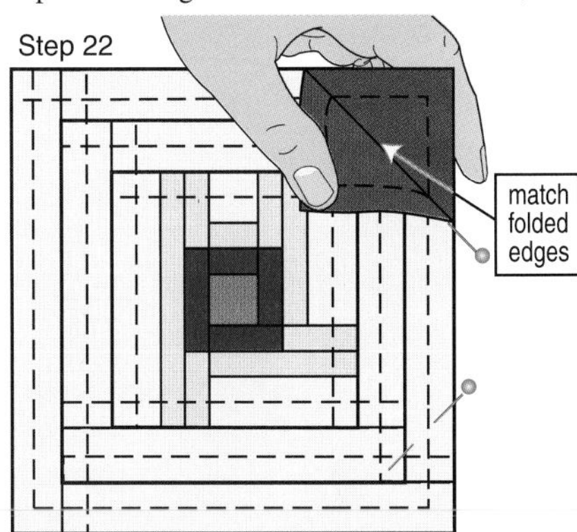

See pinning options on pages 17-18 before connecting rows. Connect rows. Press seams open.

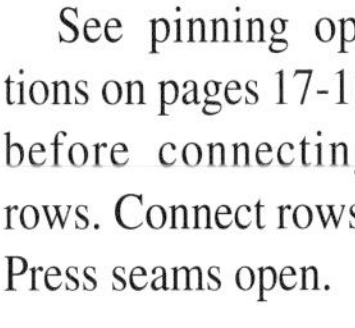

Finishing Touches

To make quilt sandwich see page 6. Because pieces are so small we decided to stitch in the ditch with a neutral thread. See diagram. To attach binding see page 7.

designed & pieced by Angela Scott

machine quilted by Marcia Stevens

Finished Size 34 1/2" x 40 1/2"

If you make each frog different buy 12 green fat quarters

If you make all frogs the same purchase 1/3 yd. of each green

2 yd. white background and backing

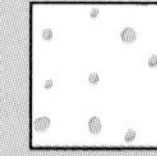

1/3 yd. sashing

1 1/2 yd. outside border and binding

FROG POND

BEGINNER

Shopping List

- QSK Quilter's Starter Kit
- Quick Grips
- Omnigrid® Rulers 6" x 24"
- Fiskars® Rotary Cutter
- IBC Glass Head Pins 0.50mm steel shaft
- Fairfield poly-fil low-loft batting
- Buttons for eyes
- Sulky® metallic thread

Read pages 2-7 before starting.

About This Quilt

Step 1. Angie got the inspiration to make this quilt while walking through my flower garden which has a pond filled with fresh lake water. It has become a perfect home for tadpoles to hatch into frogs every spring. They add so much life to the garden all summer.

Angie found the perfect border fabric first, but it took her awhile to find all greens needed for the frogs. She decided on light, medium, and dark hand dyed batiks. Batiks have texture needed to make frogs look realistic. To pull yellow out of the border she used yellow polka dots for sashing. The white on white background fabric has dragonflies, butterflies, and lady bugs printed on it.

To add interest butterflies and bugs were quilted on the background with sulky® metallic thread. Marcia stitched in the ditch around the frogs and around the frogs in the border. See Step 20 for detailed quilting suggestions. Angie put glass buttons on the frogs so they can see. We don't suggest buttons if it is going to be used as a crib quilt.

Templates from Quilter's Starter Kit were used to make this quilt. There will be special sewing and cutting instructions for eyes and in steps 7-9 on page 32. Special instructions for making feet are found in step 15 on page 33.

Step 1

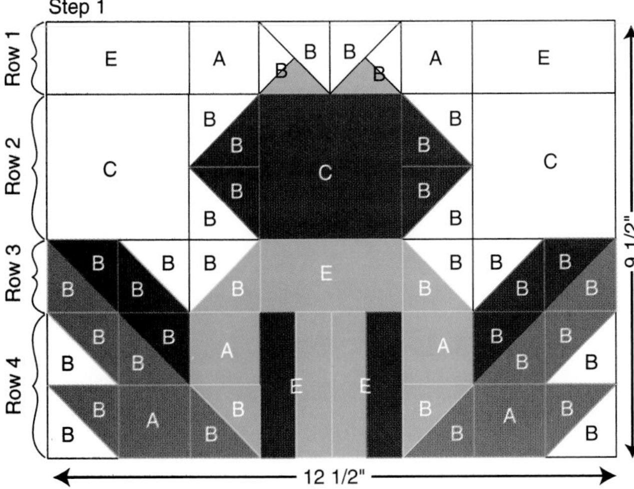

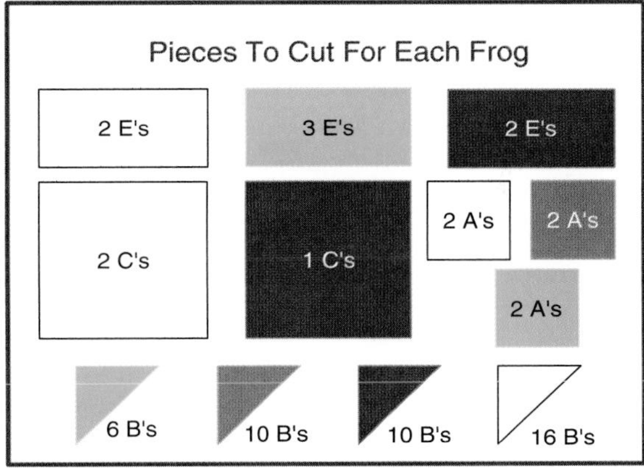

Cutting Instructions

Step 2. Cut A's and E's from same 2" strips. Bifold cut strips on top of a small 8" x 12" mat board, so it is easier to turn your work as you cut around the template. Cut 3 1/2" strips for white background C's. Cut C's needed for each frog.

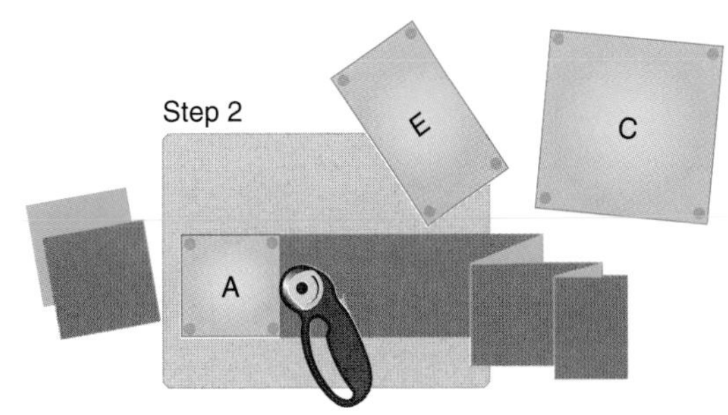

Step 3. Cut strips 2 3/8" wide for template B to get correct grain line. Bifold strips on a small mat board. Flip-flop template, cutting pieces as you go. See chart above for number of B's needed.

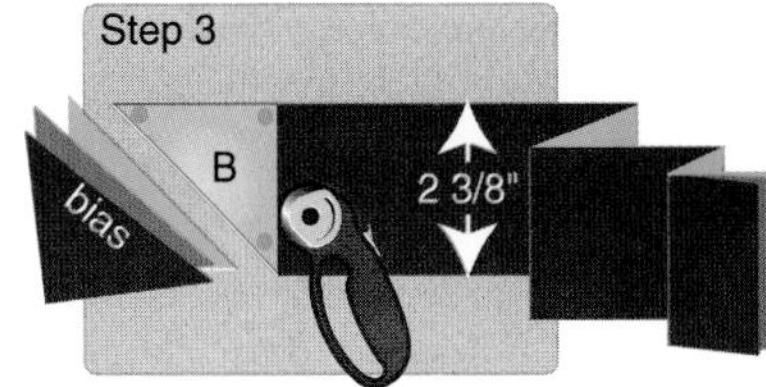

Sewing Instructions

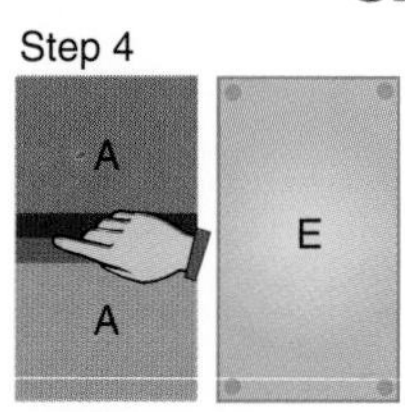

Step 4. Give yourself a sewing test before starting to chain sew. Place 2 A's right sides together and sew seam with a scant 1/4" seam allowance. Press seam open. Two A's sewn together should equal template E. If not adjust your seam allowance before continuing.

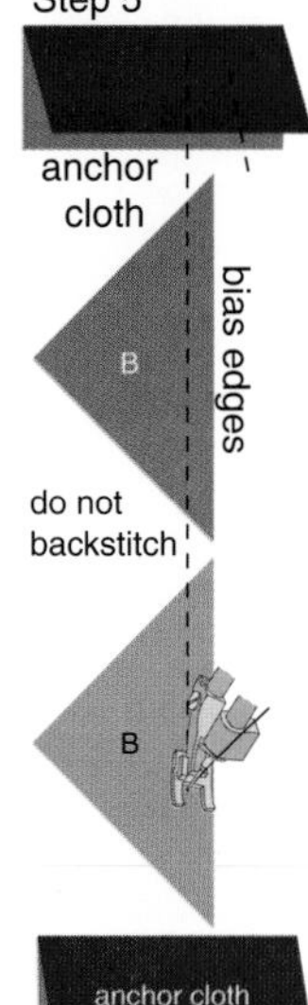

Step 5. Arrange pieces on a flannel board following diagram in Step 1. First chain sew all half-square units. Place two B's right sides together. Identical shapes are easiest shapes to sew together because there is no question about aligning them. Sew along bias edges. Do not back stitch at beginning or end of seam because it will be crossed over again. If your machine eats fabric, start and finish sewing on an anchor cloth.

Step 6. There are two ways to remove bulk in corners. Cut at a 90° angle to outside edge of block with a scissor or place a template on top of block after seams are pressed open and trim corners off with a rotary cutter. If you are a beginner and your seam allowance is too scant, extra fabric can be removed with second method.

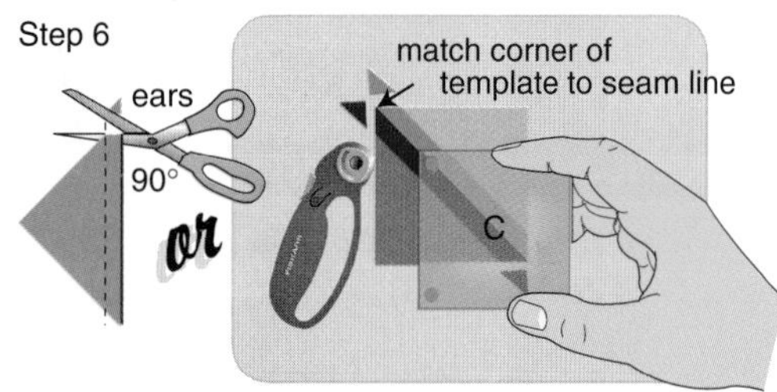

Repeat step 6 until all B units are made for each frog.

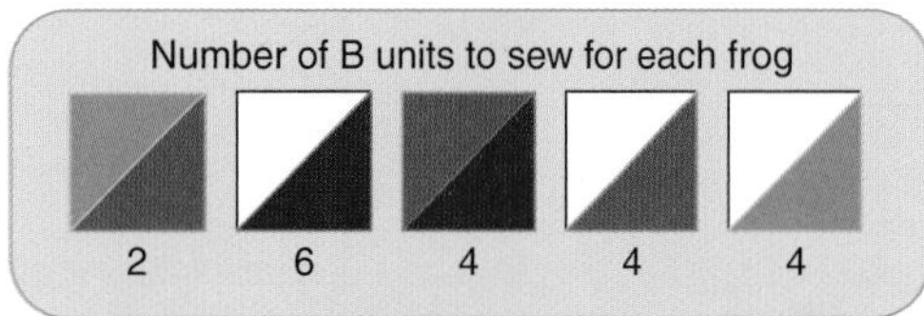

Making Frog Eyes For Top Row

Step 7. Angie came up with this fool proof way to make perfect eyes without a template for quarter-square triangles.

Place two B units made with lightest green and white made in Step 6 facing each other as shown in diagram below. Right sides together place another white B on top of each. Match 90° corners. Sew along bias edge of top B a scant 1/4" from edge. Do not back stitch at beginning or end of seam.

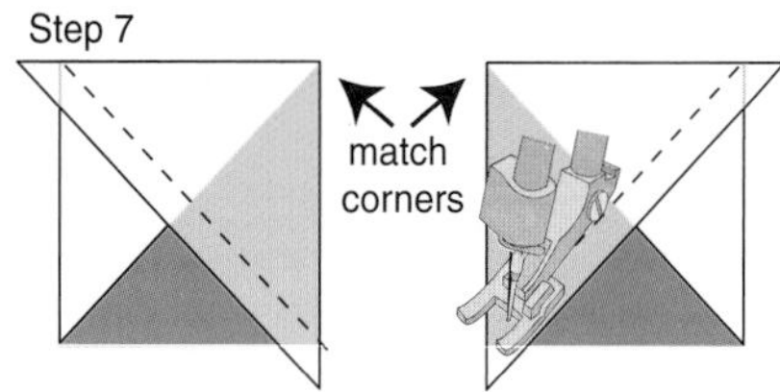

Step 8. Remove ears and extra fabric with scissor.

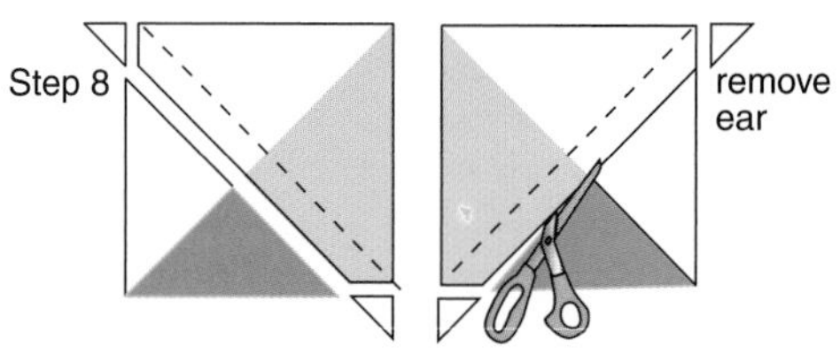

Step 9. Finger press seams open before pressing with an iron.

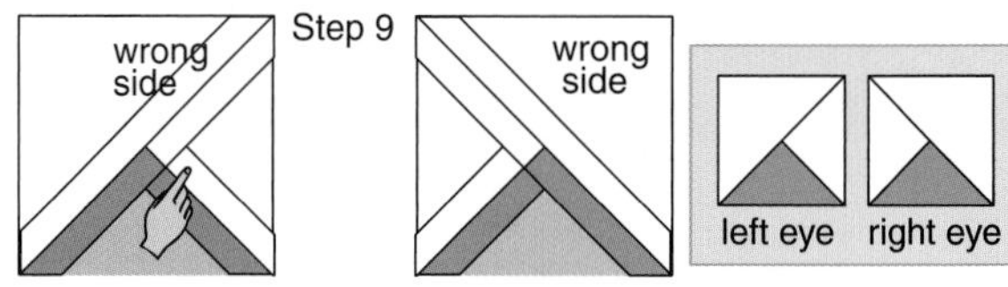

Connecting Units Of Top Row

Step 10a. Place right and left eyes right sides together as shown.

b. Insert a pin 1/4" from edge along seam line through both eyes.

c. To get perfect intersections, sew directly over point pins goes into fabric. Guide pieces in front of presser foot with stiletto to prevent uneven stitches. Do not back stitch at beginning or end.

d. Finger press seam open before pressing with an iron.

e. Intersections will be 1/4" from top and bottom edges.

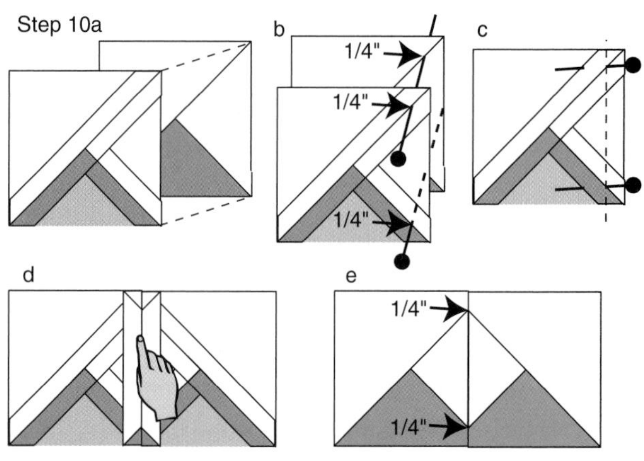

Step 11. To complete top row of frog, add a white E and A to both sides of eyes. Press seams open.

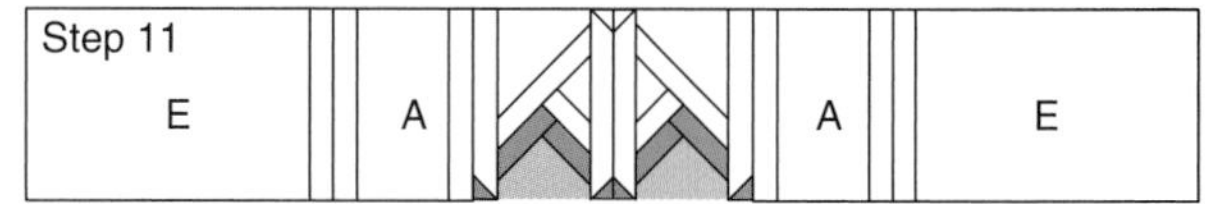

Making Frog Cheeks For Second Row

Step 12. Place a darkest green and white B unit right sides together as shown. To make a perfect intersection insert a pin 1/4" from edge along seam line through top and bottom. Sew directly over point pin goes into fabric. Press seams open. Repeat this step to make a left cheek.

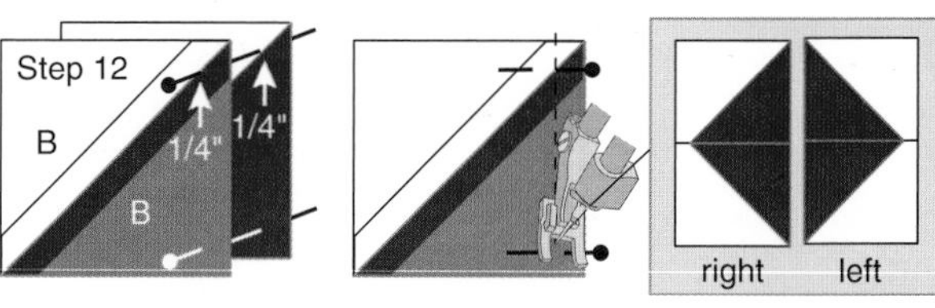

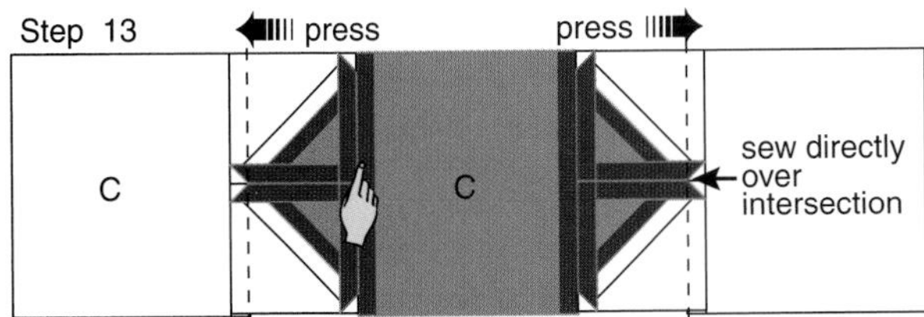

Step 13. To complete second row, add a white C on both ends and a dark C in the center. Press center seams open. Press other seams open or to one side. We decided to press ours out (see arrows).

Step 14. Third row is made up of all B units except for one E in the center. Press all seams open. Intersections should be 1/4" from edge (see red arrow) when pressed.

Cutting Frog Legs For Bottom Row

Step 15. Right sides together sew two E's together. Center template E on top and remove extra fabric on both sides with rotary cutter. Cut only one at a time. Make two leg units for each frog.

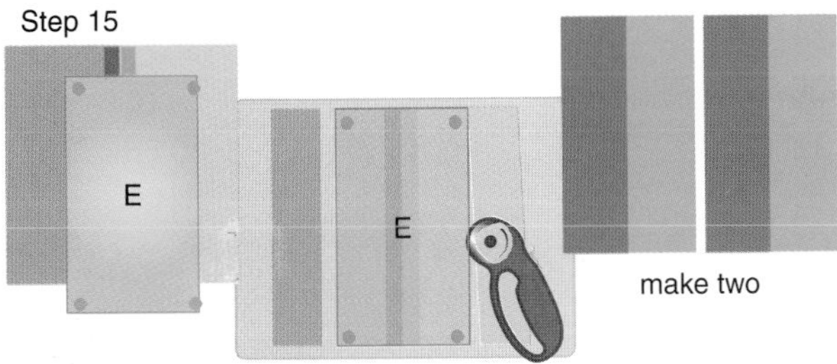

Sewing Bottom Row

Step 16. Make right and left hip of frog by arranging C's and B units into rows as shown in diagram below. They must be a mirror image of each other. Press seams open.

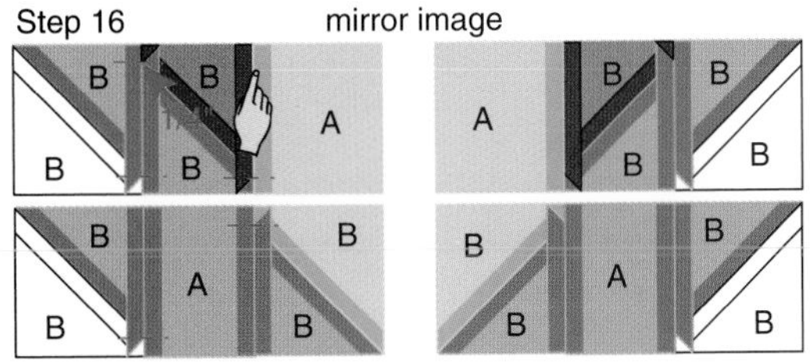

Step 17. First connect hip rows. Next connect leg units in center of row. Add hip units to both sides of legs. Press seams open. Arrange frog rows as shown below.

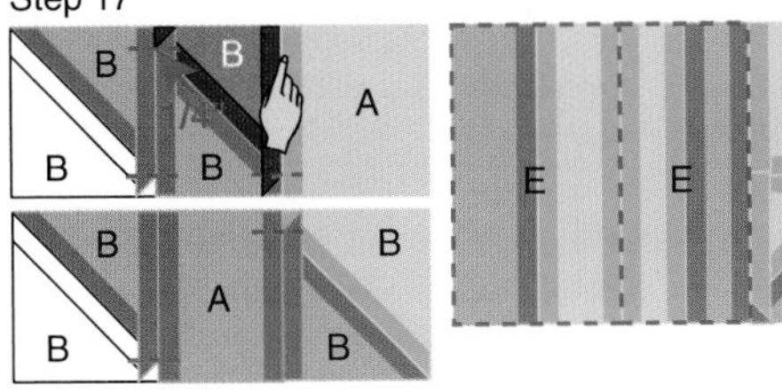

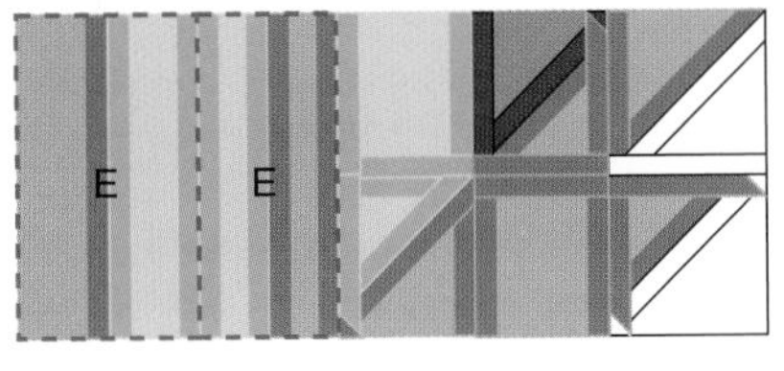

Step 18. Place rows 1 and 2 right sides together. At each intersection insert pin 1/4" from outside edge on seam lines through top and bottom row. Leave this pin standing.

On both sides of standing pin, insert another pin to hold intersection in place. Remove standing pin before sewing seam.

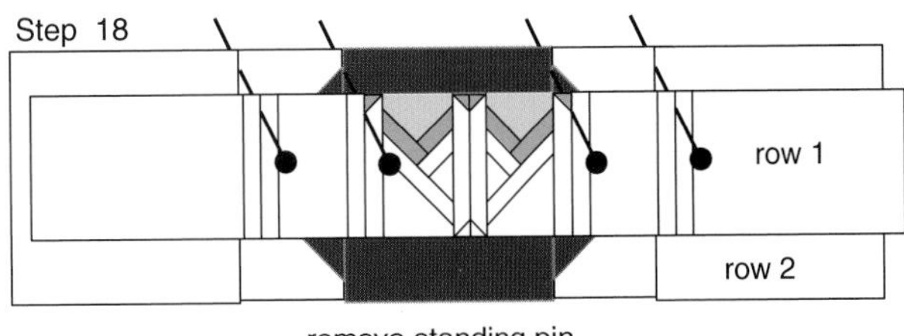

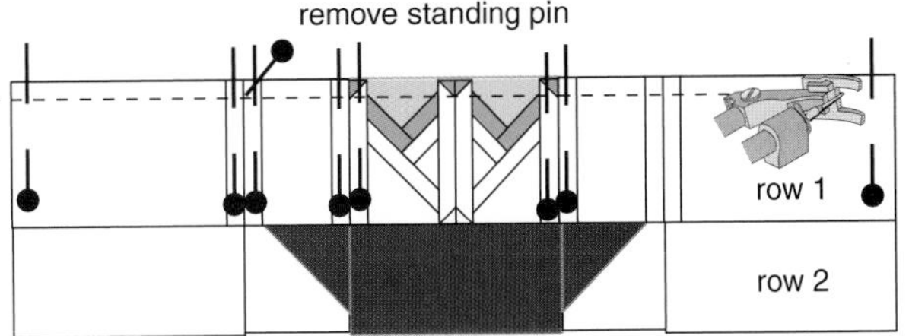

Step 19. Cut 6 strips 3 1/2"x 12 1/2" and 6 strips 3 1/2" x 9 1/2" for sashing. Cut 9 C squares for corner stones. Connect sashing to corner stones. Press seam allowance as indicated by red arrows. Connect sashing and frogs into rows. Cut outside border 5" wide and four 5" squares for corners. Add borders.

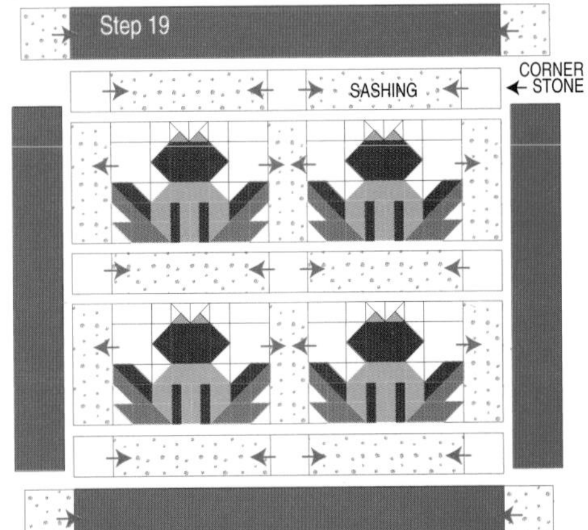

Step 20. Diagram below shows quilting ideas. See pages 6-7 to finish quilt.

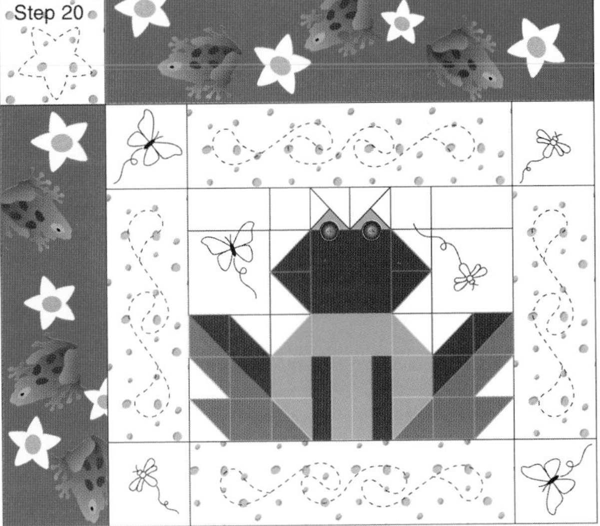

designed, pieced
& quilted by
Lindee Goodall

Shopping List

- KK2000 Embroidery Spray Adhesive
- Fun Felt or Plaid Fabric
- Omnigrid® Rulers 6" x 24"
- Quilter's Safety Pins
- Fabric Marking Pencil
- Fairfield poly-fil low-loft batting
- 40 wt. Rayon or Polyester Embroidery Thread
- Embroidery Weight Bobbin Thread
- Embroidery Card

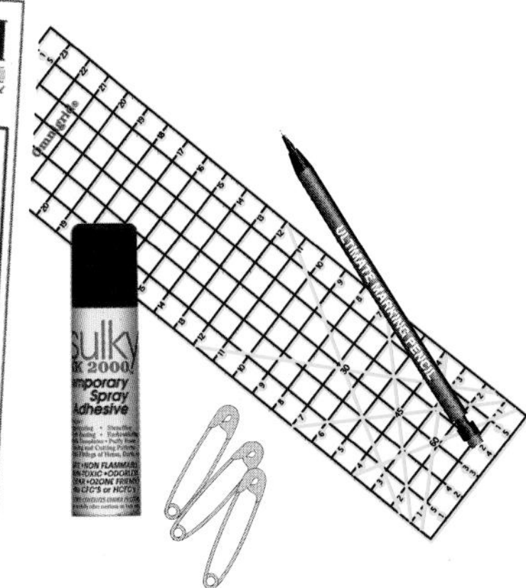

About This Quilt

This simple block quilt is made extra special through creative use of embroidery designs. Alternating blocks of yellow and blue are accented with members of the bear family. The solid blocks are embroidered tone-on-tone while the blue blocks have been appliqued with plaid bears giving a delightful cuddly texture to this small quilt. Quilting designs can be used for applique with fabrics that don't travel, such as some fake furs, polar fleece, and ultrasuede. You can add a border or finish it with a plaid binding like Lindee's.

Quilting With Your Embroidery Machine

What could be a simpler way to quilt your work than to let your sewing machine do it for you? Using your embroidery unit to sew the quilting templates is the easiest way to achieve perfect stitching. With these simple steps, you too can become a master quilter with just the touch of a button.

After piecing your top and then assembling and pin-basting your quilt sandwich, you are ready to finalize your embroidery placement. I've found the easiest way for me is to work with printed versions of my designs and move them around until I'm satisfied with their locations. Here I'll detail my method of embroidered quilting.

Step 1

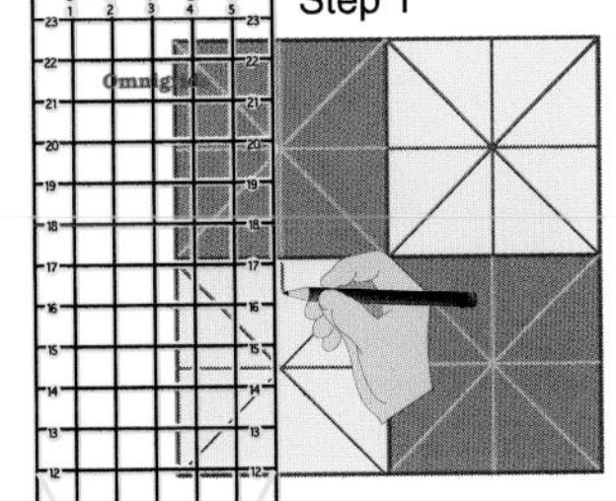

Step 1. Mark the centers of your pieced blocks. My favorite way is to bisect the box by drawing diagonal lines from corner to corner forming an "X." Then, using my gridded quilting ruler, I add vertical and horizontal lines intersecting the center point of the X. I will match these lines to those printed on my embroidery design pattern.

Step 2. Select embroidery designs you will be using to quilt. Print each design at actual size and cut out. If your software will print design with a cross hair (marking horizontal, vertical, and center of design) it will make it easy for you to get precise alignment. I printed enough designs for each placement for this quilt. Because I used four different designs, I wanted to ensure proper placement of each design ("Unembroidering" is neither fun nor easy!). I find that working with actual size designs makes placement more accurate and allows me to verify the visual balance. If I decide that a design is too large or too small for my block to suit my tastes, I can scale it to the desired size. Since most of the designs on Sharlene's disk are available in three sizes, it is easy to select one that is closest to the size I want.

Step 2

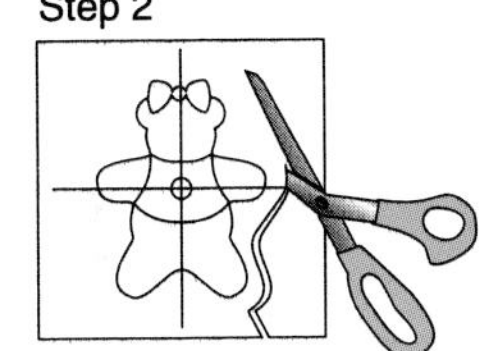

Step 3. When you are happy with your placement, pin aligned embroidery pattern, at top and bottom of paper, to your quilt. Be careful to match the grid lines. This pattern will be removed just before sewing.

Step 3

Step 4. Set up your sewing machine for embroidery and load your designs. Thread your machine with the embroidery thread of your choice. Select the smallest hoop that will accommodate your embroidery design.

Step 5. For the 'fun fur' or plaid squares, you will need to cut squares larger than actual design (at least 1" taller and wider).

Hoop Your Quilt Sandwich

Step 6. This is probably the hardest part of the whole process due to alignment. It is not necessary to use any embroidery backing (if you have used woven fabrics for your quilt top and back) because quilting designs are "low impact" designs and your quilt back adds stability.

The tricky part is getting your quilt sandwich in the hoop straight and with proper tension. If your design size is very close to maximum sewing field for your hoop, you will have to be more precise when hooping. The more free space there is around your design, within hoop, the more you can move hoop around at sewing machine to achieve proper centering.

I have found that a hooping table, such as the Embroiders Friend, can be invaluable since it holds my outer hoop in position without sliding all over the table. This gadget also has a groove down the center which helps when trying to hoop items straight. I simply follow the marked line on my quilt block with my finger right down that groove. I have also taped thin strips of spaghetti to my table to create a horizontal guide. I can precisely and quickly hoop my quilt by positioning outer hoop so its sewing center lines up over grid on my table.

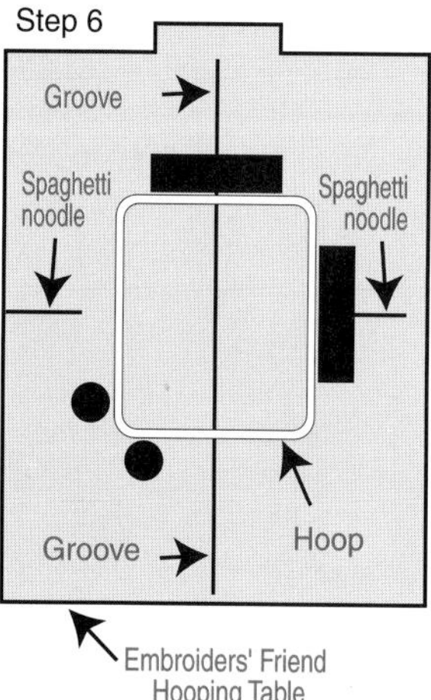

Now that we know where to hoop, how do we hoop? First, make sure you fabric is smoothed over outer hoop and centered. When you press your inner hoop into the outer hoop, it should require a fair amount of pressure resulting in a secure fit. You should not have to bounce on hoop to get it in. If you do, loosen the screw on outer hoop a bit and try again. If hoop goes in too easily, tighten screw a bit and rehoop. Tightening screw after hooping distorts tension on fabric. Also, resist the urge to tug on fabric once in hoop. If fabric is not straight or smooth and wrinkle free, rehoop it. Pulling on the fabric while it is in hoop can stretch it and pull the fabric off grain.

Attach Hoop to Embroidery Machine

Step 7. If you have a large or heavy quilt, make sure it is well supported on the table with sewing machine or table could cause the machine to sew poorly or even cause hoop to pop out of machine. Also, make sure that as hoop moves from side to side, the quilt will not interfere with its action or fall under the needle as the machine sews.

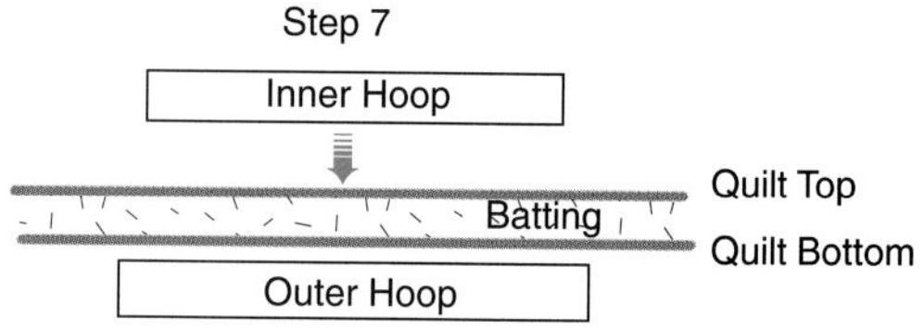

Check Design Position

Step 8. Most all domestic machines start from the center of design, whether or not design actually starts sewing there. You can take advantage of this by verifying your needle position. Turn hand wheel on sewing machine to see how close needle is to center cross hair on paper design. If necessary, use controls on your sewing machine to move hoop so needle is directly over center point. I like to, also, move needle back and forth along line to make sure my design is straight. Most machines will only rotate a design in 90° increments. If your design is crooked, you will have to stop now and rehoop. Once you are satisfied with position, remove pinned paper pattern.

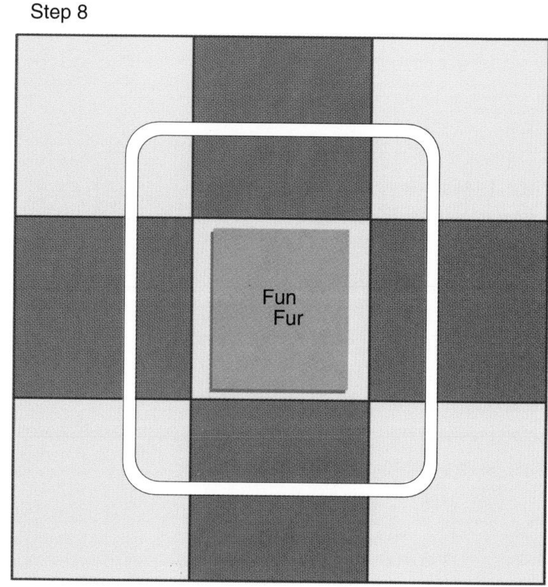

Sew The Design

Step 9. If you are sewing plain blocks, you are ready to press the start button. If you are sewing fuzzy blocks, spray back of Fun Fur with KK2000 Spray Adhesive. Make sure you spray in protected area away from your sewing machine. Since this spray is temporary, use it only when you are ready to place fabric. Center sticky fabric over guidelines on quilt. Quilt designs sew quite quickly and you'll be surprised just how fun and easy it is to finish a quilt this way.

When the embroidery design is finished, clip your threads and remove hoop from machine. To finish the bears, carefully trim away excess fabric beyond quilting lines with applique scissors.

Finishing Your Quilt

Step 10. When all embroidery is completed, finish your quilt with binding instructions on page 7.

Step 9

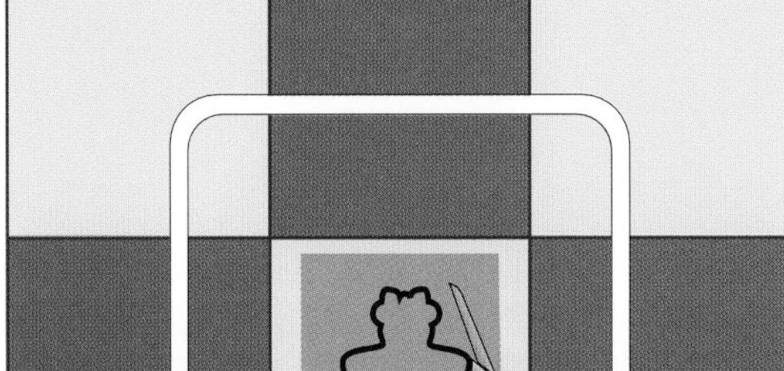

The Signature Series 12
Quilting from the Heartland Embroidery Disk
contains 37 beautiful embroidery designs
on a 3.5 diskette created specifically
for today's embroiderers.

Easy to use installer program
quickly installs the designs
for your machine.

Requires embroidery machine
with direct or indirect computer connection
for transferring design.

Color sequences and instructions for any
special techniques are included.

For more information call:
1-800-637-2541

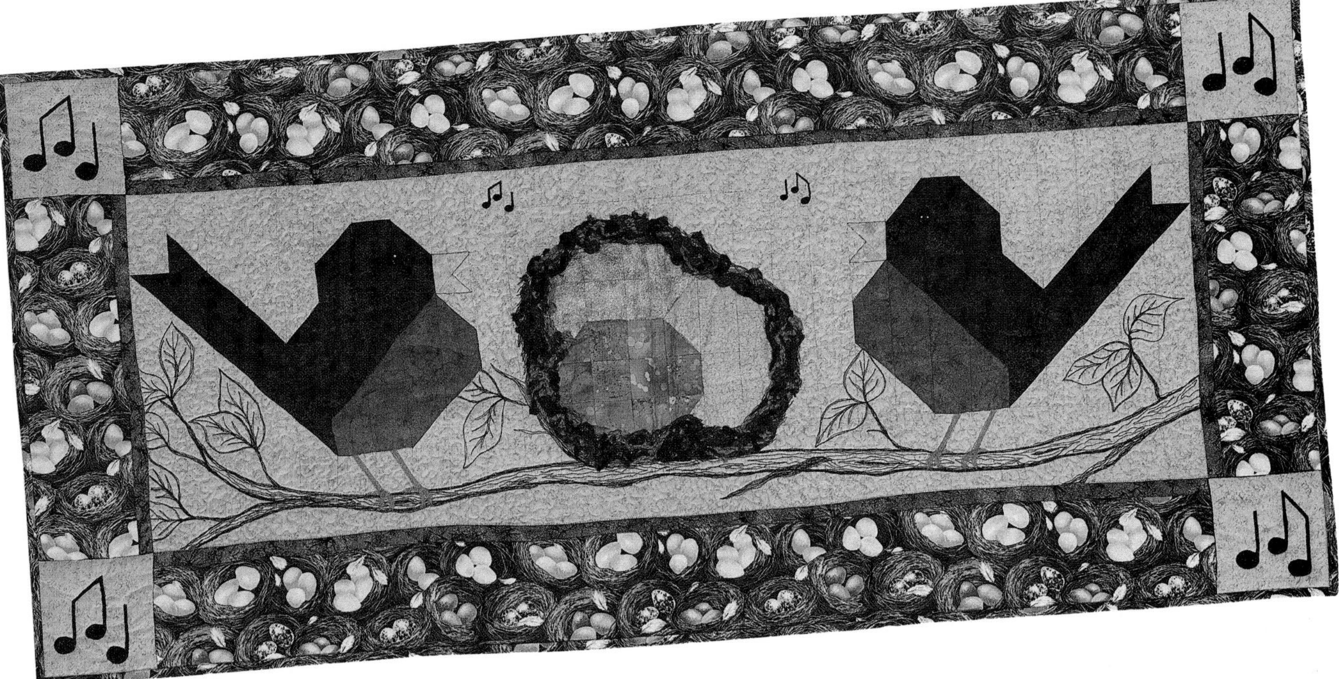

designed and pieced by
Angela Scott
machine quilted by
Phyllis Petersen &
Marcia Stevens

Yardage For Robin's Nest
Finished Size 21" x 46"

- 1/4 yd. egg
- 1/4 yd. egg
- 1/4 yd. egg
- 1/4 yd inside border
- fat quarter beaks
- 1 yd. background
- 1/4 yd. Robin
- 1/4 yd. Robin
- 2 yd. outside border and back

ROBIN'S NEST

BEGINNER

Shopping List

- QSK Quilter's Starter Kit Templates
- Quick Grips
- Omnigrid® Rulers 6" x 24"
- Fiskars® Rotary Cutter
- IBC Glass Head Pins 0.50mm steel shaft
- Fairfield poly-fil low-loft batting
- Sulky® thread
- Variegated yarn

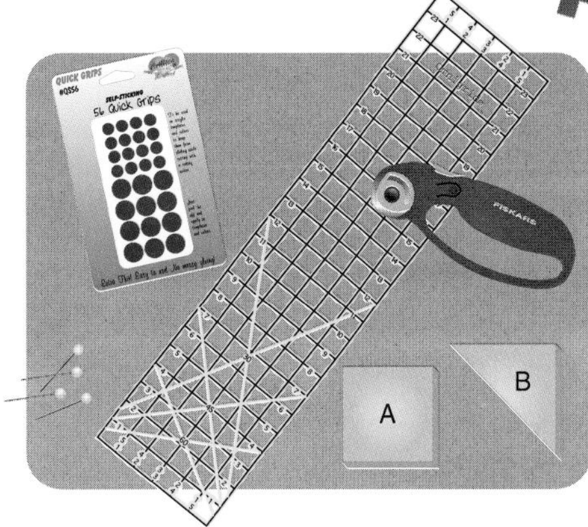

Read pages 2-7 before starting.

Read pages 2-7 before starting.

About The Robins Nest

Step 1. After a long hard Minnesota winter we get so excited when we see a Robin in the yard because it's the first sign of spring. Angie wanted to use them as the subject for her spring quilt. She found a perfect border fabric with Robin eggs at a quilt show during our winter travels. Then when spring came she waited for the Robins to come into the yard so she could pick the right colors. She found three contrasting blues to match eggs in the border fabric.

Step 1

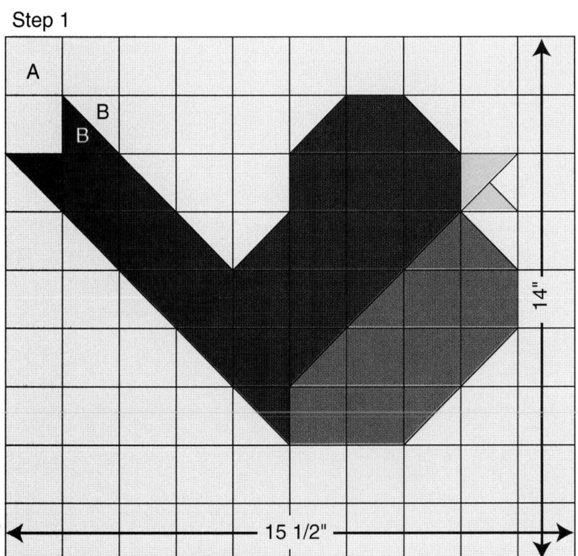

There isn't a lot of texture in the prints, but there is a contrast in color. The quilting shows up so much on fabrics that read as a solid. Marcia Stevens did a beautiful job machine quilting branches and leaves for the Robins to perch on. She gave the Robins legs and built their nest with a combination of variegated yarn and Sulky® thread. Because the Robin is a song bird music notes were perfect in the corner blocks.

There are only two blocks in the quilt made with templates A and B from the Quilters Starter Kit. There will be special sewing and cutting instructions for making Robin beaks and two units in the egg blocks in step 6-8 on page 40

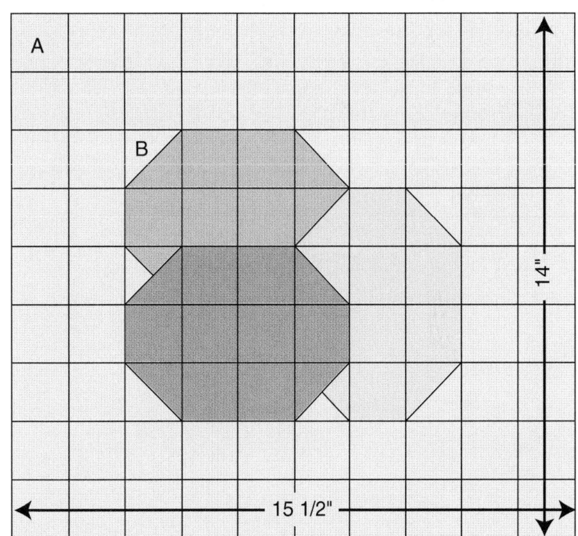

Cutting Instructions

Step 2. Cut 2" strips of each color needed. Bifold strips on top of a small 8' x 12" mat board, so it is easier to turn your work as you cut around the template. See chart below for amount needed.

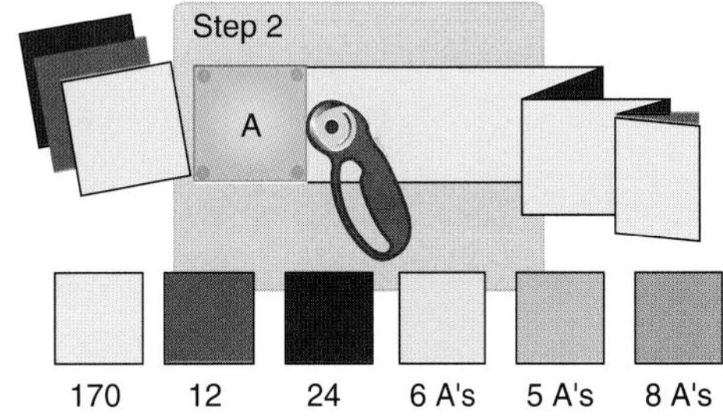

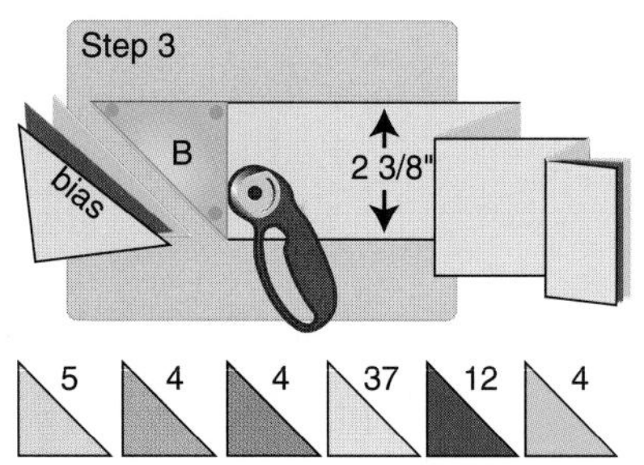

Step 3. Cut strips 2 3/8" wide for template B to get correct grain line. Bifold strips on small mat board. Flip-flop template, cutting pieces as you go. See chart above for number of B's needed.

Step 4. See page 32 Step 4 for instructions to take a sewing test.

Step 5. See Step 5 and Step 6 on page 32 for instructions to chain sew and trim ears off B's.

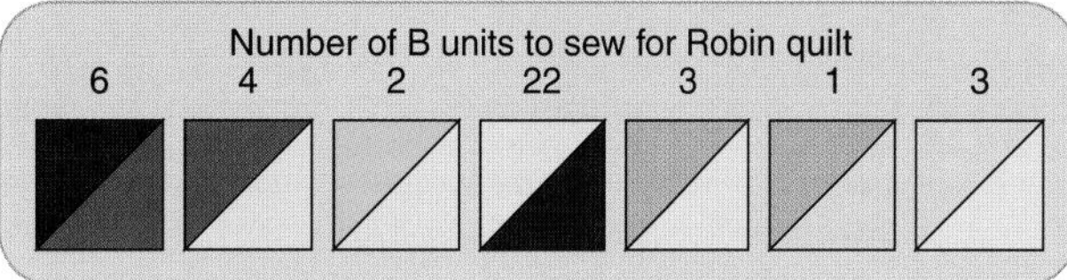

Making Beaks for Robins

Step 6. Place two B units made with gold and ivory made in Step 5 facing each other. Right sides together place another gold B on top of each. Match 90° corners. Sew along bias edge of top B a scant 1/4" from edge. Do not back stitch at beginning or end of seam.

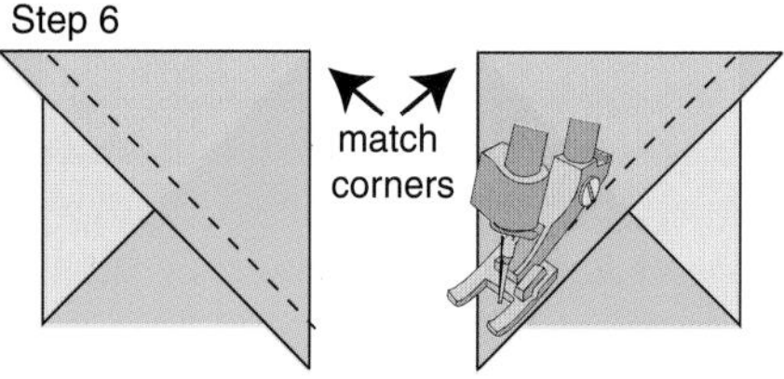

Step 7. Remove ears and extra fabric with scissor.

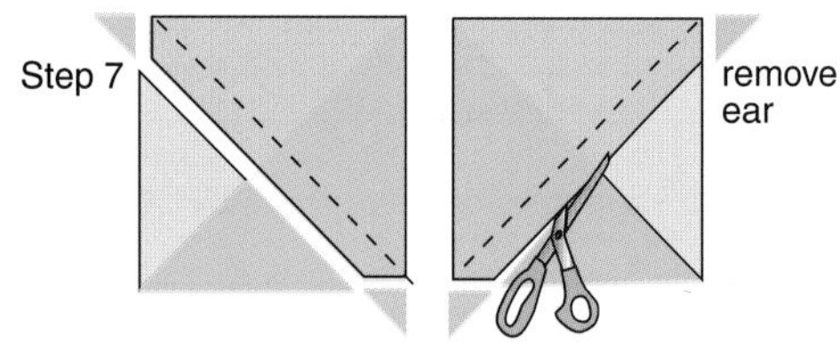

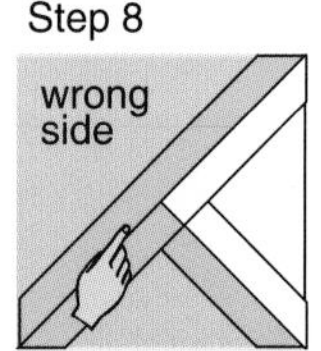

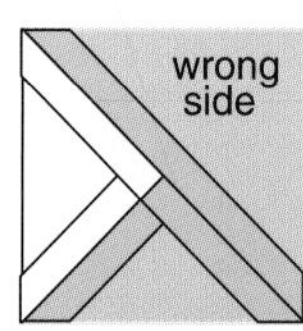

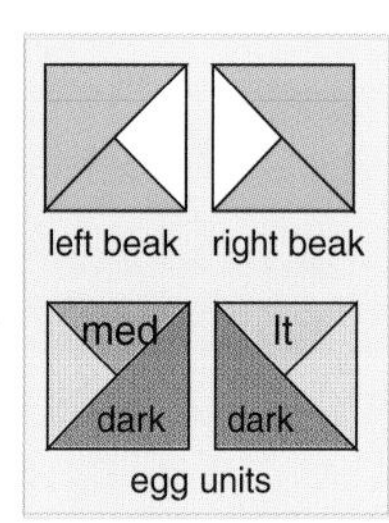

Step 8. Finger press seams open before pressing with an iron. Repeat steps 6-7 to make egg units with light, medium, and dark blues.

Connecting Pieces Into Rows

Step 9. Follow diagram below when arranging pieces on a flannel board. Make sure triangles are turned in right direction when connecting units together. Sew with a scant 1/4" seam allowance. Finger press seams open before pressing with an iron. Intersections should be 1/4" from edge when sewn.

Step 10. Place rows 1 and 2 right sides together. At each intersection insert a pin 1/4" from outside edge on seam line through top and bottom row. Leave this pin standing.

On one or both sides of standing pin, insert another pin to hold intersection in place. Remove standing pin before sewing seam. Add remaining rows and press seams open. When I use only one pin, I prefer to put it on left side of seam. For more pinning options see page 17.

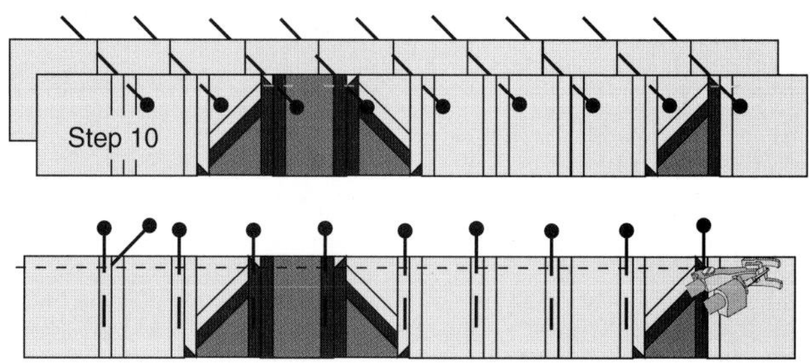

Repeat Steps 9 - 10 to make second robin block. Second block has to be a mirror image of the first one. Make one egg block following diagram on page 39.

Attaching Borders

Step 11. Attach a Robin block to each side of egg block. Press seams open.

Cut inside border strips 1" wide and outside border 4 1/4" wide. Our border fabric was a directional print so the sides borders were cut lengthwise and the top and bottom were cut from selvage to selvage. Angie sewed the inner border to outside border before attaching it to each end of the quilt. Cut four 4 3/4" squares. Attach squares to both ends of top and bottom border. Press seams open. After borders are added see page 6 for instructions to make quilt sandwich.

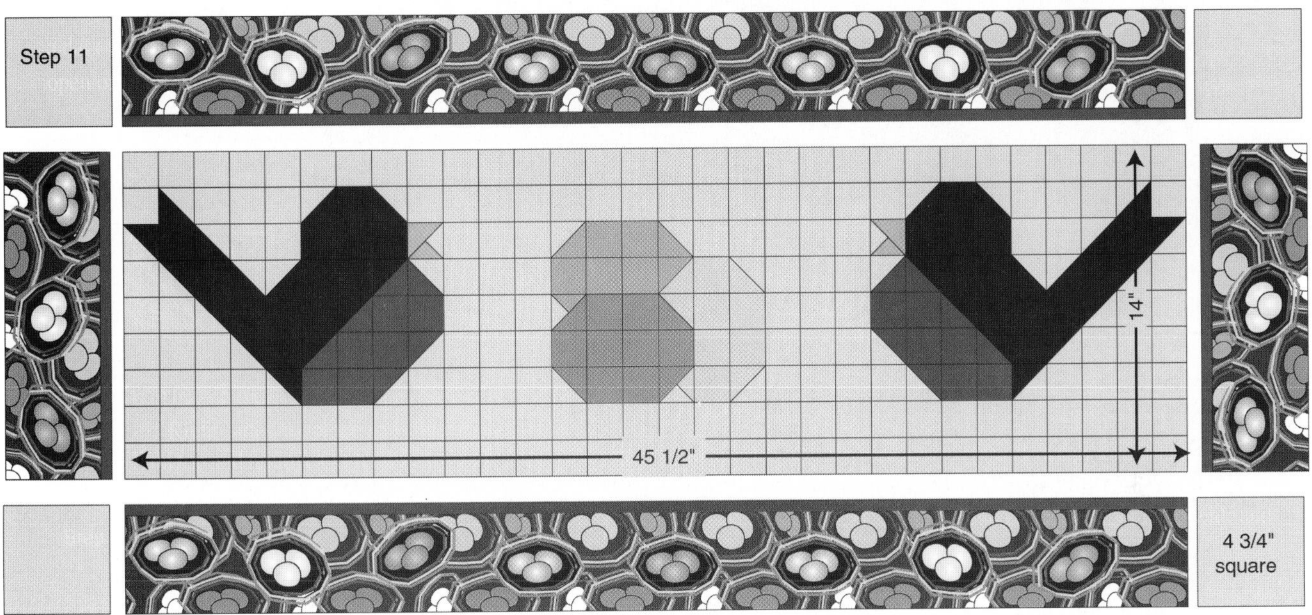

Quilting instructions

Draw quilting designs onto quilt top with a fabric marking pencil. Since there isn't a stencil for these designs you will have to enlarge them on a copy machine or draw them free hand like Marcia did. Remember your design doesn't have to be exactly like ours. You can machine or hand quilt. You can hand quilt 1/4" from edge of each color in the Robin and eggs. We chose to machine quilt in the ditch around each egg and around each color of the Robins. Small meandering was done over the light background. Add buttons for eyes. See page 7 to attach binding. Green thread was used for leaves and brown for branches. Notes and legs of Robins were machine quilted. Notes were filled in by sewing in a continuous circular motion. To create wider lines on notes and Robins legs continue going over same area until you have desired width.

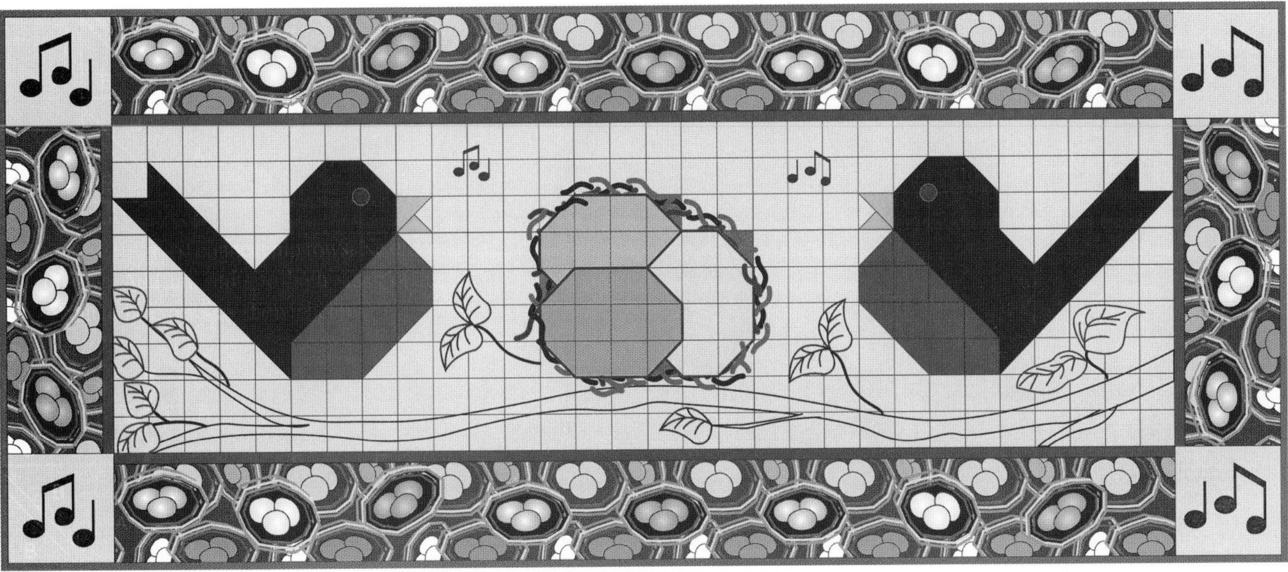

Cat Sampler

designed & pieced by three generations

Sharlene Jorgenson
Angela Scott
Brittany Tostenson

machine quilted by
Lin Grinde

YARDAGE
finished size 70" x 58"

2 yds. gold background
4 yd. backing

1/2 yd. for each cat

1/4 yd. each of 4 fabrics for stars

1/2 yd. striped inner border
2 yds. if not piecing

2 1/4 yd. outer border

YARDAGE
finished size 34" x 39"

2/3 yd. gold background
1 1/4 yd. backing

1/4 yd. for each cat

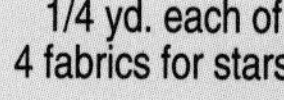
1/4 yd. each of 4 fabrics for stars

1/4 yd. striped inner border

1 1/2 yd. outer border

Shopping List

- QSK Quilter's Starter Kit Templates
- Quick Grips
- Omnigrid® Rulers 6" x 24"
- Fiskars® Rotary Cutter
- IBC Glass Head Pins 0.50mm steel shaft
- Fairfield poly-fil low-loft batting
- Buttons for eyes (optional)
- Continuous Line Star Stencil ST-S

Read pages 2-7 before starting.

About The Cat Sampler

Step 1. Three generations came together to build this quilt. Angie picked the wild fabrics. Both Brittany and I are more conservative, but we let her have her way this time. Brittany says the cats in the border look like they have had too much caffeine. The inner border has a stripe which repeats the stripe in the cats tails. We used vibrant colors of batiks for the cats to match the colors in the outer border. We called it a cat sampler because every cat has a different star in the center. We decided the cats looked better facing each other instead of all looking the same direction.

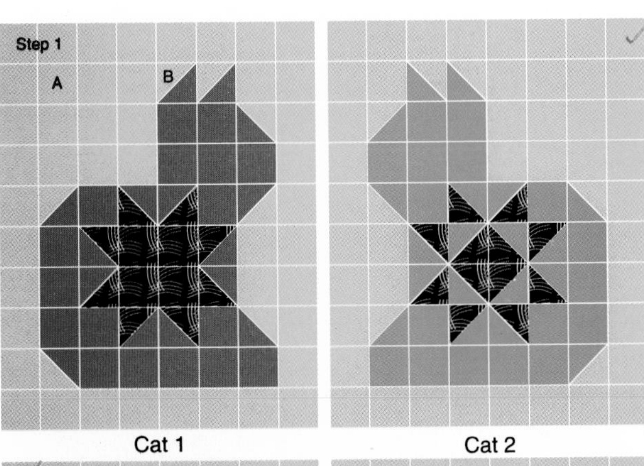

Cat 1 Cat 2

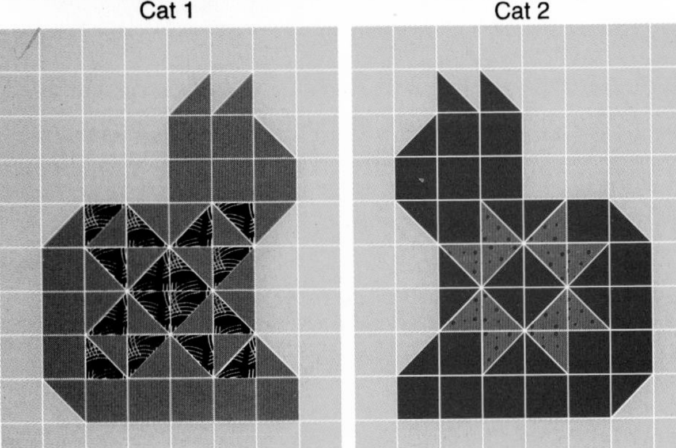

Cat 3 Cat 4

I never dreamt I would consider a yellow background for a quilt, but it was the perfect color this time. Challenge yourself to make a quilt with wild colors. It might shock you in the end like it did me. We liked the finished quilt so much it became the cover.

Cutting Instructions

This is definitely a quilt for beginners to make. Only two shapes were used from the Quilter's Starter Kit to build the whole quilt. It can be made in two sizes. *Use templates A and B to make 12" x 15" blocks or C and D to make 24" x 30" blocks.*

Step 2. Cut strips 2" wide for template A, or 3 1/2" wide for template C. Bi fold strips on a small mat board, so it is easier to turn your work as you cut around the template. See chart below for amount needed.

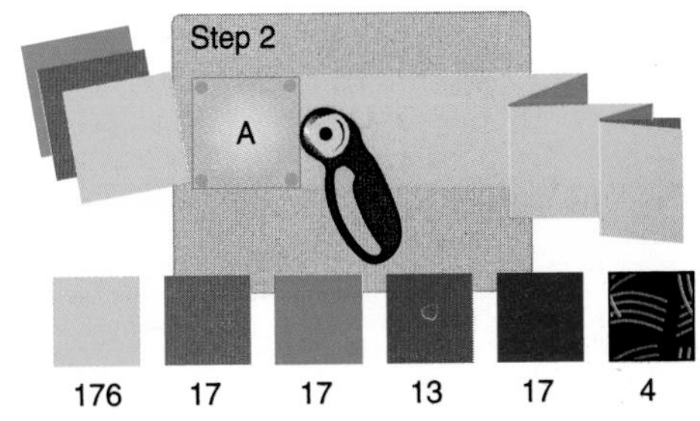

Step 3. Cut strips 2 3/8" wide for template B, or 3 7/8" wide for template D. Flip-flop template cutting pieces as you go. See chart below for number needed.

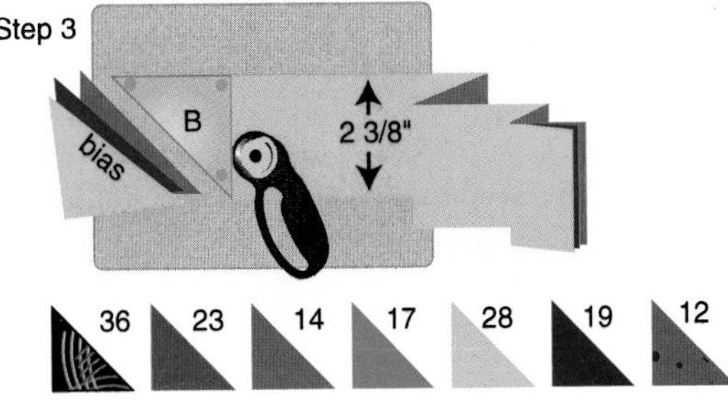

You might want to make different stars in your cats. Brittany designed her stars after she had some half-square triangles sewn together. Just keep turning triangle units until you like what you have. The star fabrics should have a different texture and be a high contrast to the cat. After following exercises 1-4 below you will be amazed how many new stars you can create.

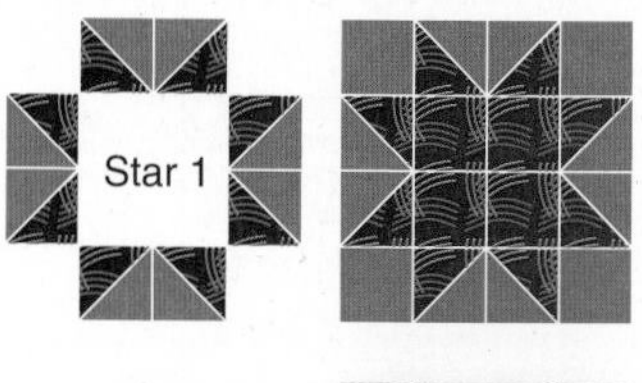

Star 1. Begin each star by arranging half-square triangles as shown to the left. Star 1 is completed with four dark squares in the center and pink corner squares.

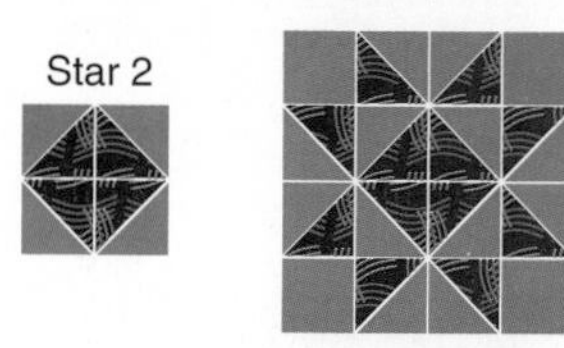

Star 2. To make this star different from the first one, we substituted the four center squares with half-square triangle units.

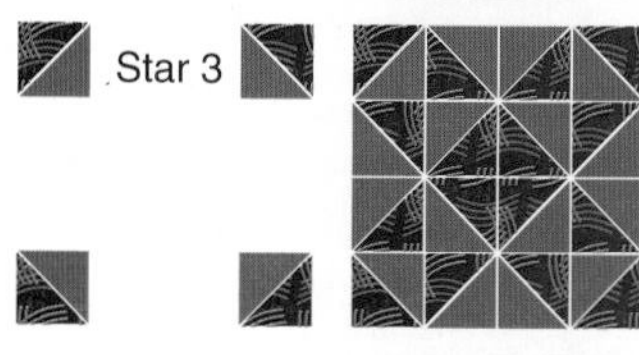

Star 3. This star is the same as star 2 except for the outside corners which have half-square triangle units.

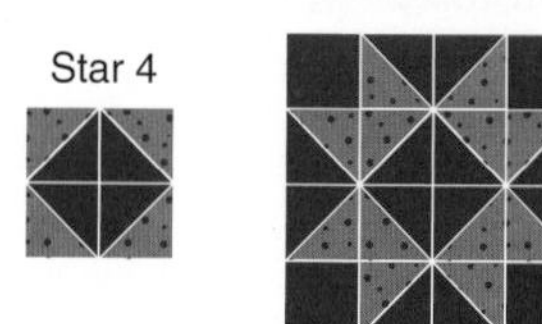

Star 4. To make this star we just turned each half-square triangles in the center of the second star 180°.

Sewing Instructions

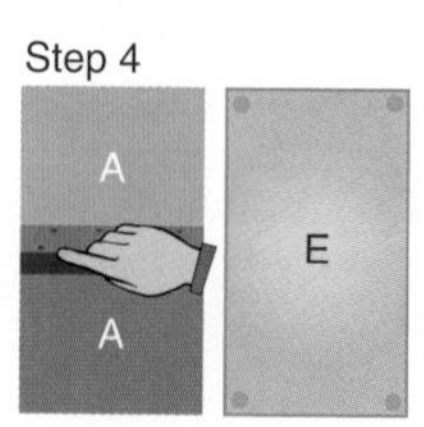

Step 4. Give yourself a sewing test before starting to chain sew. Place two A's right sides together and sew seam with a scant 1/4" seam allowance. We get better results finger pressing seams open on a hard surface. Two A's sewn together should equal E template. If not adjust your seam allowance before continuing.

Step 5. Arrange pieces on a flannel board following cat #1 in Step 1. First chain sew all half-square units. Place 2 B's or (2 D's large) right sides together. Sew along bias edges. To avoid bulk in corners do not back stitch at beginning or end of seam. If your machine eats fabric, start and end sewing on an anchor cloth.

To make stars like ours, follow chart below for amount of half-square triangle units needed.

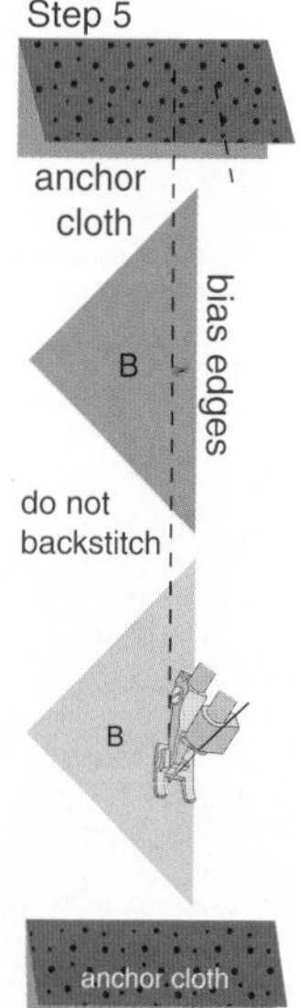

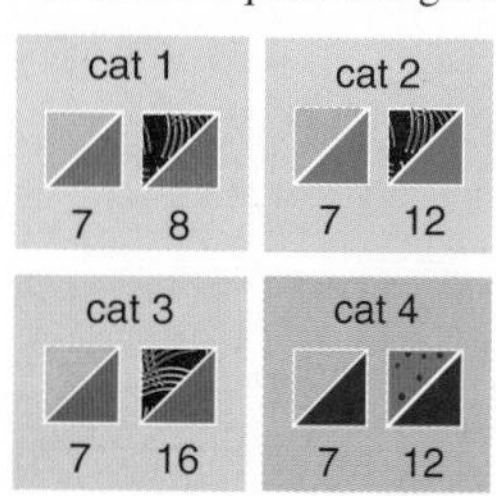

Step 6. There are two ways to remove bulk in corners. Cut at a 90° angle to outside edge of block with a scissor or place a template on top of block after seams are pressed open and trim corners off with a rotary cutter. If you are a beginner and your seam allowance is too scant, extra fabric can be removed with second method.

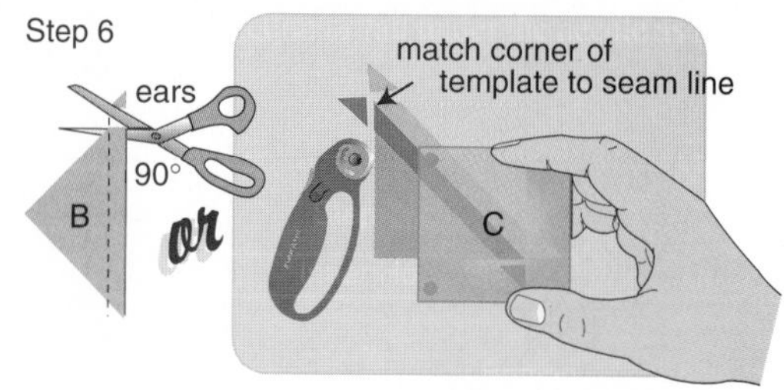

Connect Units Into Rows

Step 7. See diagram in Step 8. It shows the back side of cat #1 made into rows. Connect 8 A's to make the top row. Sew with a scant 1/4" seam allowance. Make sure B triangle units (D triangles large) are turned right direction (see diagram below) when connecting ears together in second row. Insert a pin 1/4' from edge on seam line through both ears as shown. Guide pieces in front of presser foot with stiletto to prevent uneven seams. Do not back stitch at beginning or end of seam.

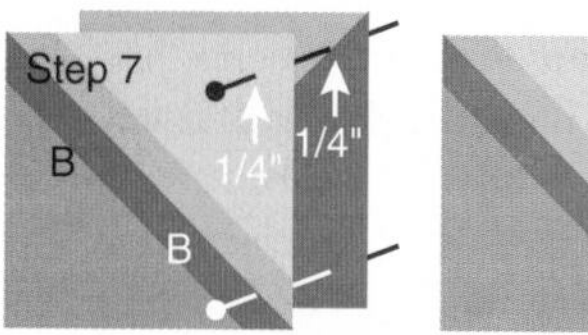

Step 8. Intersections should be 1/4" from top and bottom edges. Finger press seams open before pressing with iron to prevent wells in seam line. Complete all 10 rows as shown below.

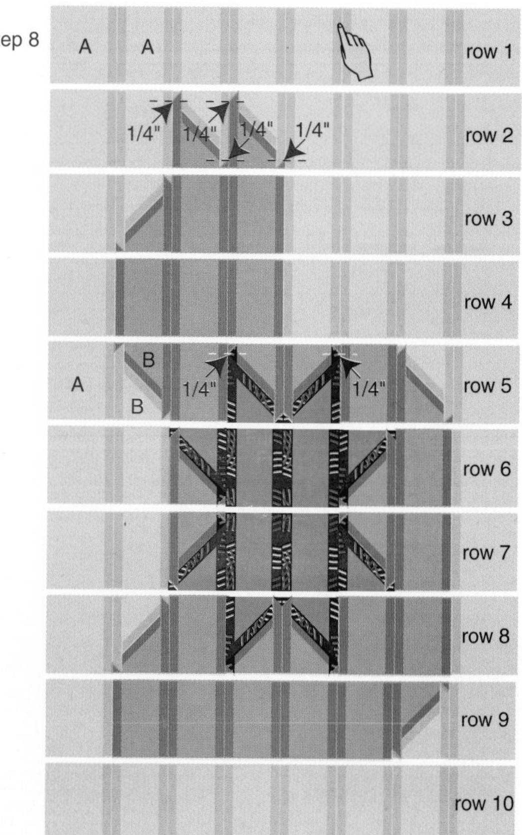

Step 9. Place rows 1 and 2 right sides together. At each intersection insert a pin 1/4" from outside edge on seam line through top and bottom row. Leave this pin standing.

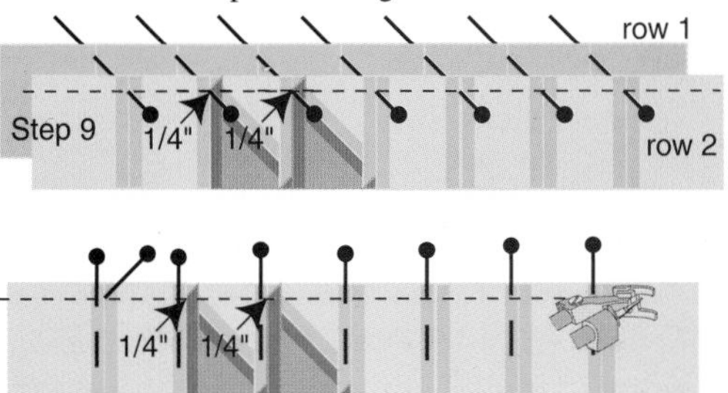

On both sides of standing pin, insert another pin to hold intersection in place. Remove standing pin before sewing seam. Add rest of rows and press seams open. When we use only one pin we prefer to put it on left side of seam. For more pinning options see page 17. Add rest of rows and press seams open.

Repeat steps 5 - 9 and make three more cats. If you are using many colors like we did, distribute colors until they are pleasing to look at.

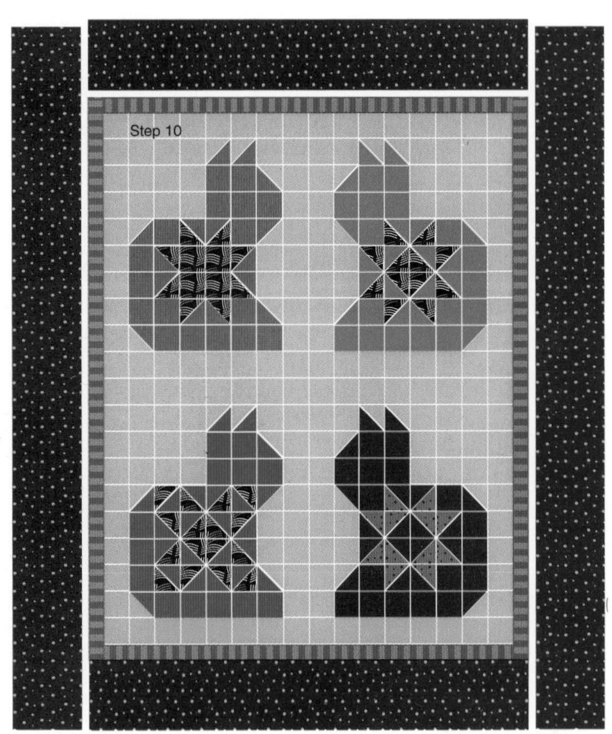

Step 10. Connect cats and press seams open. See photo on page 42 before cutting strips for inside border. We decided the stripe looks best when running horizontal on each side and vertical on top and bottom. Cut strips for inside border 1" wide. Add inside border.

Cut strips for outside border 5" wide. Our border fabric was a directional print so top and bottom borders were cut going from selvage to selvage. To prevent cats from facing wrong direction we cut side borders from length of fabric.

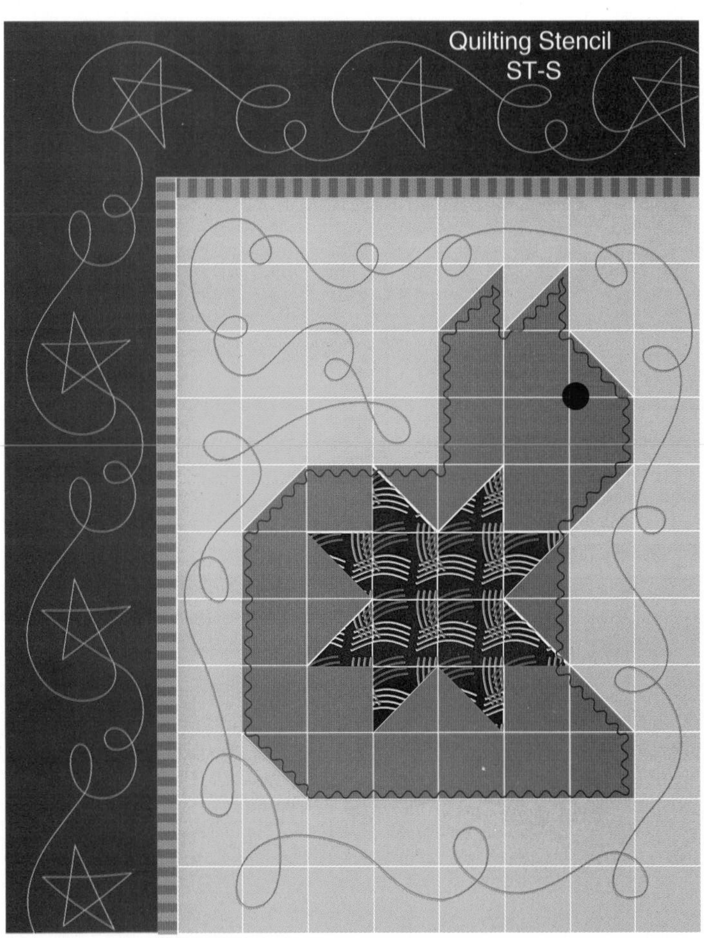

Finishing Touches

After borders have been added see page 6 for instructions to make quilt sandwich.

Lin Grinde did a fantastic job with the machine quilting. She stitched a continuous wave along the edge of each cat and star. The gold background is filled with a continuous loop that resembles yarn the cat might have gotten into. The outside border has a continuous loop with an occasional star. We liked this design so much, because it repeated the idea of stars found in each cat and also the small stars in the border fabric. We don't recommend adding buttons for eyes if it is a crib quilt. To add the binding see page 7.

With Lin's permission we slightly changed the quilting design in the outside border and made it into a quilting stencil every one can enjoy using.

Give Lin a call if you want her
to machine quilt your cat quilt.

320-235-7576
Lin Grinde
DarLin Quilts
6691 Hwy 71 NE
Willmar, MN 56201

designed and pieced by
Angela Scott
machine quilted by
Lin Grinde

Lady Bug Quilt Yardage
Finished size 36" x 36"

- 1 yd. white background
- 3/4 yd. white background
- 1/2 yd. white background
- 1 1/4 yd. white back
- 1 1/4 yd. border & binding

Lady Bug Picnic

Shopping List

- QS 15 Pandora's Box
- QS 27 Add On To Pandora's Box
- Quick Grips
- Omnigrid® Rulers 6" x 24"
- Fiskars® Rotary Cutter
- IBC Glass Head Pins 0.50mm steel shaft
- Fairfield poly-fil low-loft batting
- Velvet buttons (16 small 20 large)

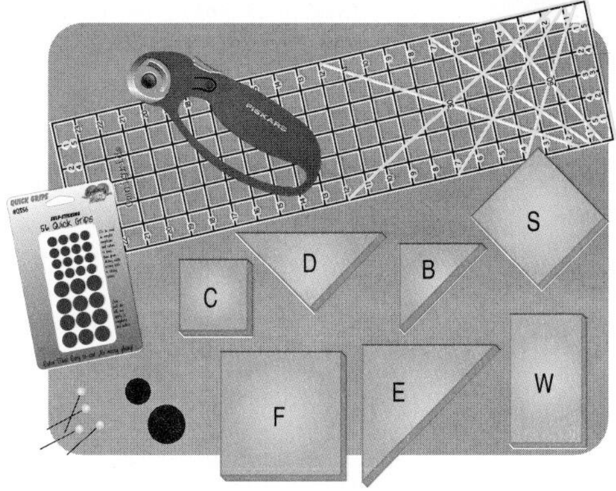

Read pages 2-7 before starting.

About The Lady Bug Picnic

Angie captured bright colors from the Lady Bug border fabric which was the inspiration for this whimsical design filled with energy. It was easy for her to pick fabrics for lady bugs after seeing the border print. She needed only two fabrics with very little texture to make the bugs. She decided on red and black batiks that look like solids. The background fabric was perfect because it is a white on white print filled with butterflies, lady bugs, and dragonflies.

Angie put a checker board block in the center and repeated the same idea in the corners to make it look like the Lady bugs were resting on a picnic cloth. Corner bugs look like they are just landing and center bugs have already started having their lunch.

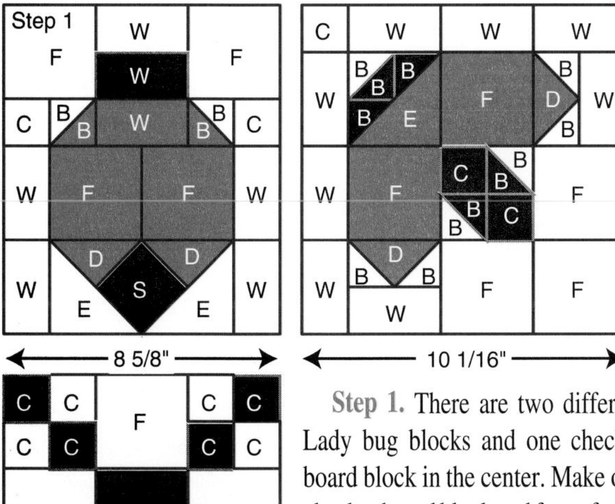

Step 1. There are two different Lady bug blocks and one checker board block in the center. Make one checker board block and four of each Lady bug block. Angie used the same three fabrics for all Lady Bugs and the same white and black for center checker board block.

Cutting Instructions

Templates B, C, D, E, and F from Pandora's Box and templates S and W from Add On To Pandora's Box were used.

Arrows in diagram indicate straight of grain needed for each piece. Cut strips width needed to get correct grain line. Flip-flop template, cutting pieces as you go. Follow diagram for number needed. Repeat step to cut squares and rectangles.

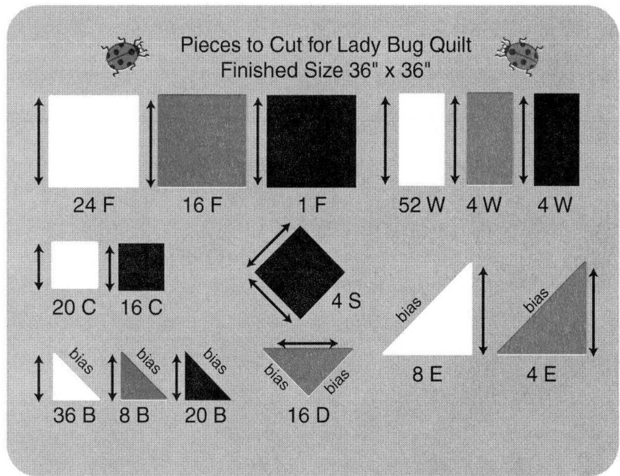

Step 2. See page 2 to prepare fabric and page 3 to straighten fabric. Arrows in diagram indicate straight of grain needed for each piece. Cut strips width needed to get correct grain line. Flip-flop template, cutting pieces as you go. Follow diagram above for number needed.

Repeat step to cut squares and rectangles.

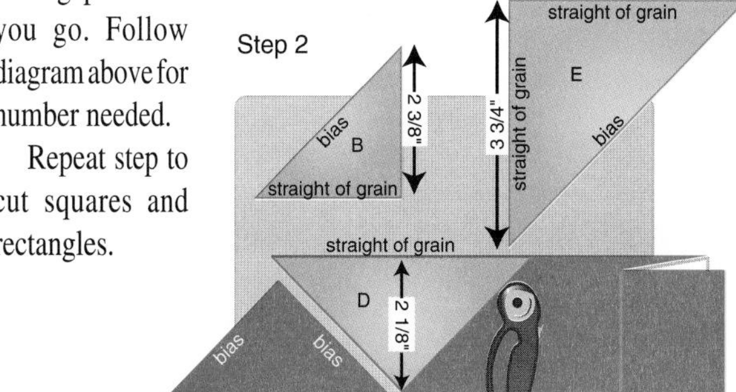

Sewing Instructions

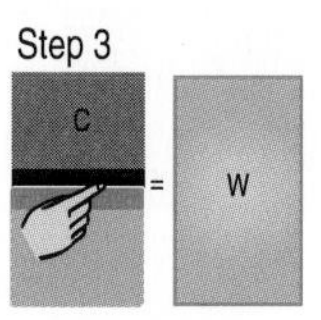

Step 3. Before starting to sew, give yourself a sewing test. Squares are easiest to sew together for sewing test because there is no doubt how to line them up. Place 2 C's right sides together and sew seam with a scant 1/4' seam allowance. Finger press seam open, then press with an iron. Two C's sewn together should equal the W. If not adjust before continuing.

Step 4a. Arrange pieces for each Lady Bug on a flannel board.

b. Chain sew B's together. Do not back stitch at beginning or end of seam. When using an anchor cloth beginning stitches on patchwork will be more secure and won't fall apart as easily as first stitches sewn. If you guide pieces in front of presser foot with a stiletto you don't have to worry about pieces scooting to one side at end of seam. Save time and thread by sewing off onto a second anchor cloth.

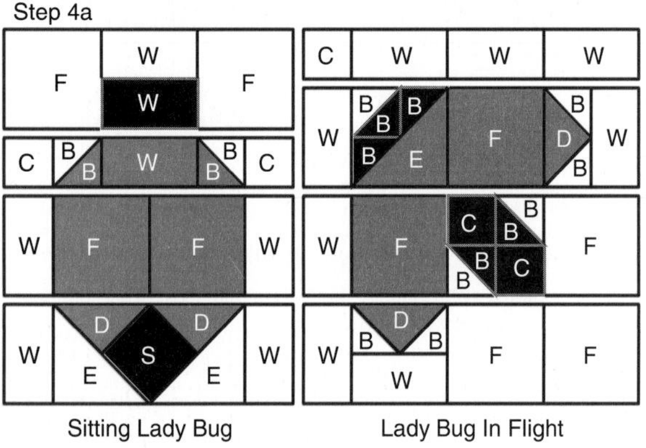

c. Finger press seams open, before pressing with an iron.

d. There are two ways to remove bulk in corners. Cut at a 90° angle to outside edge of block with a scissor or place template on top of block after seams are pressed open and trim corners off with a rotary cutter. If you are a beginner and seam allowance is too scant, it can be corrected with second method.

Connecting Units Into Rows

Step 5. Connect units for sitting Lady Bug into rows. Press all seams open. See steps 6a-6h to make tail unit needed in fourth row.

Step 6a. Right sides together, put a red D on top of an S square. Match corners. This seam will not end in crevice. There will be a couple of stitches on D. Guide fabric with stiletto. See step 4b. Do not back stitch at either end of seam.

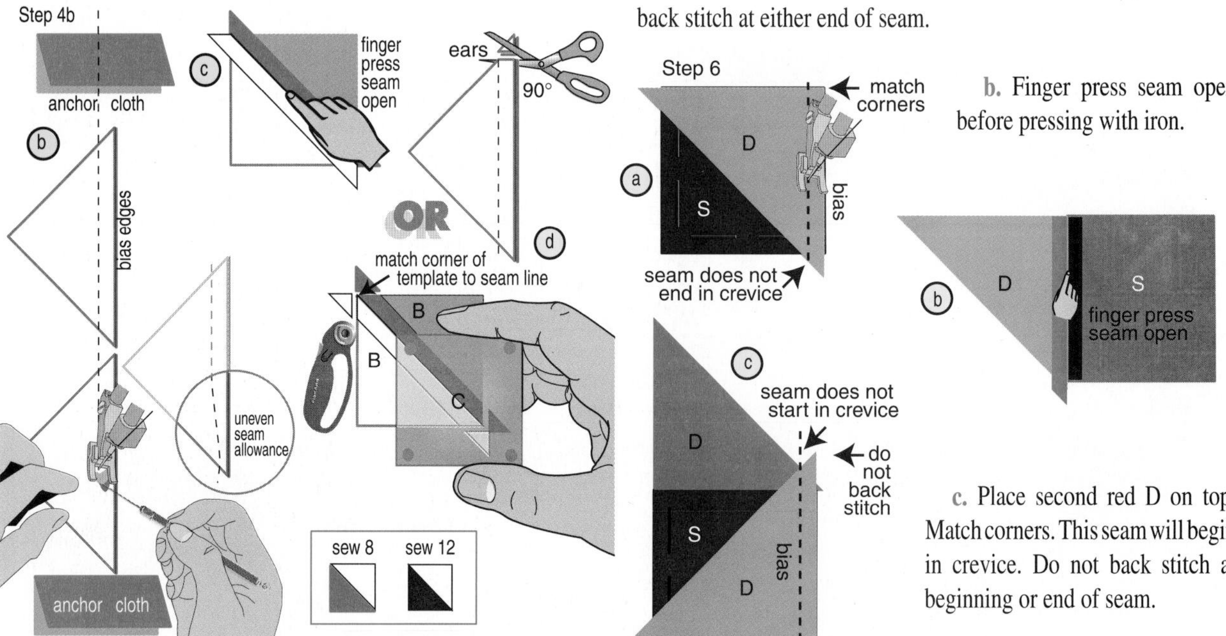

b. Finger press seam open before pressing with iron.

c. Place second red D on top. Match corners. This seam will begin in crevice. Do not back stitch at beginning or end of seam.

d. Press seam open and remove ears.

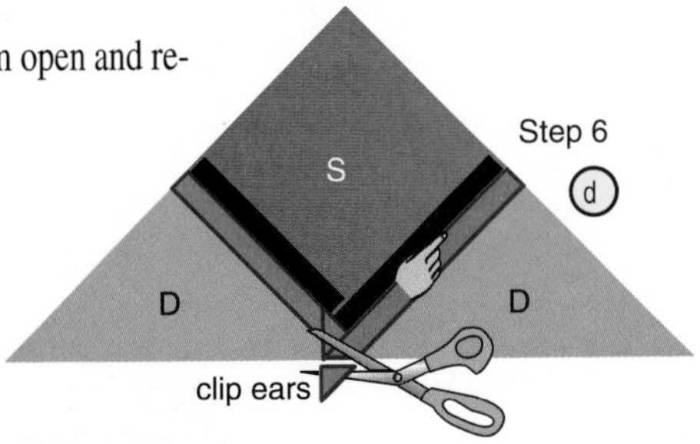

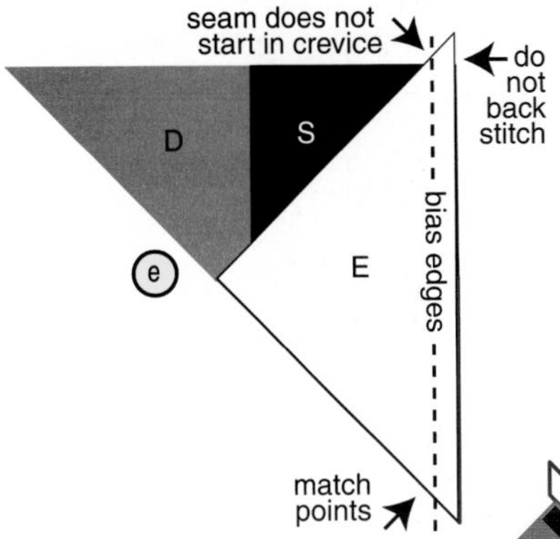

e. Put white E on top of unit. Match points. This seam does not start in crevice.

f. Press seam open.

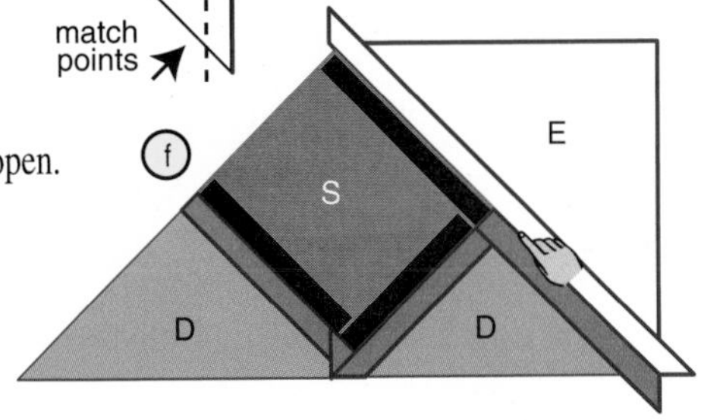

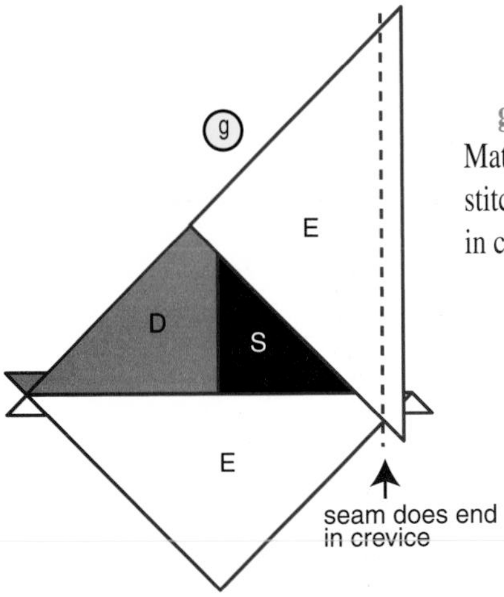

g. Add second white E. Match points. Do not back stitch. This seam will end in crevice.

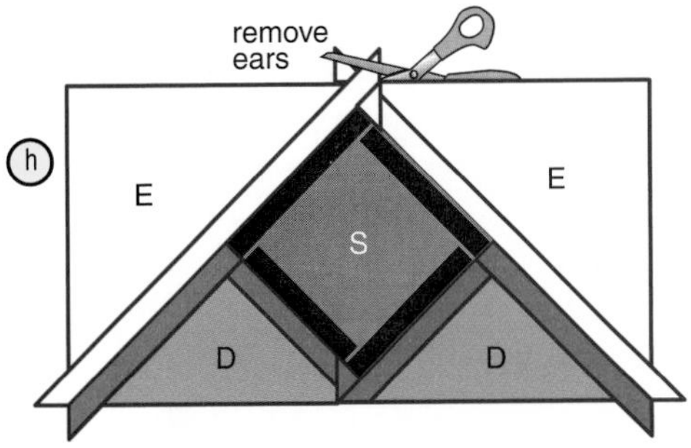

h. Press seam open. Remove ears. To complete this row add a W to both ends of this unit. See diagram in Step 5.

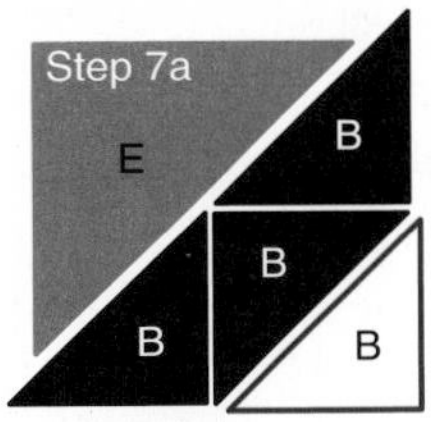

Sewing Lady Bug In Flight

Step 7a. Arrange units for head of Lady Bug as shown in diagram to left. Use one of the black and white B units made in steps 4a - 4d in the bottom right corner.

b. Place another black B on top as shown. Make sure black and white B's are turned in right direction. Match corners. This seam will not end in crevice. Do not back stitch at beginning or end of seam.

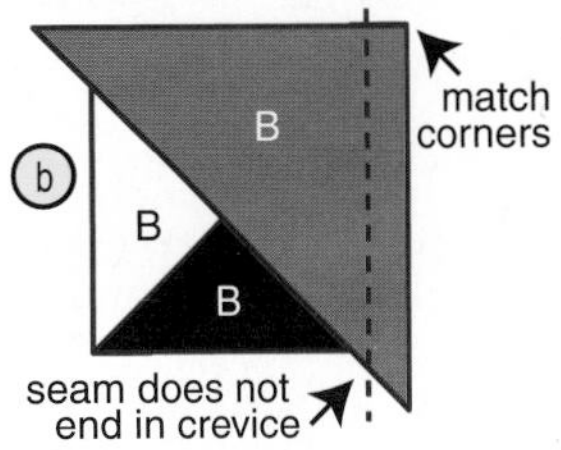

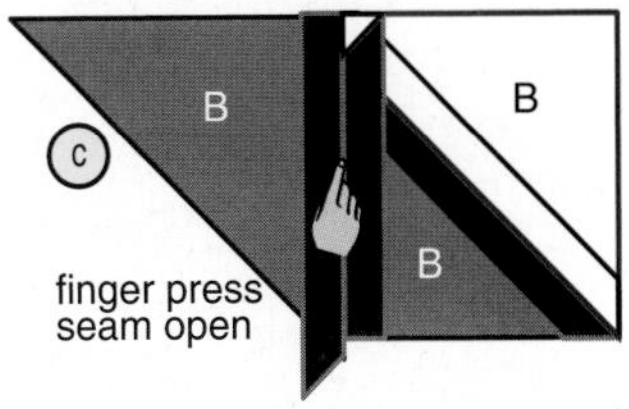

c. Finger press seam open.

d. Right sides together add another black B. This seam starts in crevice. Do not back stitch at beginning or end of seam.

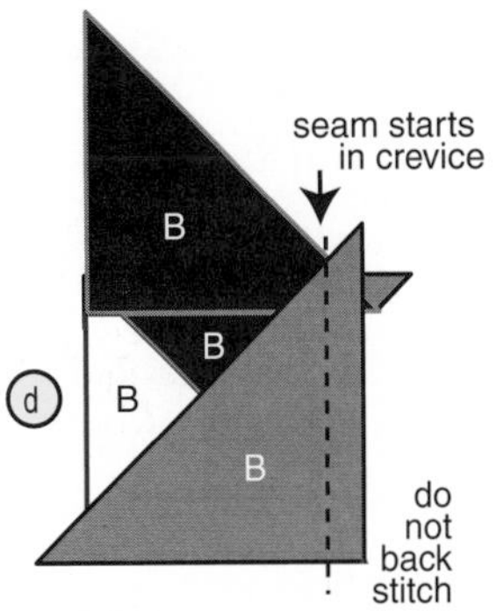

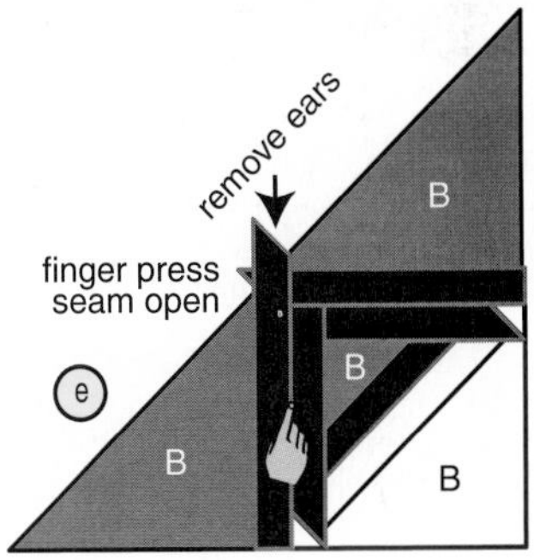

e. Finger press seam open.

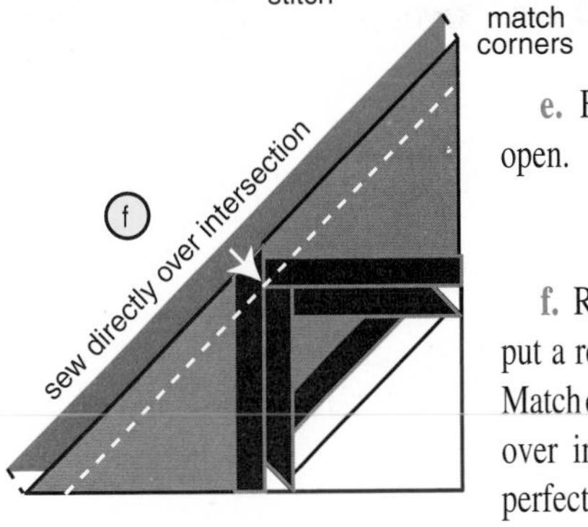

f. Right sides together put a red E on the bottom. Match corners. Sew directly over intersection to get a perfect point on right side.

Step 7g. Press seam open. Intersections along outside edge will be 1/4" from edge. Trim corners of block. These units sewn together should equal the F template. This completes the head unit of Lady Bug in flight. Make four.

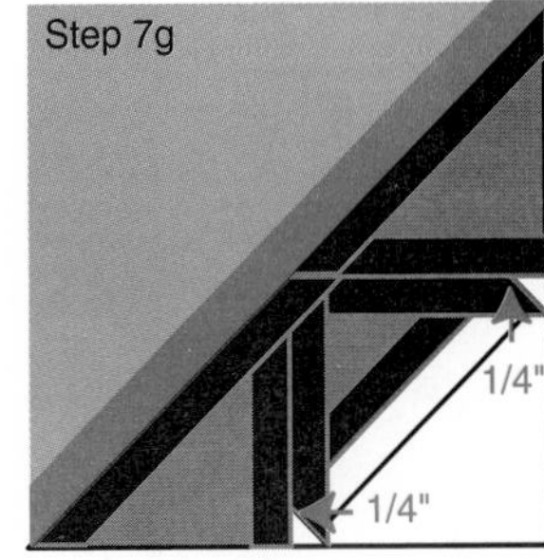

Step 8a. Two flying geese units are used in wings of each lady bug in flight. They are both the same color combination. One is used in second row and the other is used in fourth row. See Step 4a.

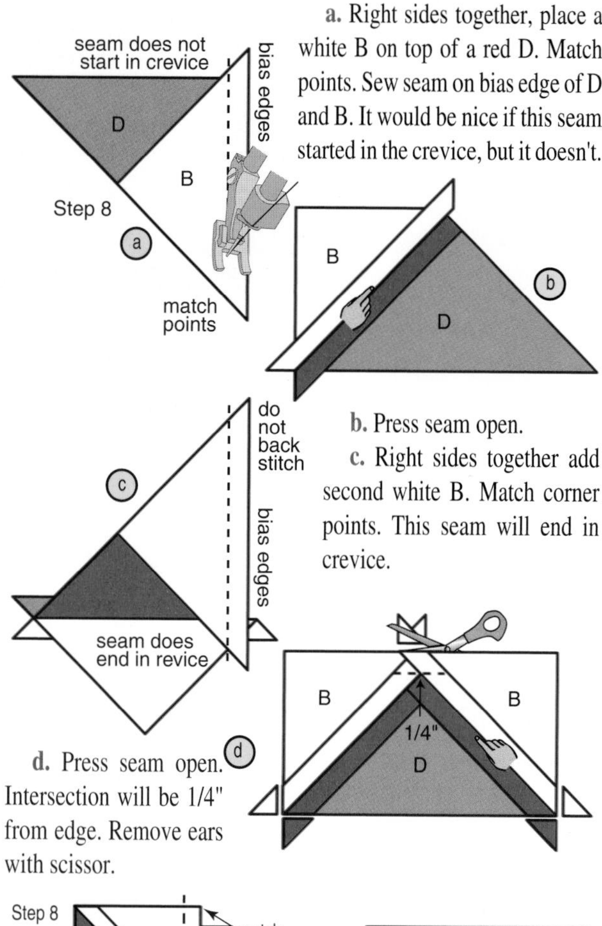

a. Right sides together, place a white B on top of a red D. Match points. Sew seam on bias edge of D and B. It would be nice if this seam started in the crevice, but it doesn't.

b. Press seam open.

c. Right sides together add second white B. Match corner points. This seam will end in crevice.

d. Press seam open. Intersection will be 1/4" from edge. Remove ears with scissor.

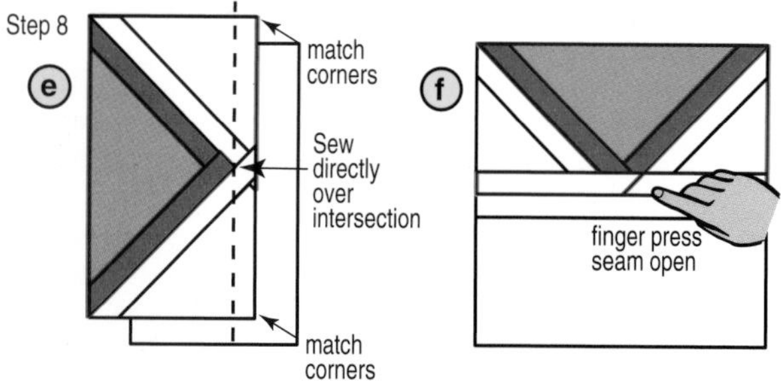

e. Right sides together, put a white W on bottom of flying geese unit. Match corners and sew directly over intersection.

f. Press seam open. Repeat Steps 8a - 8f and make a total of eight.

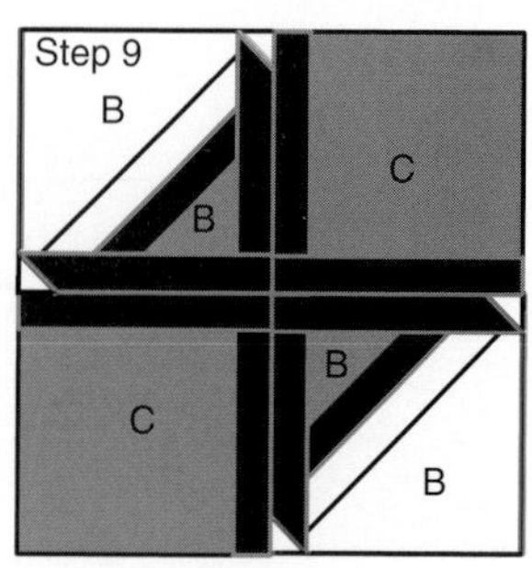

Step 9. To make tail section of Lady Bug in Flight, connect black and white B units to black C's into two rows as shown. Press seam open. Connect rows. Make four exactly alike.

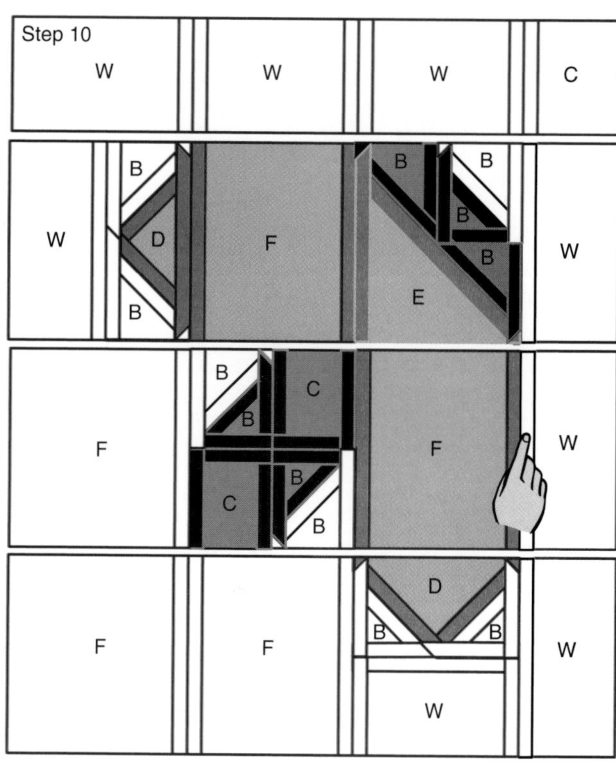

Step 10. Connect units for Lady Bug in flight into rows. Flying geese units are used in second and fourth row. Make sure they are turned in right direction. The tail unit is used in third row. Press all seams open after rows are made.

Connect all rows. Make four of these bugs.

Next follow diagram in Step 1 to make one checker board block.

Step 11. Arrange blocks as shown with the checker board block in the center. Connect blocks into rows as shown in diagram below. Press seams open.

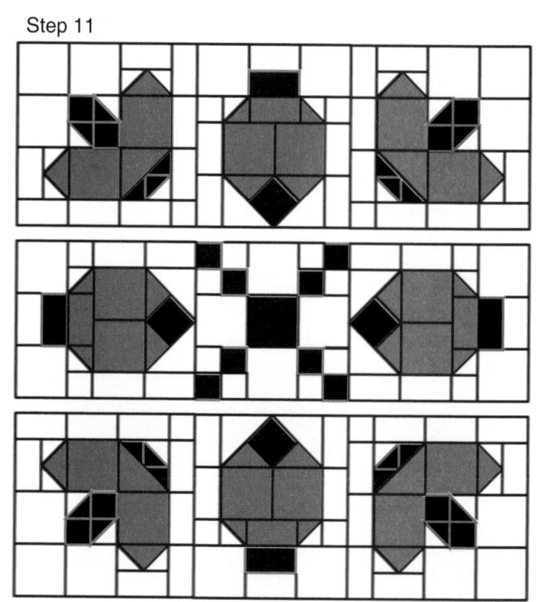

Sashing and Cornerstones

Step 12. Use template C to make four black and white nine-patch blocks for corners. Press seams open. Measure the length of all sides of quilt and take the average measurement. Cut four strips of border fabric length of quilt edges and width of your corner blocks.

Put sashing on bottom when attaching it to the quilt so seams you want to sew over are visible. Press seam allowance towards the sashing. Attach corner blocks to both ends of top and bottom sashing. Press these seams towards sashing. Attach top and bottom border.

To prepare quilt back and sandwich see page 7.

Finishing Touches

Sometimes it is hard to figure out which quilting designs would look best after the top is finished. Lin Grinde was very creative when she machine quilted this one. To add life to lady bugs, she used red thread to sew a continuous line loop on wings and backs. Around all black parts she stitched a black continuous wave. The machine did a three forward, two backward (cha cha) stitch with black thread to make it look like the legs and antennas were hand embroidered. Small meandering with white thread was done over the white background and a green continuous leaf was put in the border.

In the eleventh hour we got help from Margaret Lykins, Beth Love, and Betty Smith to decide where to put the buttons. They decided to use small buttons for heads. They also thought it looked best to use two small and two large buttons on backs of corner bugs. Three large buttons were put on backs of center bugs. I think you would agree, anyone would love to own this quilt.

designed & pieced by
Angela Scott
machine quilted by
Marcia Stevens
faces painted by
Jill McCoy

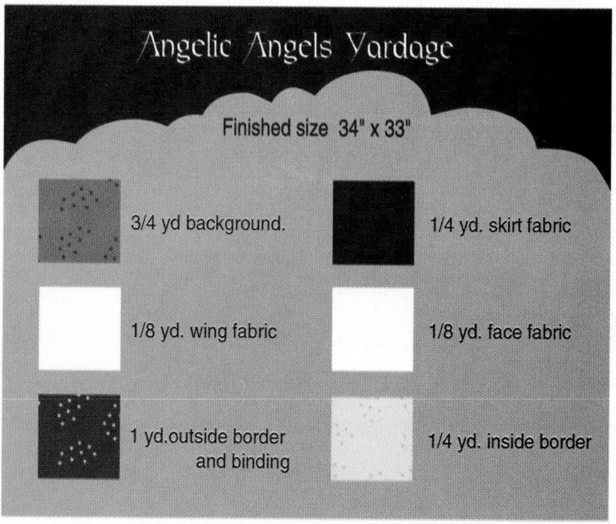
Angelic Angels Yardage
Finished size 34" x 33"
3/4 yd background.
1/4 yd. skirt fabric
1/8 yd. wing fabric
1/8 yd. face fabric
1 yd.outside border and binding
1/4 yd. inside border

INTERMEDIATE

Shopping List

- QS 15 Pandora's Box templates (L, M, N, O, J, and G)
- QS 27 Add On To Pandora's Box template (Q)
- Quick Grips
- Omnigrid® Rulers 6" x 24"
- Fiskars® Rotary Cutter
- IBC Glass Head Pins 0.50mm steel shaft
- ST-S continuous line star stencil
- Fairfield poly-fil low-loft batting
- Pigma permanent marking pencils
- Angel hair and 8 iron on stars

Read pages 2-7 before starting.

About Angelic Angels

Angie has been collecting celestial fabrics as well as all types of angels for years. She learned the hard way that you need to pick the border fabric first. After she had the main part of her first angel quilt finished we were unable to find the right border fabric. This gives us a good excuse to keep going to more fabric stores.

The second time she made an angel quilt she chose the border print first. It is a dark print filled with angels and stars. The angels look best made out of a fabric that looks like a solid. We were lucky to find a fabric that looks like it has silver angel dust all over it to add even more sparkle. The background and inner border fabrics are the same print, but in different colors. They have small clusters of stars covered with silver metallic speckles.

Cutting Instructions

Step 1. Bi- fold strips on a small mat board. Flip-flop template cutting pieces as you go until you have the number needed.

- Cut one strip 2" wide for M from background fabric.
- Cut one strip 3 1/4" wide for N from background and wing fabric.
- Cut one strip 5 3/4" for O from skirt fabric.
- Cut one strip 2" wide for L from background.

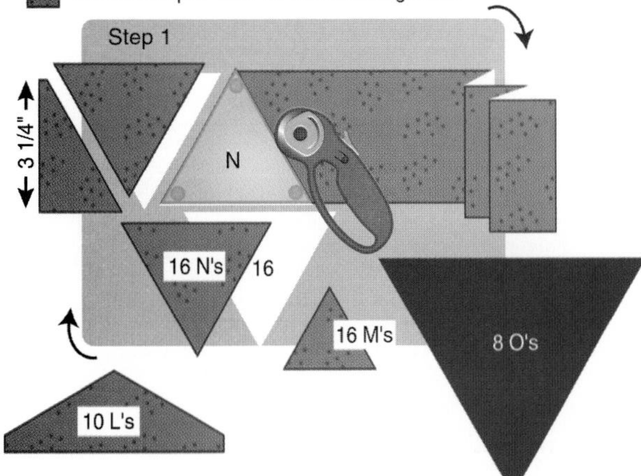

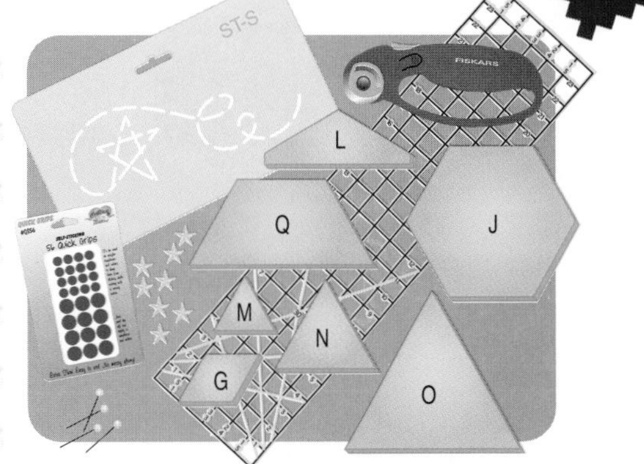

- Cut one strip 1 3/4" wide for G from face fabric.
- Cut one strip 3" wide for Q from background fabric.
- Cut one strip 5 1/2" for J from background fabric.

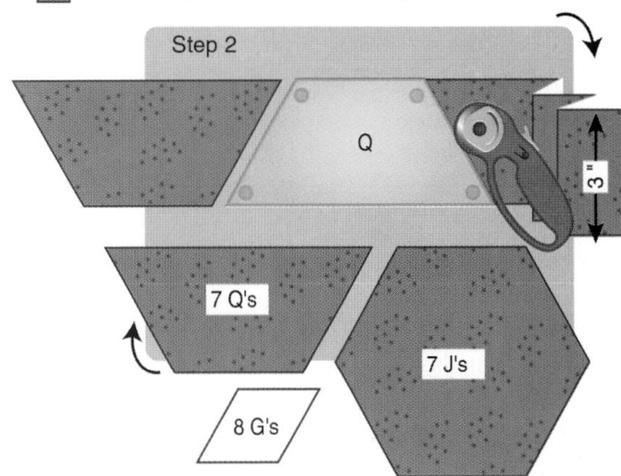

Step 3. Follow this step if you are not comfortable drawing faces on angels after the top is finished. Place white fabric on top of our pattern and trace features with different colors of permanent marking pencils. Our pattern is actual size. Center template G on top of face and fussy cut one at a time.

Make 8 faces.

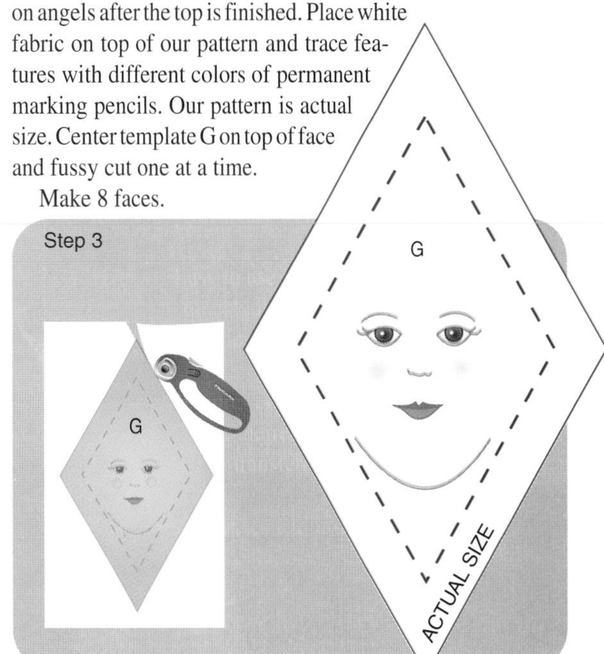

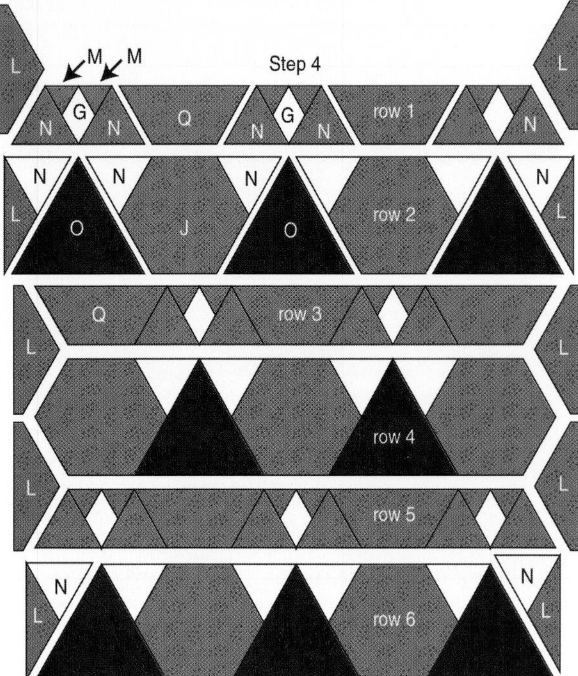

Step 4. Angie was able to arrange difficult shapes into rows making this a fast and easy quilt to make. Arrange pieces on a flannel board as shown in diagram above.

Sewing Instructions

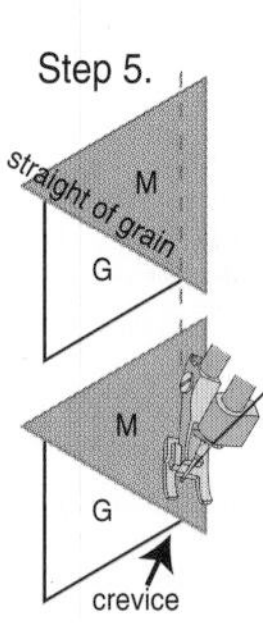

Step 5. Start with head units. Make *only one* and pass sewing test in step 7 before starting to chain sew. Use G's with painted faces if you don't want to draw on finished quilt.

Tip! Put straight of grain of M piece as shown in diagram to stabilize bottom of head unit.

Put an M and G right sides together. They are easy to match because points match on one corner. It's not necessary to pin. Sew with a scant 1/4" seam allowance. Seam ends in crevice. Do not back stitch at beginning or end of seam because they will be crossed over again. Chain sew 8.

Step 6
G
M
right side
straight of grain

Step 6. It is easier to finger press seams open on a hard surface. Press with an iron after seams have been finger pressed open.

Step 7a. Right sides together, place an M on top. Seam will start in crevice and points will match at bottom of seam.

b. Intersection will be 1/4" from edge. Press seams open.

c. These pieces sewn together will equal template N.

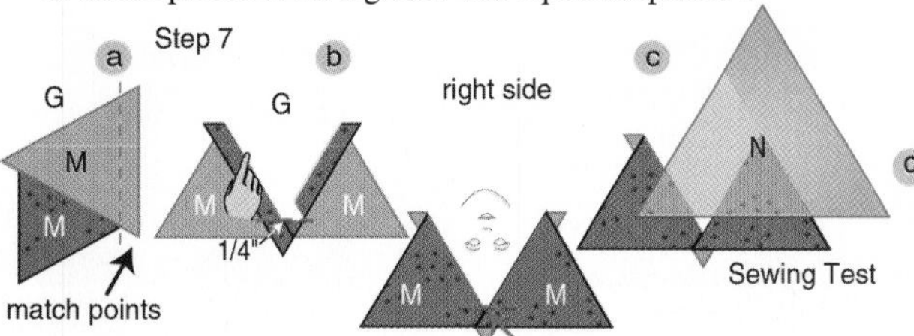

Connect Units In Rows 1, 3, and 5

Step 8a. Right sides together place an N on bottom of head unit as shown. Points will match.

b. Do not back stitch at beginning or end of seam.

c. Finger press seam open.

d. Add second N to opposite side.

e. Right sides together place a Q on the bottom as shown. Match ears at beginning of seam. Seam will end in crevice.

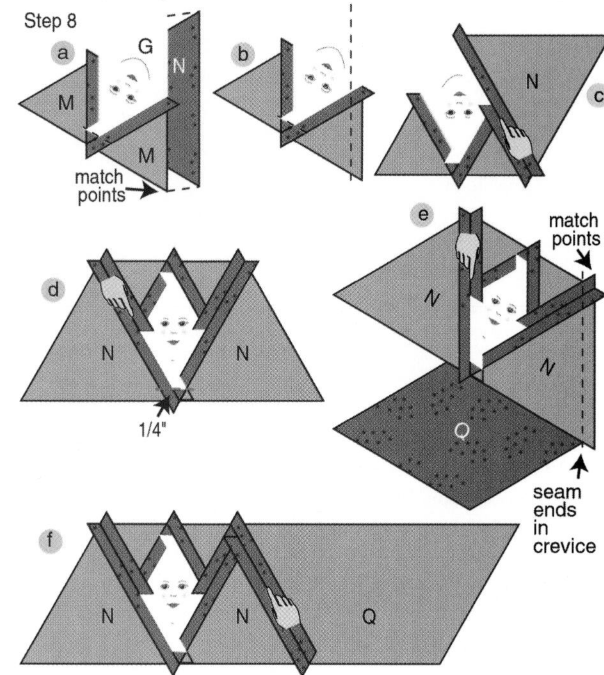

f. Finger press seam open. Follow diagram in Step 4 when connecting pieces together. Row 1 and 5 are the same. Because there are two angels in middle of quilt row 3 starts and ends with a Q.

Connecting Units In Rows 2, 4, and 6

Step 9a. Right sides together place white wing (N) on top of (L) as shown. A *small ear* from L should extend behind N at beginning of seam.

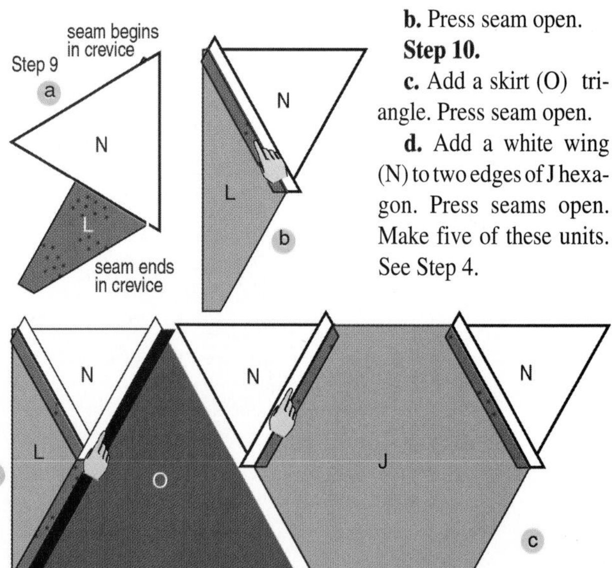

b. Press seam open.

Step 10.

c. Add a skirt (O) triangle. Press seam open.

d. Add a white wing (N) to two edges of J hexagon. Press seams open. Make five of these units. See Step 4.

Step 11

row 1

row 2

row 3

NOTE:
The faces will not be on back of quilt, as shown in diagrams. They are there only for reference to show direction of faces on front of quilt.

Step 11. Connect all units into rows 1-6 as shown.

Press seams open.

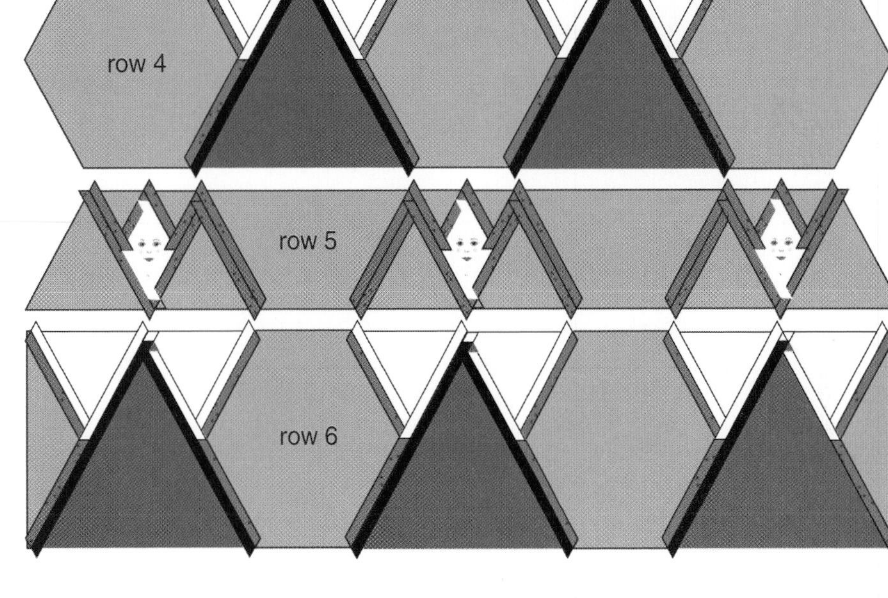

Step 12. Right sides together, put row 1 on top of row 2. Insert a pin at each intersection 1/4" from edge through top and bottom row. Sew directly over point pin goes into seam.

Press seams open.

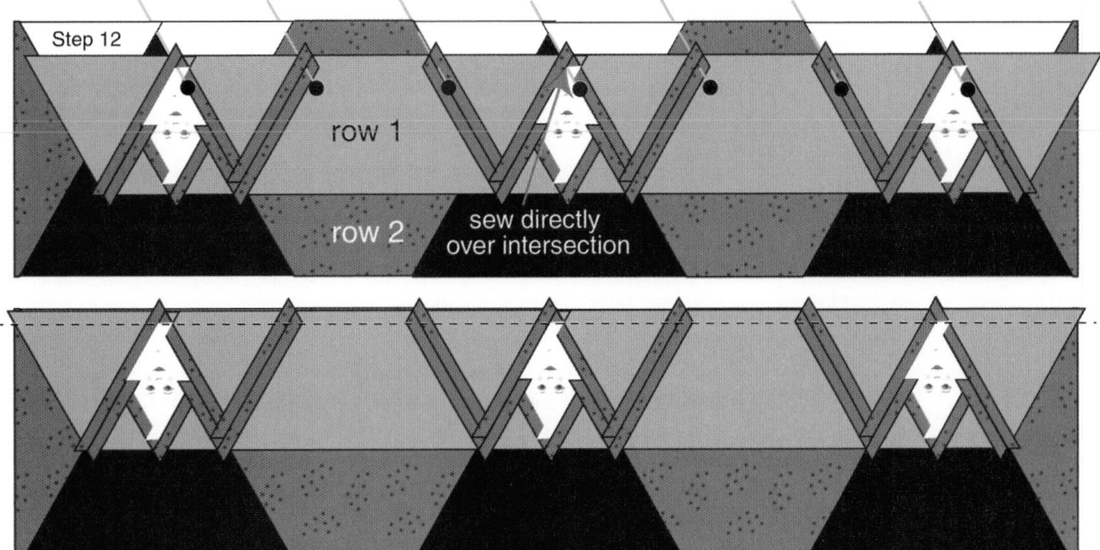

Step 13. Use L triangles to straighten side edges. Right sides together *place L on bottom of quilt so intersection you want to pivot on is visible.* Start sewing at outside edge. Stop sewing at intersection with needle in down position. Lift presser foot. Readjust fabric, drop presser foot and sew to other end. Use L triangles to square up top corners of quilt. Remove extra with scissor.

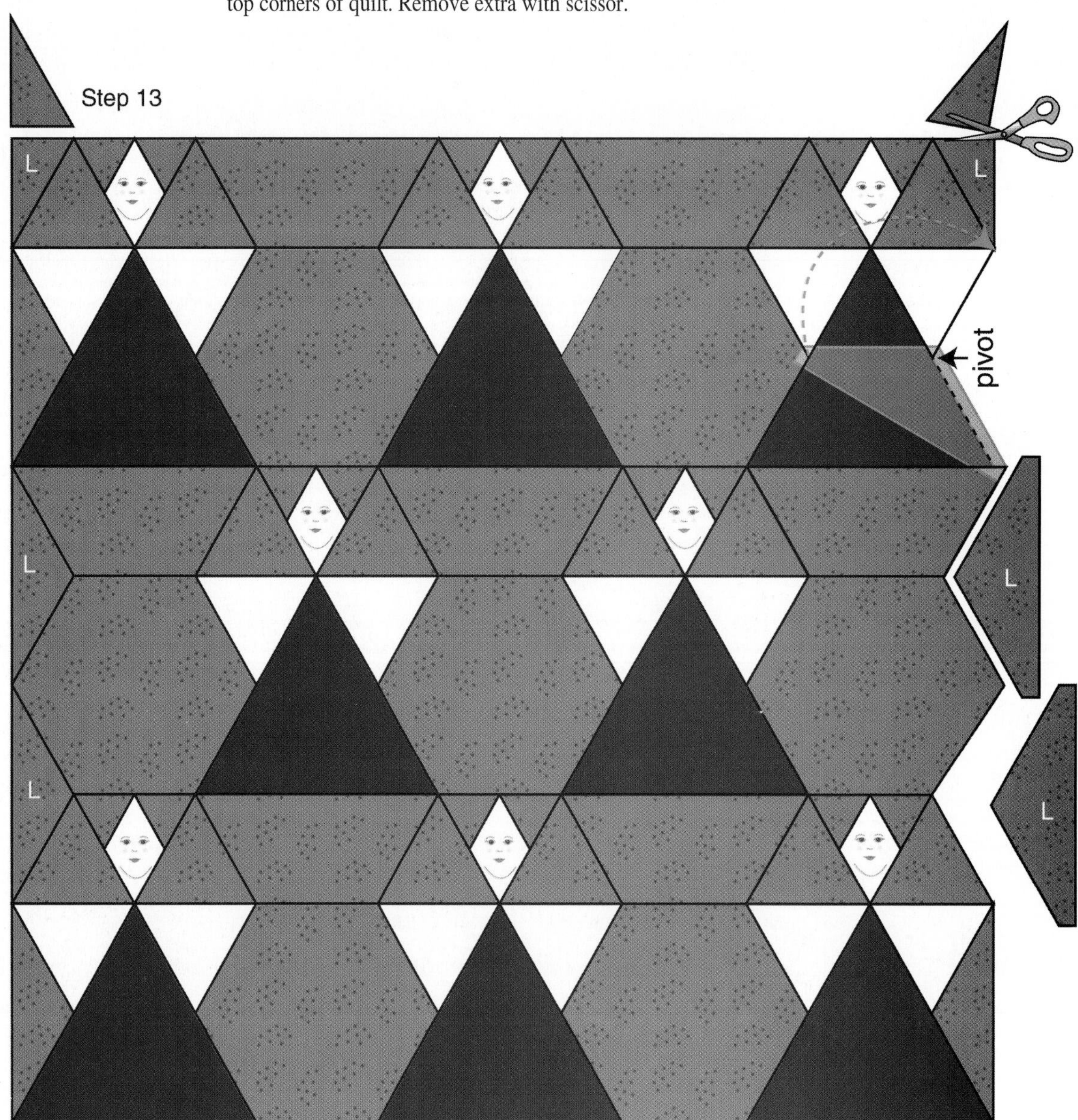

Step 14. Cut strips for inside border 1" wide. Cut strips for outside border 5" wide. Too add borders see page 5.

ST-S continuous line star stencil

Finishing touches

It's important to choose quilting designs that complement the quilt. In keeping with the celestial theme Marcia Stevens added wings and folds in the skirt with Sulky® silver metallic thread. She added stars and clouds in the background. Marcia filled in the area around the face with gold hair. To create a full head of hair she sewed back and forth over same area with gold Sulky® thread. The continuous line *ST-S star stencil* was used in the outside border.

Jill McCoy created angelic faces with fabric paints. Each face is a little different. I found fuzzy thread for the halo that was hand tacked in place. The iron on star was added last to the center of the halo. I think you will agree, this quilt will put everyone in the holiday spirit.

designed & pieced by
Angela Scott
machine quilted by
Marcia Stevens

Shopping List

- QSK Quilter's Starter Kit
- Quick Grips
- Omnigrid® Rulers 6" x 24"
- Fiskars® Rotary Cutter
- IBC Glass Head Pins 0.50mm steel shaft
- Fairfield poly-fil low-loft batting
- Sulky® metallic thread

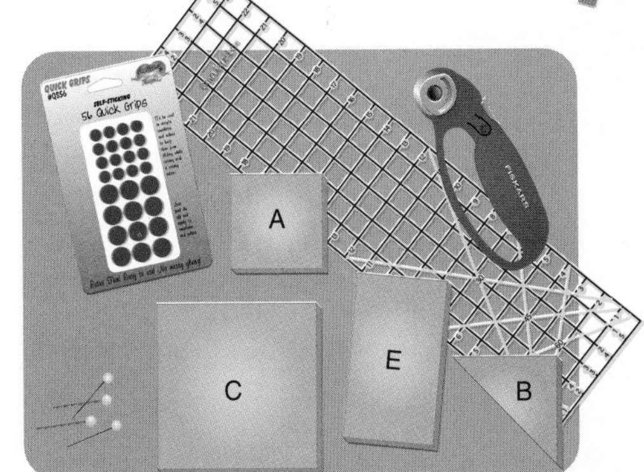

Read pages 2-7 before starting.

About Dragon Fly Fantasy

The "Fantasies" print by Hoffman used in border, generated the inspiration for Angela's Dragonfly quilt. The dragonflies, stars and leaves in the border were recreated in the quilt itself. The blue and yellow dragonflies are set in a darker background to give a dramatic evening feel. The yellow sashing creates an important visual separation between the background and border. The only fabric that has much texture and design is the border print. The rest of the fabrics are a tone on tone that look like solids in the quilt.

Marcia Stevens brought feeling and movement to the quilt with her stunning work. The dragonfly and leaves look more realistic using thread a shade darker to enhance the dragonflies body and veins of the leaves. The wings, twinkling stars and tiny fireflies glow quilted with sulky metallic thread. Eyes legs and a nose finish this fantasy insect. Designer thread by On-the-Surface was used to connect the leaves. The dragonflies were outlined in the border connected with a general meandering. A linear design quilted on the background creates a gentle evening breeze. The dark blue cornerstones are quilted with a simple continuous line motif created by Marcia.

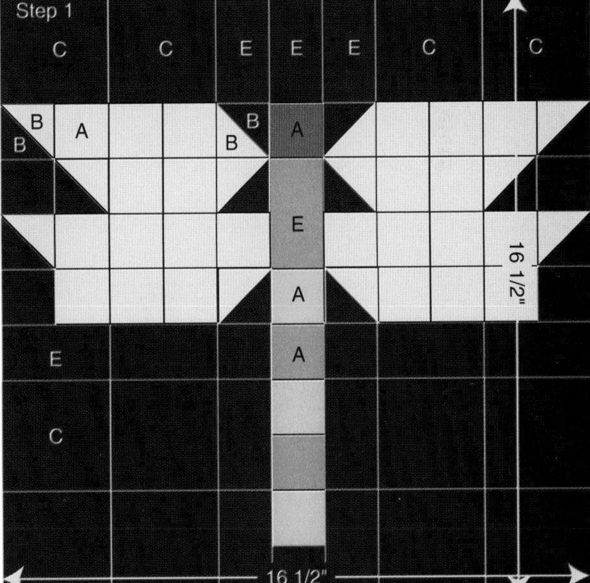

Cutting Instructions

Templates A, B, C, and E from the Quilter's Starter Kit were used to create the whole quilt. It amazes me how simple shapes combined with the right fabrics can turn into something so beautiful.

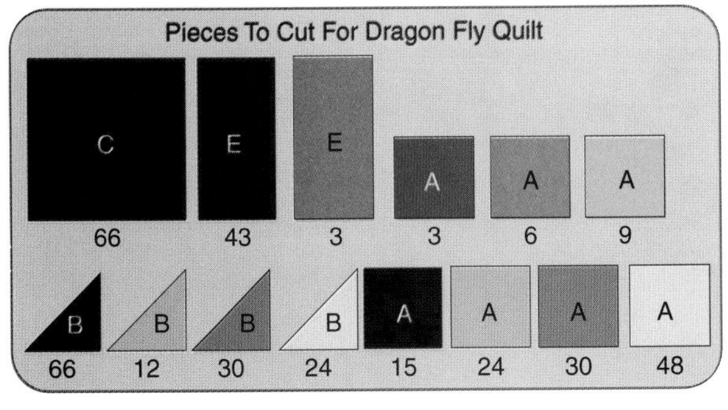

Step 1. There are only two blocks in the whole quilt.

Make two gold dragon fly blocks.

Make one blue dragon fly block.

Make three leaf blocks.

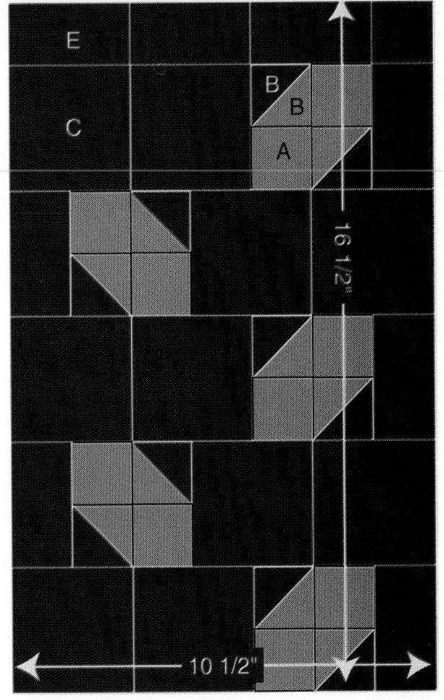

Cutting Instructions

Step 2. Cut A's and E's from 2" strips. Bi fold strips on top of a small mat board, so it is easy to turn work as you cut around the template. Cut 3 1/2' strips for background C's. See chart on page 59 for number needed.

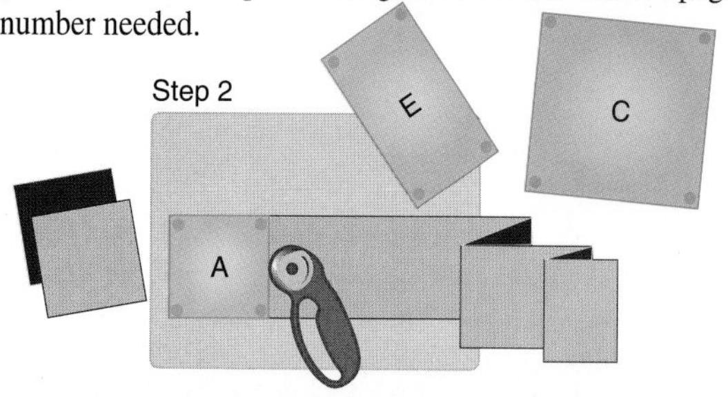

Step 3. Cut strips 2 3/8" wide for template B to get correct grain line. Bi fold strips on a small mat board. Flip-flop template cutting pieces as you go. See chart on page 59 for number of B's needed of each color.

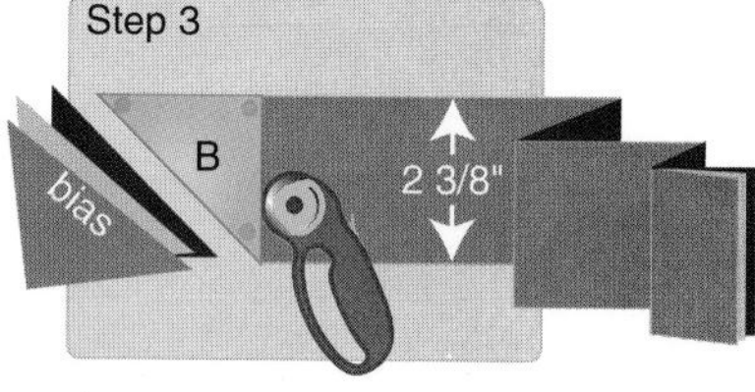

Step 4. See page 32, Step 4 to take sewing test before continuing.

Step 5. Arrange pieces on a flannel board following diagram on page 59. See page 32, Step 5 to chain sew B's together.

Step 6. See page 32, Step 6 to remove bulk in corners.

Repeat step 6 on page 32 until 24 pale yellow, 12 pale blue and 30 green B units are made.

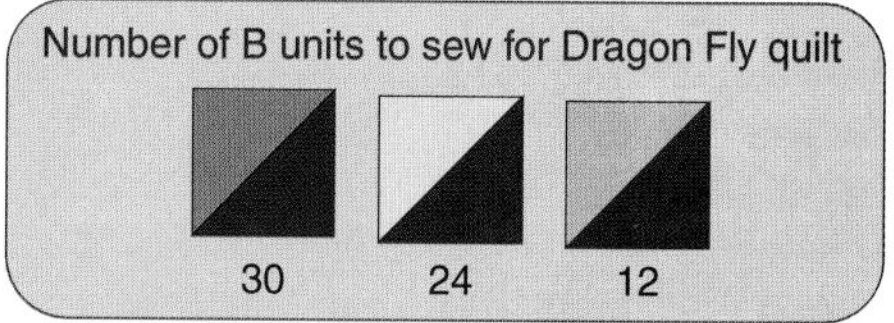

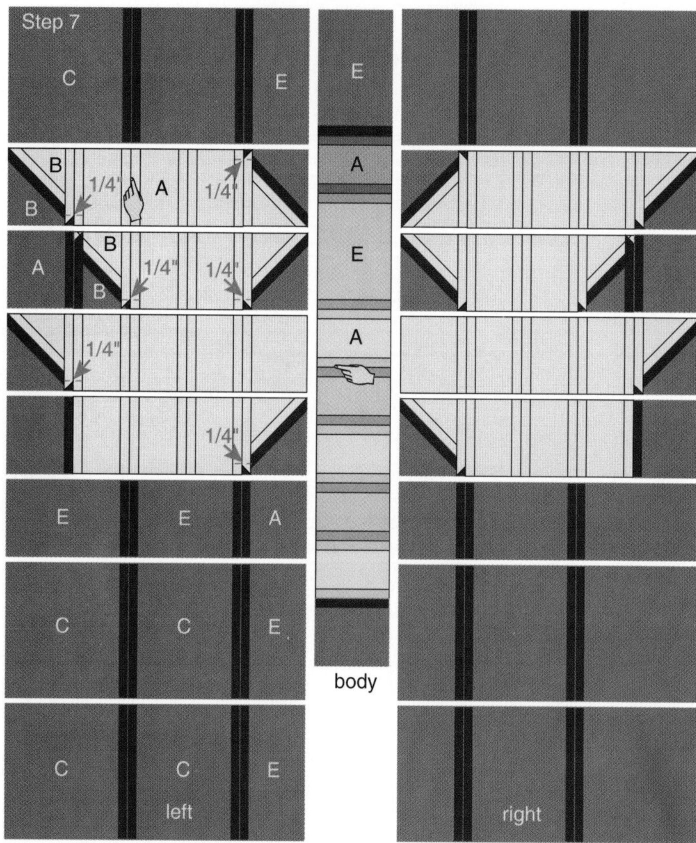

Connect Units Into Rows

Step 7. Connect units into rows for one dragon fly at a time. Right side is a mirror image of left side.

It is easier to finger press seams open on a hard surface. After seams have been finger pressed open, press them again with an iron.

Center row (body) of dragon fly is sewn together in a separate row of it's own. Center row is perpendicular to other rows.

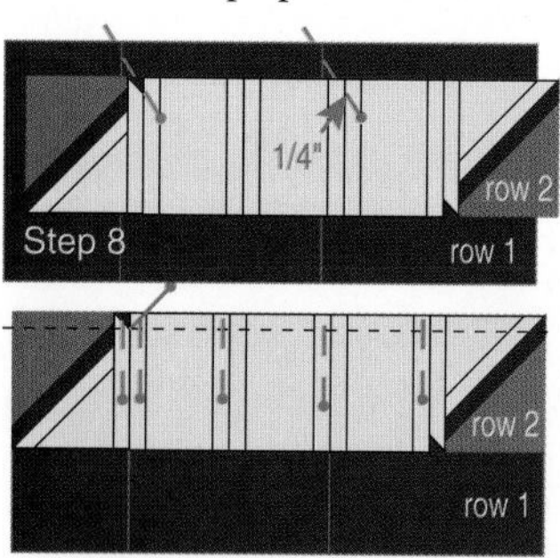

Step 8. Right sides together place row 2 of wing on top of row 1. Insert a pin 1/4" from edge through top and bottom at matching seams. Leave this pin standing.

Insert another pin on both sides of standing pin. Remove standing pin.. After seam is sewn press seam open. See page 17 for more pinning techniques. Continue to add rows until both right and left sides are complete. Add body and one dragonfly is complete.

Step 8b

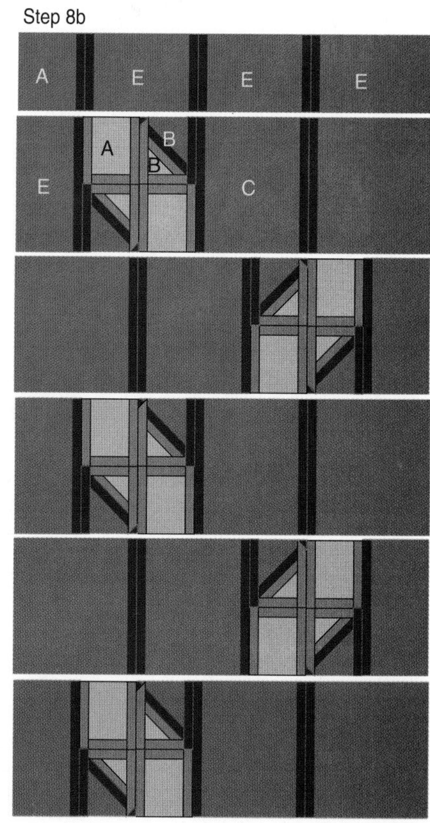

Step 8b. Arrange pieces to make leaf blocks as shown in Step 1 or as shown above. Connect units into rows. Press seams open before connecting rows. Each block has five leaves. Make three blocks.

Connecting Blocks

Step 9. Just one Dragon Fly makes a nice pillow or continue to add rows. I also like a shorter version of the quilt using only two Dragon Flies and two leaf blocks. It is easier to decide on finished size when you know where it is going to hang. Connect the blocks into rows. Press seams open. Then connect the rows.

Finishing Touches

Cut strips for inside border 1 1/4" wide. Cut strips for outside border 5 3/4" wide. See page 5 for more ideas when adding borders. See pages 6-7 to make quilt back and quilt sandwich. Description of the machine quilting is found on page 59.

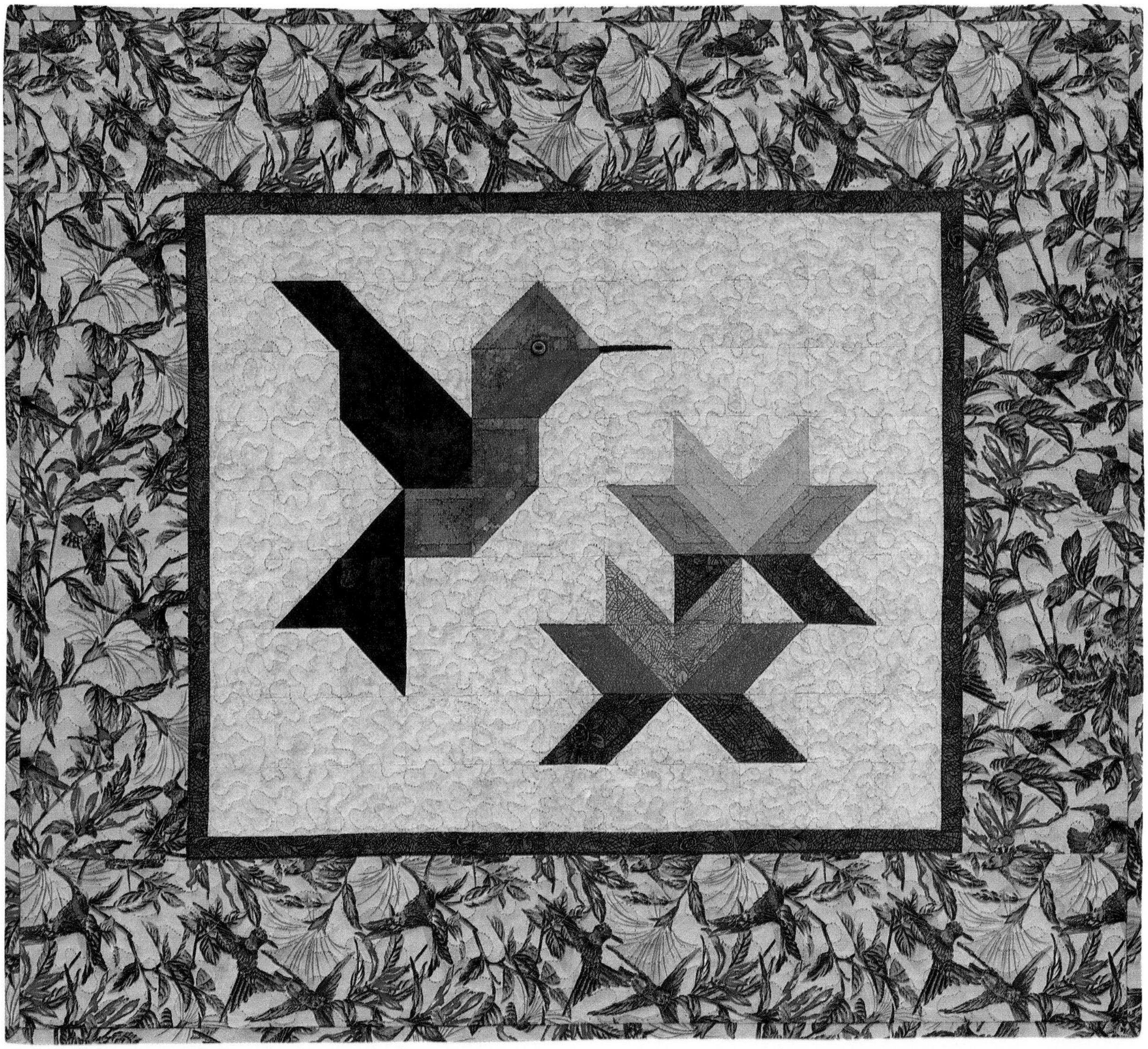

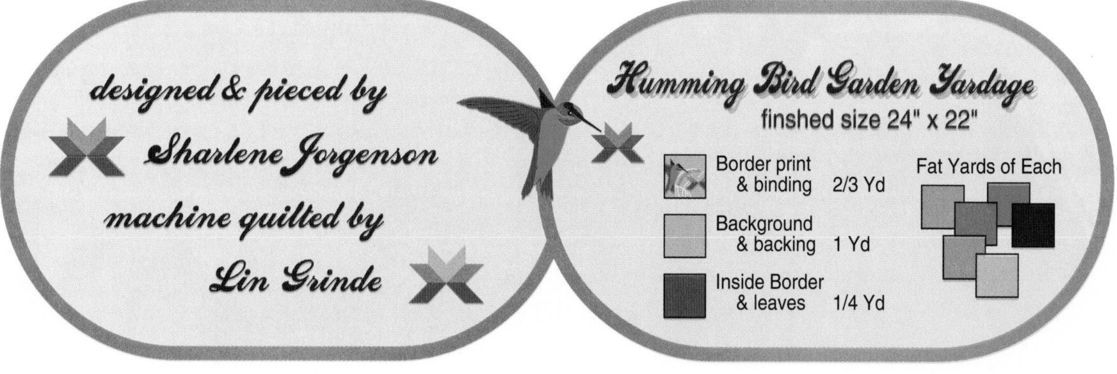
designed & pieced by
Sharlene Jorgenson
machine quilted by
Lin Grinde
Humming Bird Garden Yardage
finshed size 24" x 22"
Border print & binding 2/3 Yd
Background & backing 1 Yd
Inside Border & leaves 1/4 Yd
Fat Yards of Each

Humming Bird Garden

BEGINNER

Shopping List

- QSK Quilter's Starter Kit
- Quick Grips
- Omnigrid® Rulers 6" x 24"
- Fiskars® Rotary Cutter
- IBC Glass Head Pins 0.50mm steel shaft
- Fairfield poly-fil low-loft batting
- Button for eye
- STBF-B Butterfly stencil

Read pages 2-7 before starting.

About The Humming Bird Garden

There were many places to look for design ideas when working on the hummingbird. I found a drawing of a bluebird in an old 1969 McCall's Needlework magazine and kept it for reference when designing this wall quilt. Then I found a small book with colored pictures of all the different humming birds. I suggest you pick the border fabric before starting to pick any of the other fabrics. The main source of inspiration came from the Hummingbird border fabric by Timeless Treasures for Hi-Fashion Fabrics.

After border fabric has been decided on, choose background. The background is a soft blue which sets off the vibrant colors of the Hummingbird and Flowers.

Benertex has an assortment of colors and textures that made it easy to design the little helicopter. Fabrics with a very slight texture were chosen to enhance rather than distract from the design. I pulled colors with high contrast from the border to create definition in the flowers and the hummingbirds wings, body, neck and head.

I don't always like what I make the first time. I experimented with many color combinations and made several birds over a period of three days. To pick fabric for the first block I looked at the border fabric and chose the blue Humming Bird with the yellow neck. Then I made a couple of different ones with shades of pink. I wasn't completely happy until I switched to shades of green for the body and made a pink neck. I pulled yellow out of the border by putting it into one of the flowers. The same green from the flowers is used for the small inside border.

Cutting Instructions

This is definitely a quilt for beginners to make. Only two shapes were used from the Quilter's Starter Kit to build the whole quilt. It can be made in two sizes. *Use templates A and B to make 12" x 15" blocks or C and D to make 24" x 30" blocks. I used template A and B.*

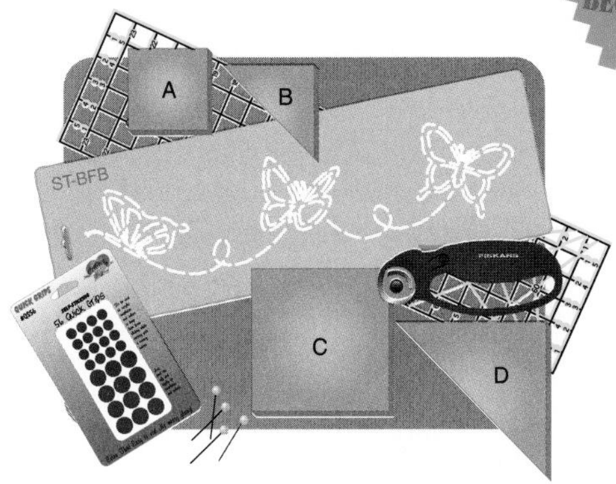

Step 1. Cut strips 2" wide for template A, or 3 1/2" wide for template C. Bi fold strips on a small mat board, so it is easier to turn your work as you cut around the template. See chart below for amount needed.

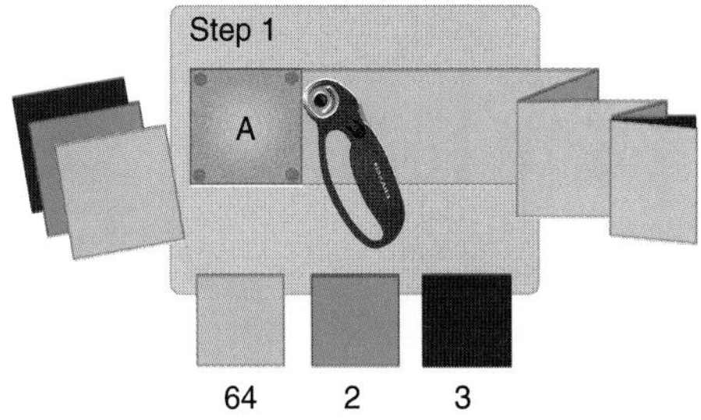

Step 2. Cut strips 2 3/8" wide for template B, or 3 7/8" wide for template D. Flip-flop template cutting pieces as you go. See chart below for number needed.

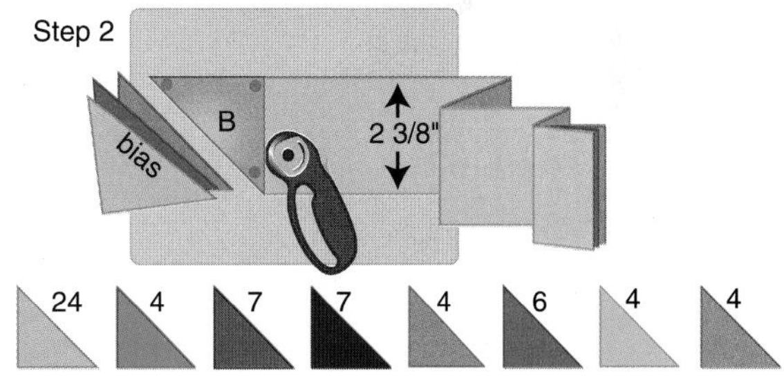

Step 3-6. See page 32, Step 4 to take a sewing test before starting to chain sew. Arrange pieces on a flannel board following diagram on page 64. See page 32, Step 5 and 6 to chain sew the B units together and remove bulk in the corners. Repeat step 6 until you have connected all the B's needed.

Step 7. Follow diagram on page 64 when connecting B's together. Make sure they are turned in right direction before sewing. Do not back stitch at beginning or end of seam. To make a perfect intersection insert a pin 1/4" from edge along seam line through top and bottom. Sew directly over point pin goes into fabric. Press seams open.

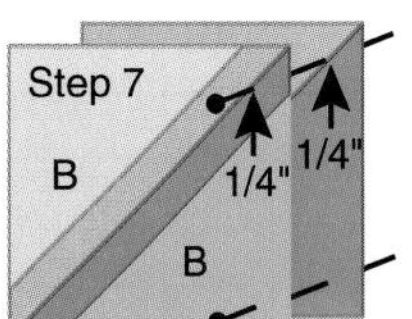

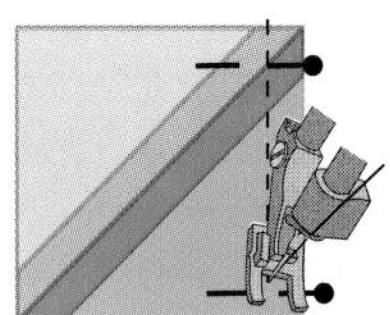

Connect Units Into Rows

Follow diagram at right and connect units into nine rows. This diagram shows the wrong side. Finger press seams open before pressing with an iron. Intersections should be 1/4" from edge.

The diagram below shows the right side of rows.

See pinning options on pages 17-18 before connecting rows together.

Finished size of each block is 16 1/2" wide x 13 1/2" long.

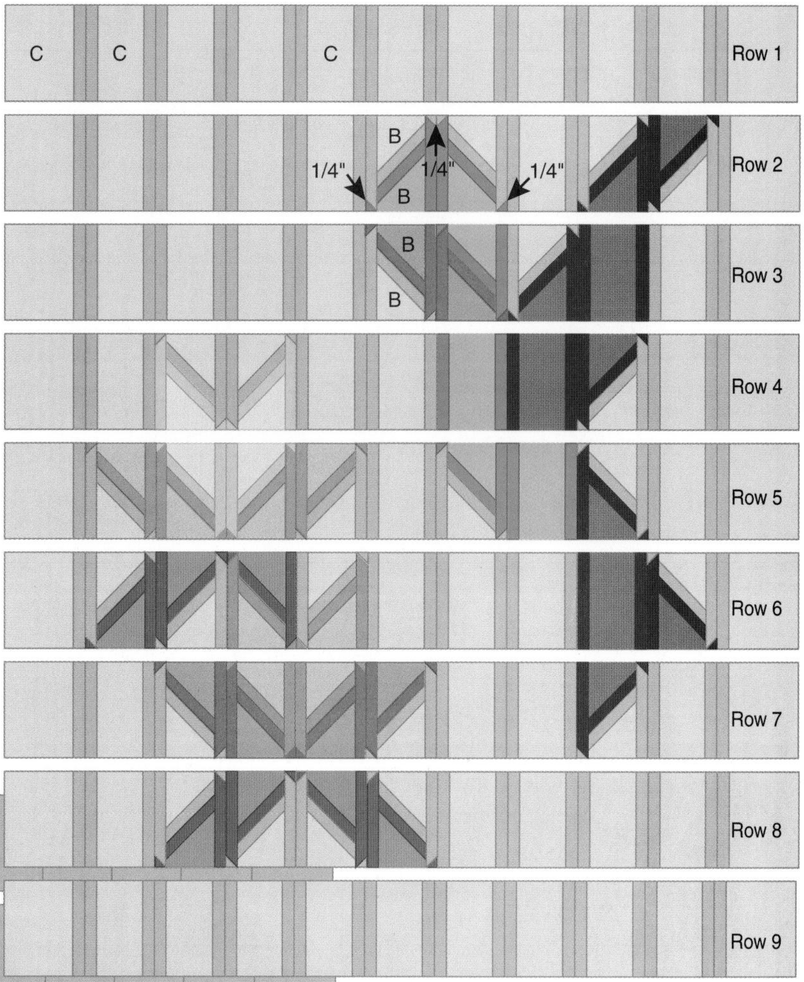

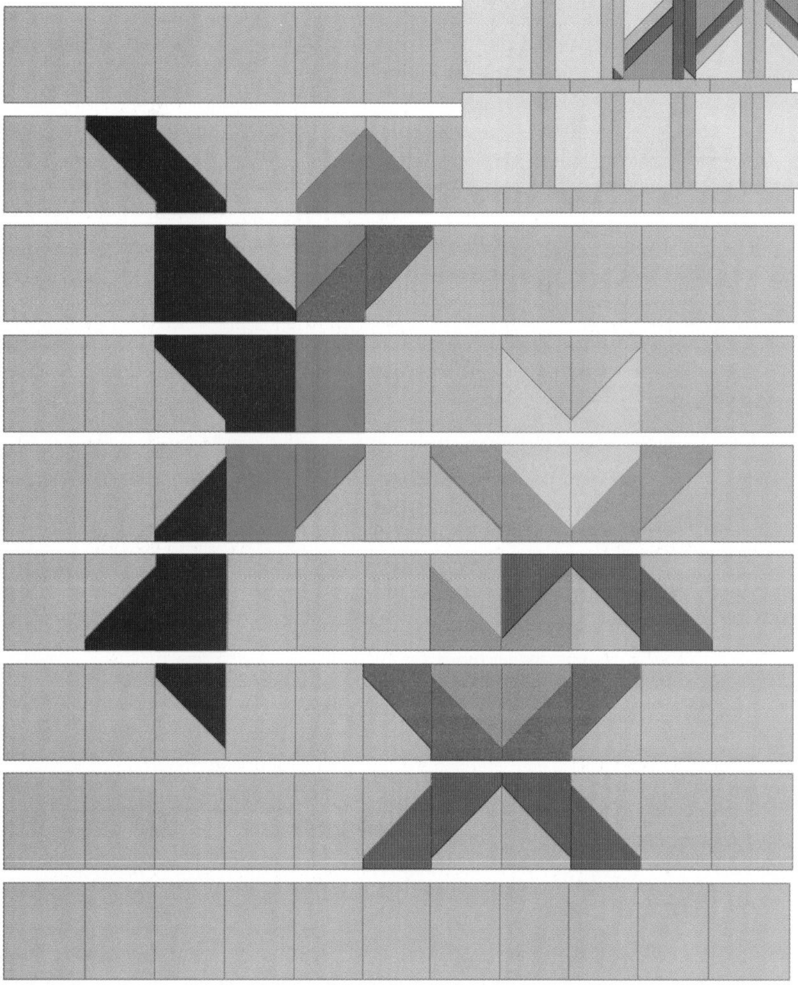

I made only one block for my quilt because it was perfect for the area I wanted to use it in. It would be easy to turn this design into a bed size quilt by making more blocks.

Finishing Touches

See page 5 for instructions to add border. I cut strips 1" wide for inside border and 4 1/2" wide for outside border.

See pages 6-7 to make quilt back and quilt sandwich.

The border is quilted in an overall meandering with a flower appearing from time to time. The smaller frame around the background has a small meandering stitch with a leaf here and there and the background is a larger meandering stitch. A butterfly and colorful center in each flower would be a nice touch. Each segment of hummingbird and flower look good outlined with a gently waving stitch in matching thread or a straight stitch 1/4" from edge of each color.

The button was added for the eye and a beak was stitched after quilting was finished. See page 7 to attach binding.

designed
& pieced by
Brittany Tostenson

machine quilted by
Phyllis Petersen

Shopping List

- ✶ QSK Quilter's Starter Kit Templates A, B & E
- ✶ Quick Grips
- ✶ Omnigrid® Rulers 6" x 24"
- ✶ Omnigrid® Ruler 6 1/2" x 6 1/2"
- ✶ Fiskars® Rotary Cutter
- ✶ IBC Glass Head Pins 0.50mm steel shaft
- ✶ Fairfield poly-fil low-loft batting
- ✶ Continuous line star stencil ST-S

Read pages 2-7 before starting.

About Brittany's Millennium Quilt

Step 1. Brittany chose a border print that gives a lot of motion to her Millennium quilt. The stars and planets are surrounded by a milky way of metallic gold. The star block has a light gold background with a small star, the medium red legs have a larger metallic star print, and the dark solid blue points make it appear as though the star is spinning. The alternate block is the same dark blue found in the star block.

This is a great quilt for a beginner to make because you only have to learn how to make one block. Each block is a 6 1/2" (6" finished) square before used in quilt top.

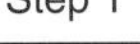

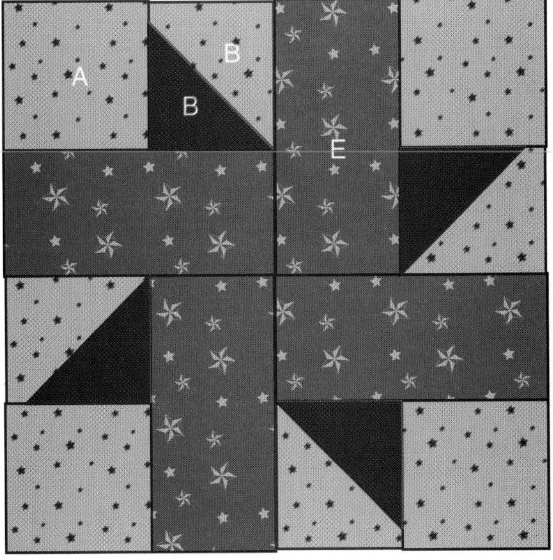

Cutting Instructions

Use templates A, B and E from the Quilter's Starter Kit.

Step 2. Cut strips 2" wide for templates A and E. Bi fold strips on a small mat board base, so it is easy to turn your work as you cut around the template. Cut 52 E's and 52 A's.

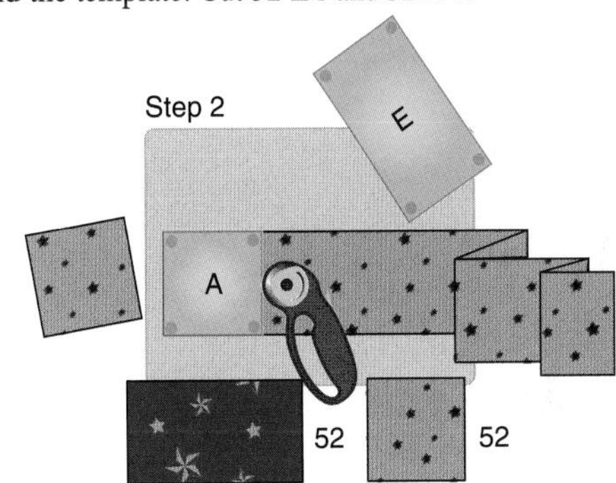

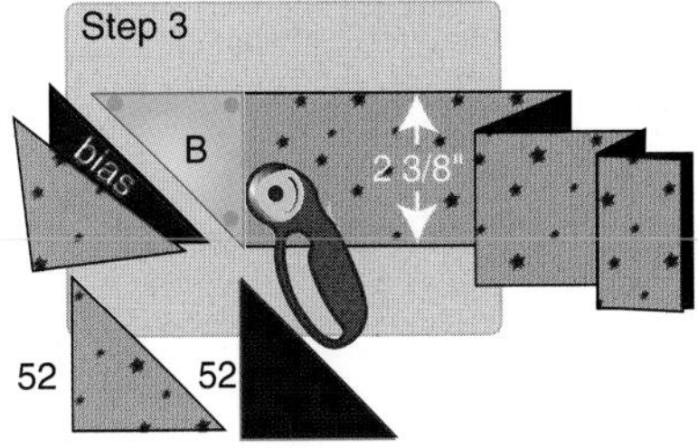

Step 3. Cut strips 2 3/8" wide from two fabrics for template B. Flip flop template cutting pieces as you go. Cut 52 of each color.

Step 4. See page 32, Step 4 to take a sewing test before starting to chain sew. Arrange pieces on a flannel board for one block following diagram in step 1. See page 32 Steps 5-6 to chain sew B units together and remove bulk in corners. Repeat Step 6 until you have connected 52 B units.

Step 4

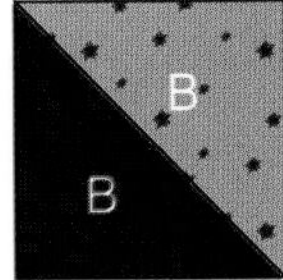

52

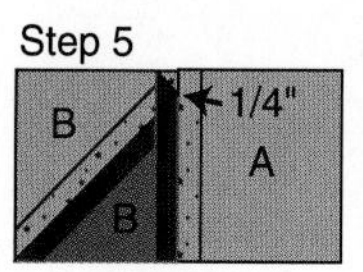

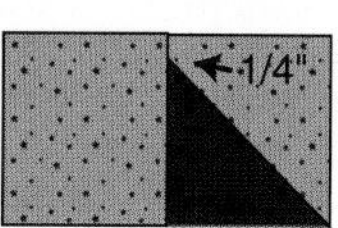

Step 5 Right sides together place B units on top of A. *If you don't make them all the same the stars won't spin in same direction.* Finger press seams open before pressing with an iron. Make 52.

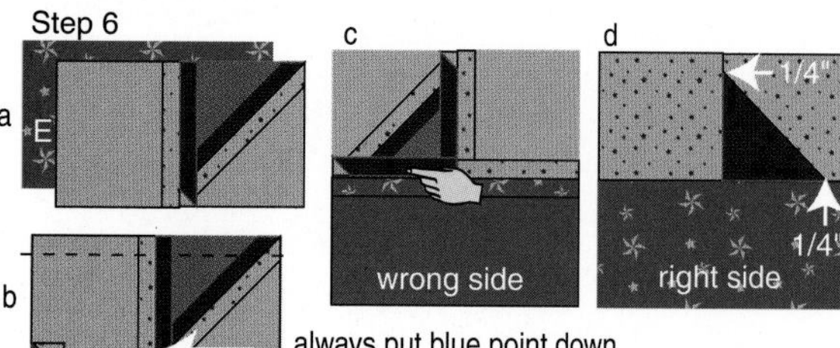

Step 6a. Right sides together place an E on the bottom.
b. Always put blue point of star pointing down.
c. Finger press seams open before pressing with an iron.
d. Intersections should be 1/4" from edge. *Make 52 the same.*

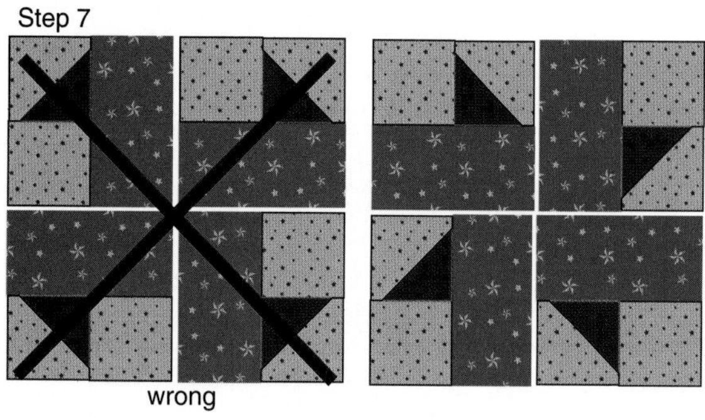

Step 7. Arrange four units made in Step 6 as shown in diagram. Be careful! It is easy to make the wrong design.

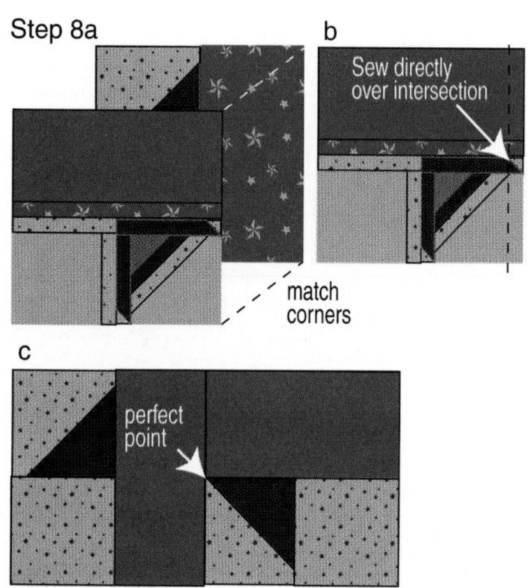

Step 8a. Sew two units together. Match corners.
b. Sew directly over intersection to get a perfect point.
c. Make 26 exactly the same.

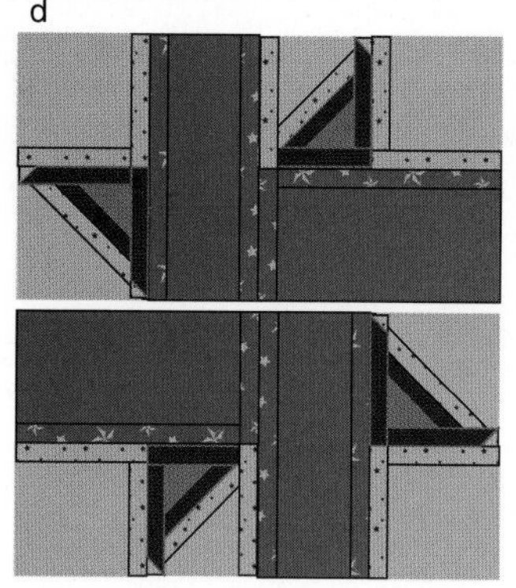

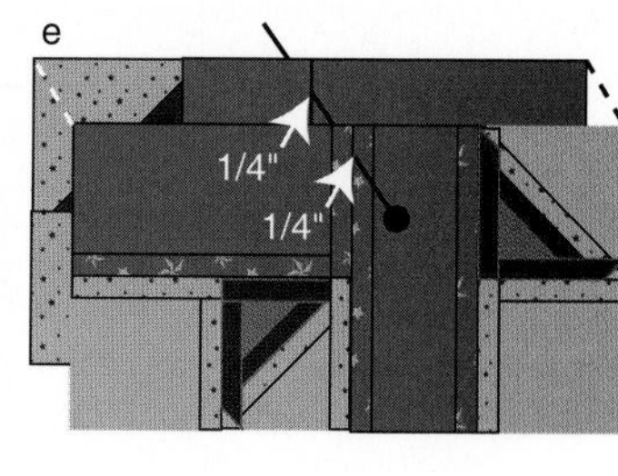

d. Arrange two rows as shown.

e. Match corners. Insert a pin on seam line 1/4" from edge through top and bottom. Finger press seam open.

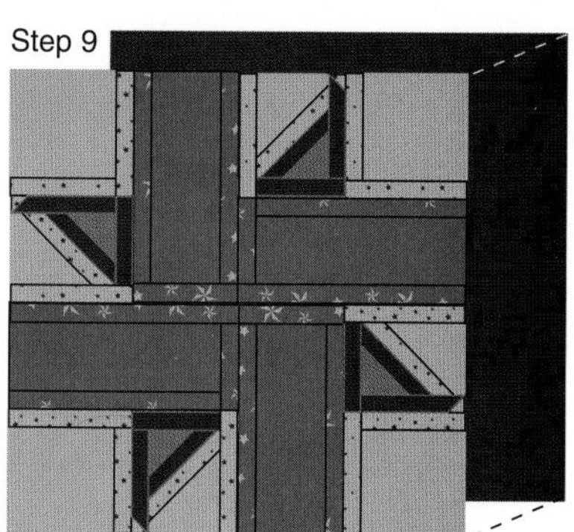

Step 9. Cut twelve 6 1/2" dark blue squares to use for alternate blocks. Right sides together start connecting blocks to alternate blocks to make rows. Sew directly over intersections. Press seams open.

Step 10. Every other row starts with an alternate block. The width of the quilt is determined by the number of blocks in a row. The length is determined by the number of rows.

Connect rows and press seams open.

ST-S
Continuous Star Stencil

Finishing Touches

Cut strips for inside border 1 1/4" wide.

Cut strips for outside border 5 1/2" wide.

A coordinating, lightly textured red separates the quilt from the border. The quilting in the alternate block adds to the motion generated by the border with a continuous line of spinning stars in gold thread. The border is quilted with an overall meandering stitch, the gold in the star block is quilted with a small meandering stitch, and red logs are quilted 1/4" from seam.

See pages 6 and 7 to see how to finish quilt.

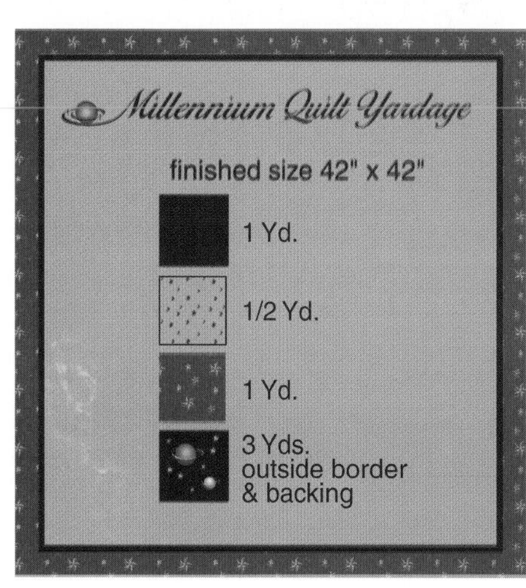

UNBELIEVABLE!

Designer I is a completely new sewing experience from Husqvarna Viking with exclusive features that make the impossible possible, the unbelievable believable, and the limited unlimited.

Our dedicated team of engineers worked tirelessly to bring you the ultimate in sewing and embroidery. What they developed will astound you: Eight fantastic new features that will turn your passion for sewing into an obsession. Not to be outdone, our creative team of educators put together an inspirational support package that will ensure you get the most out of your new Designer I. So visit your local Husqvarna Viking Dealer today for a demonstration and a free sewing booklet. For a brochure and the dealer nearest you, call 1-800-358-0001 or visit our web site at http://www.husqvarnaviking.com

Husqvarna VIKING

KEEPING THE WORLD SEWING

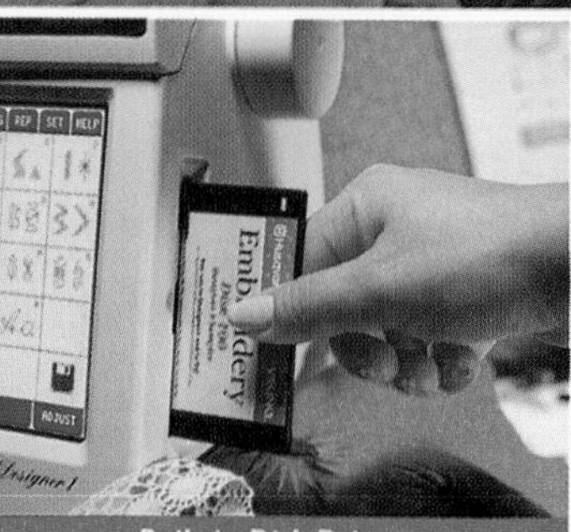

Built-in Disk Drive

* *Designs come on a standard 3.5-inch floppy computer disk*
* *Transfer designs from your PC*
* *Quick updates via the Internet*

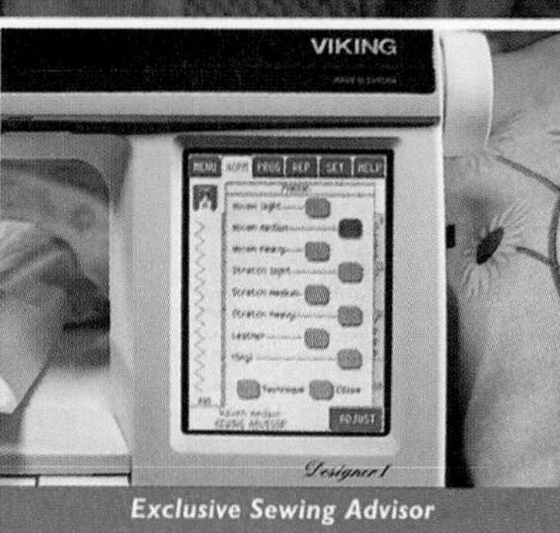

Exclusive Sewing Advisor

* *Automatically selects the best stitch, stitch width, stitch length, tension and sewing speed according to your fabric and technique*
* *Help menu tells you everything you need to know to sew*
* *Patented Sw pat 419 658, 420 328*

Color Touch Screen, Built-in Customizing

* *Everything is right at your fingertips*
* *See designs in full color before sewing*
* *Easy to use menus and windows*
* *Combine designs right on screen*
* *Personalize designs with lettering*
* *Custom embroidery in a flash*

Sensor Foot Lift, Sensor Foot Pressure

* *Raises and lowers automatically for every sewing technique*
* *Four positions: Up, extra lift, pivot, and down*
* *Hands are free to guide sewing*
* *Patented Sw pat 507 831*
* *Glides from thick to thin automatically*
* *Get perfect results thanks to even feeding*
* *Patented Sw pat 507 831*

All statements valid at time of Designer I introduction

QS 28
Log Cabin
D

QS 28
Log Cabin
E

QS 28
Log Cabin
F

QS 28
Log Cabin
G

QS 28
Log Cabin
C

QS 28
Log Cabin
B

QS 28
Log Cabin
A

QS33
Miniature
Log Cabin
K

QS-28
LOG CABIN
H

QS33
A

QS33 - Miniature Log Cabin
H

QS33
B

QS33 - Miniature Log Cabin
G

QS-28
LOG CABIN
I

QS33
C

QS33 - Miniature Log Cabin
F

QS33 - Miniature Log Cabin
D

QS33 - Miniature Log Cabin
E

QS33
J

QS33 - Miniature Log Cabin
I

QS15
Pandora's Box
B

QS15
Pandora's Box
N

QS15
Pandora's Box
M

FISKARS founded in 1649
1649
Fiskars began manufacturing cast iron and forged products.
1657
Hot chocolate was introduced in England.
1662
Pencils were mass-produced in Nuremberg, Germany.
1670's
Fiskars made nails, wire, knives, hoes, reinforced wheels and cast iron pots. Most were shipped to Sweden.
1677
Ice cream became the fashionable dessert item in Paris.
1706
First use of π, (the 16th letter of the Greek alphabet and first letter of the Greek word for perimeter) as the symbol for the ratio of the circumference to the diameter of a circle.
1723
Earliest commercial valentines were decorated papers for writing personal messages.
1750
With 56 employees, Fiskars began refining copper.
1760
Modern sandwich was created in England when notorious fourth Earl of Sandwich refuses to leave his gaming tables to eat. He insisted that meat and cheese be brought to him between pieces of bread.
1762
Charcoal was used to fire the blast furnaces and forges at Fiskars Ironworks.
1776
HISTORICAL HIGHLIGHT
Betsy Ross designed a flag which was adopted by the United States — 13 alternating red and white stripes and 13 stars.
1784
Benjamin Franklin invented bifocal eyeglasses.
1789
Charcoal made from burning wood in kilns was used by Fiskars in blast furnaces.
1837
Fiskars founded Finland's first machine workshop. Steam powered vehicles were produced at this facility.
1840
Blackboards were introduced.
ABC
1851
First commercial home sewing machine invented and marketed by US inventor, Issac Singer.
1860
Fiskars plough, to be drawn by two horses, was awarded a prize at the St. Petersburg exhibition.
1880
Fiskars Tailor's scissors were introduced.
1888
Kodak marketed its first "Home Camera."
1880-97
Fiskars began Puukko Knife production.
1900
Paper Clip was patented.
1940
Fiskars founded a spring factory.
1940
Mars, Inc. developed M&M's chocolate candy (intended for GI's; candy designed to resist melting in the field).
1960
Fiskars created the first ergonomic orange-handled scissors.
1980
Microcomputers began to appear in US classrooms.
1990
Fiskars® for kids Scissors step into the classroom.
1992
Fiskars® Softouch® Multi-Purpose Scissors reduce cutting fatigue.
1993
Fiskars® 45mm Rotary Cutter brings ergonomic comfort to quilters and sewers.
1994
Fiskars® Paper Edgers were introduced.
1996
Fiskars® Personal Paper Trimmer set the standard for paper cutters.
1999
Fiskars® Oval Cutter was the first of its kind to cut and draw.
2000+
2000 and beyond, history in the making!
FISKARS
Making History
Since 1649
Give your hands the royal treatment with Fiskars® Softgrip® Scissors. Their soft, cushion-grip handles allow for endless cutting....with less fatigue. Fiskars® Softgrip® Bent Scissors feature offset handles for easier cutting along flat surfaces. Fiskars® Softgrip® Craft Scissors have special Micro-Tip® blades, perfect for detailed cutting. Fiskars® Softgrip® Pinking Shears have an extended lower blade to keep material between blades for better cutting efficiency. Perfect for finishing or adding decorative edges.
For more information on all of Fiskars craft products visit, www.fiskars.com/crafts.
GOT TALENT? We'd love to see what you can create with Fiskars tools. For more information, write to the address below c/o Education Dept., PAC.
FISKARS INC. • 7811 W. STEWART AVE • WAUSAU, WI 54401 • WWW.FISKARS.COM
13121.c

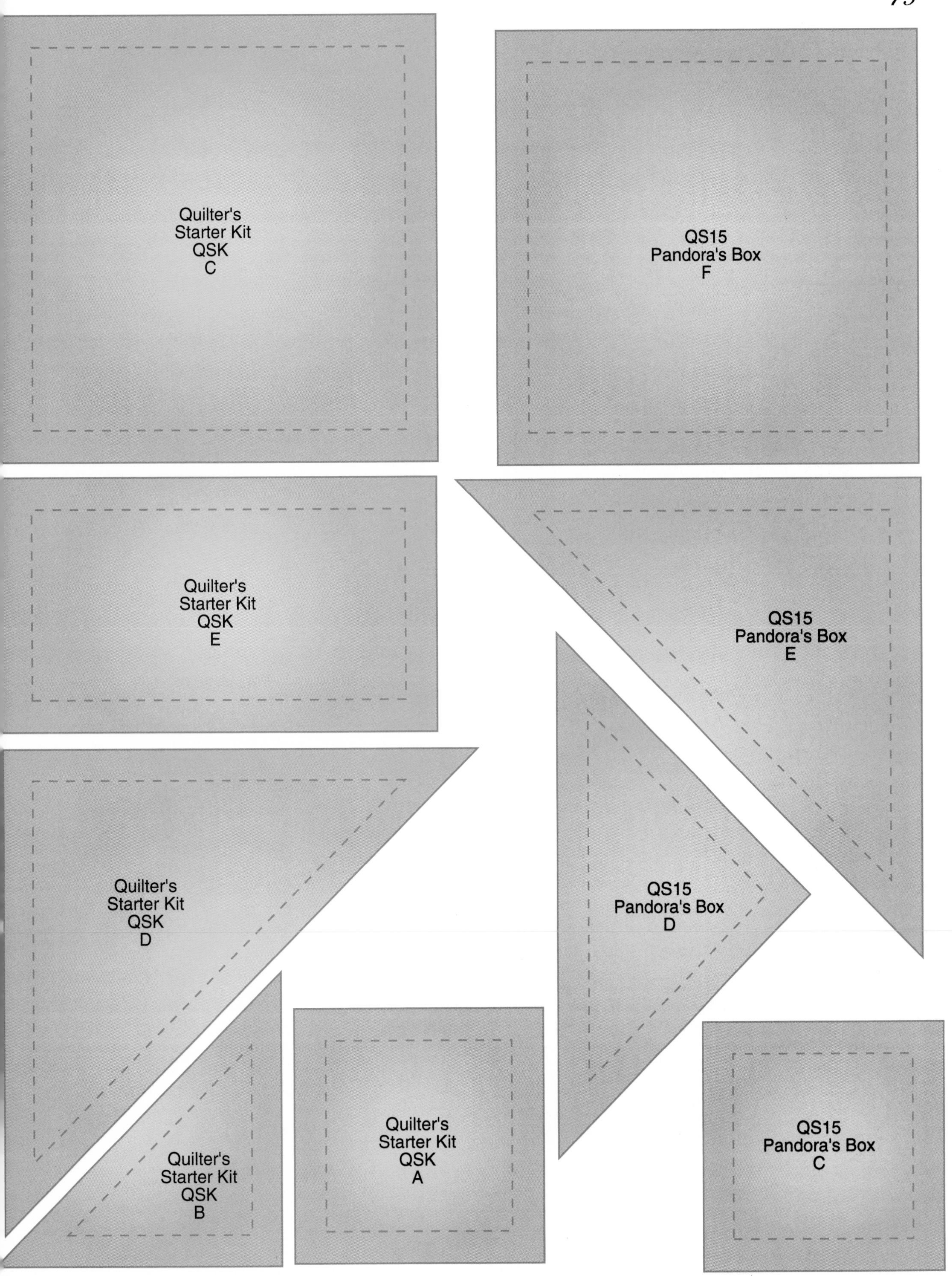
Quilter's
Starter Kit
QSK
C
QS15
Pandora's Box
F
Quilter's
Starter Kit
QSK
E
QS15
Pandora's Box
E
Quilter's
Starter Kit
QSK
D
QS15
Pandora's Box
D
Quilter's
Starter Kit
QSK
B
Quilter's
Starter Kit
QSK
A
QS15
Pandora's Box
C

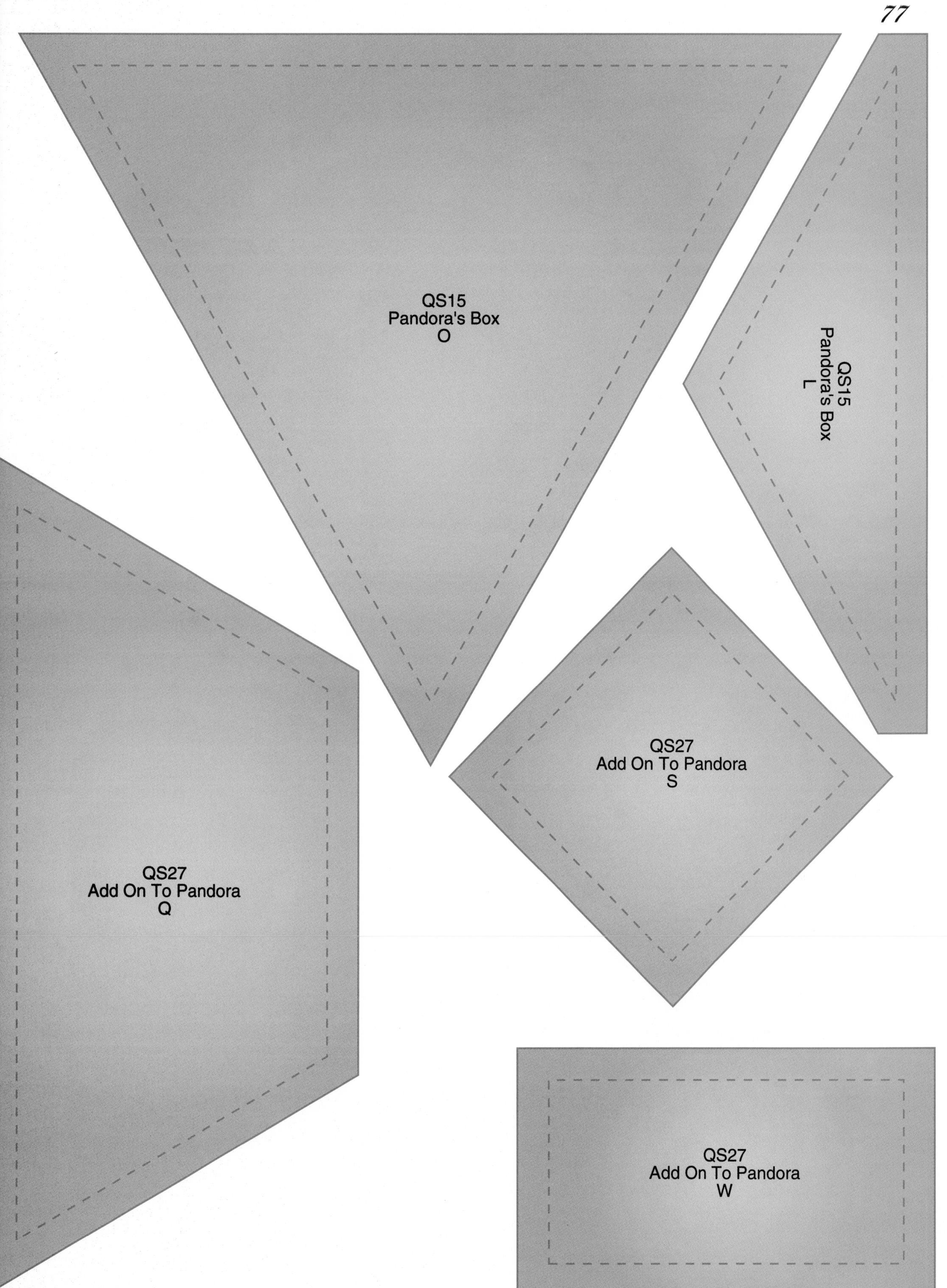
QS15
Pandora's Box
O
QS15
Pandora's Box
L
QS27
Add On To Pandora
S
QS27
Add On To Pandora
Q
QS27
Add On To Pandora
W

QS15
Pandora's Box
J

QS1
DOUBLE
WEDDING
RING
B

QS15
Pandora's Box
G

QS1
DOUBLE
WEDDING
RING
F

QS1
E

Straight of grain

Fold

When making the E template place this line on the fold of the paper.

QS1
DOUBLE
WEDDING
RING
H

QS1
DOUBLE
WEDDING
RING
D

QS1
DOUBLE
WEDDING
RING
C

QS1
DOUBLE
WEDDING
RING
G

QS1
DOUBLE
WEDDING
RING
A